WORLD ENCYCLOPEDIA OF INDOOR PLANTS & FLOWERS

Dear John,

Happy Birthday and I hope you enjoy this book.

Always,

Helen and Craig Mom

WORLD ENCYCLOPEDIA OF
INDOOR PLANTS & FLOWERS

Edited by Joanna Kelly

CHARTWELL
BOOKS INC.

Contents

First published in the USA by
Chartwell Books, Inc.
A division of Book Sales, Inc.
110 Enterprise Avenue
Secaucus, New Jersey 07094

© 1977 Octopus Books Limited

ISBN 0 7064 0585 4

Produced by Mandarin Publishers Limited
22A Westlands Road
Quarry Bay, Hong Kong

Printed in Hong Kong

Introduction

Decoration with growing plants has always been popular and although we sometimes read of 'contemporary' plants, the pot plant in the home is no recent introduction. It is the way that plants are used that has changed so tremendously during the past two decades. A plant is no longer an afterthought. It is an embellishment, an applied decoration, lasting longer than fresh cut flowers and in so many senses, serving a fuller purpose. Plants are a necessity. They add to our happiness and our tranquillity. They are living things and so easy to live with.

Where at one time plants seemed to stand isolated in a home, usually on a sill or in a window, having no real share in the homely things around them, they now play an important decorative role. In this book we shall see how plants can be used both with and in lieu of furnishings. We shall see how to draw them into the general theme of home decoration. How to place them, how to use them to advantage in more ways than one, how to mix them and arrange them and, of course, how to buy, grow and care for them.

Most people begin by buying their plants. Some continue to do so but there are others who discover that they would like to raise some plants of their own. This subject will also be discussed – fortunately, so many house plants can be raised easily from cuttings.

Not all house plants bloom and not all of those which do have conspicuous or even beautiful flowers, at least not when seen with the naked eye. However most people want flowers as well as leaves around them. So after describing the house plants we can grow well, we shall go on to discuss how fresh flowers can be arranged and used to the greatest advantage. And from the display of fresh flowers, whose lives alas are so fleeting, it is a short, logical step to arranging dried flowers.

These, like today's plants, also play a new role. With plants, dried flowers share the estimable quality of remaining lovely for long periods in warm interiors – in rooms which often are responsible for cut flowers maturing and so fading, too quickly. Central heating calls for its own kind of decoration!

Dried flowers can look as attractive as any other kind. Gone is the Victorian dust-trapping birds' nest type of bouquet of immortelles and grasses and in its place we can have both modern and classically styled flower arrangements, montage and all kinds of decorative designs, if these are required. In these, the old favourite flowers are combined with a wealth of new 'perpetuelles' now drawn from all parts of the globe and on sale everywhere. Dried flowers are delightful complements to green, living plants and they can stand between a plant and some source of dry heat, an attractive but effective barrier, protecting the plant in a convenient manner since so many plants need a humid atmosphere.

Once you have arranged flowers many times it will become natural to think also of arranging plants. These can be treated in much the same way as flowers and grouped together still in their pots in temporary arrangements or else given a more permanent value and beauty by transplanting them and mixing them in a larger container.

Once you have seen how attractive such arrangements can be you will not hesitate to take that short step to making pot-et-fleur, mixing plants and cut flowers. Indeed you might begin unprompted simply by enlivening a bowl of plants which look past their best. You will soon appreciate that this is another fascinating form of flower arrangement in its widest sense.

Throughout this book are examples of many ways in which all these subjects have been and can be used. While it is hoped that the reader will find them attractive and appealing enough to want to copy them, it is also hoped that this book will become an inspiration to all who love plants and who would like to arrange them instead in his or her own special individual way. Through it we hope to promote a much wider use of plants and flowers in the home.

Plant Guide

Achimenes (Hot Water Plant)
This summer-flowering, compact houseplant has many trumpet-shaped blooms in all shades.
LOCATION: Light, airy window when in flower.
CULTIVATION: Moist but not saturated peat-based mixture, constant warmth and regular feeding will keep this plant healthy. Dry off the tubers when flowering finishes in September and store them in frost-free conditions until starting new growth. Immersing the plant pot in hot water when encouraging dormant tubers into growth in February will promote rapid development.
PROPAGATION: Seeds sown early in the year; from cuttings; from splitting rhizome growth.

Aconite, Winter see **Eranthus**
African Violet see **Saintpaulia**

Alchemilla mollis (Lady's Mantle)
The leaves of this summer-flowering, hardy perennial are soft green in colour, downy and perfectly round with deep incisions and scallop-edges. The flowers, clusters of tiny sulphur-green, are produced in June and July.
LOCATION: Sun or shade in containers.
CULTIVATION: A moist soil mixture of most varieties and only a little care will see the clumps of Alchemilla seeding freely and spreading happily over their container.
PROPAGATION: By division of crowded clumps in autumn and spring.

Amaryllis see **Hippeastrum**

Anthurium scherzerianum (Flamingo Flower or Piggy-Tail Plant)
Though naturally spring-flowering this plant can be seen in bloom at almost any time of the year. With large, dark green lanceolate leaves and brilliant scarlet flowers with coiled spadex, it makes a most stunning plant for the home or patio.
LOCATION: Good light out of draughts. It dislikes dryness.
CULTIVATION: This plant is an aroid and therefore enjoys humid conditions with moderate warmth. The growing medium should include a high proportion of peat; this could beneficially be plunged into a large peat- or moss-filled container in order to maintain constant moisture and humidity. This plant should be watered with rainwater if possible, but always with the chill taken off. Watering should be moderate in winter and generous in the growing season.
PROPAGATION: By splitting up the old plant or by seed sown in peat.

Aphelandra
This plant can flower throughout most of the year. The two most popular varieties, *A. squarrosa*, a free-flowering variety that grows to 60cm (2ft) tall, and *A. dania*, a smaller, less productive plant with more silvery leaves, are prized both for attractive foliage and colourful flowers. The leaves are green with prominent white stripes. Flowers are yellow spikes.
LOCATION: Shaded from strong sunlight in summer but away from draughts to avoid leaf-loss. The pot is best plunged in a larger, peat-filled container.
CULTIVATION: It is essential that the soil be permanently moist and that feeding is regular with a balanced liquid fertilizer in amounts that can safely exceed the manufacturer's recommended dosage. The thick mass of roots makes this extra feeding and constant watering necessary and demands a loam-based soil when potting on annually in spring.
PROPAGATION: Remove dead flowers when flowering finishes and cut back the main stem to the first pair of sound leaves. When new growth develops at the axis and two pairs of leaves have formed, remove this and put it in a peat and sand mixture in individual small pots. This will root in six weeks in a heated propagator.

Azalea indicum (Indian azalea)—otherwise known as **Rhododendron simsii**
This small, winter-flowering, shrub produces its abundant red, pink or white blooms to grace the December festivities.
LOCATION: This plant may be grown outdoors during the summer and then under glass, or indoors from autumn till flowering in December. Indoors it needs a good cool, light situation. After flowering it may be put out in the garden again, for the summer, where it should be kept moist and sprayed periodically.
CULTIVATION: When buying new plants look for those with an abundance of buds, as backward plants may never flower satisfactorily indoors. It is most important to keep the potting mixture permanently wet, as any drying out will result in wilting. When flowering, it is best to plunge the pot in a bucket of rainwater once or twice each week. After flowering, plants may be put out in the garden for the summer where they should be kept moist and sprayed occasionally. The soil mixture must be composed almost entirely of leafmould and peat; these are lime-hating plants.
PROPAGATION: By cuttings taken from old wood during the summer months, inserted in equal parts peat and sharp sand mixture. Maintain a temperature in the region of 15°C (60°F) until the new plants are established.

Left
Begonia semperflorens is a fibrous-rooted species which blooms for many months of the year.

9

Begonia (see also *Foliage Plants* for **Begonia Rex**)
There are many varieties of this tuberous or rhizome-rooted plant. *B. semperflorens*, as the name indicates, is always-flowering. These are tender annuals of green or bronze foliage with fibrous roots, glossy leaves of bright green, brown or purple and flowers of white, pink or red. *B. hybrida pendula* are the pendulous, summer-flowering begonias; these are tuberous plants of yellow, pink and red which are ideal for hanging baskets. The *B. tuberhybrida* is a huge, double-flowered variety for bedding or outdoor pots, in colours ranging from white to yellow and red, many with frilled petals. The Multiflora Begonias are also tuberous rooted and form compact, bushy plants and almost rival the *semperflorens* for continuous flowers. These blooms are double or semi-double and sometimes almost rosebud in form. There are many other varieties.
LOCATION: All begonias will take some shade but most prefer at least a few hours of sunshine, the tuberous sorts enjoy cool shade the best. *B. semperflorens* does better in dryer, sunny conditions.
CULTIVATION: Keep all begonias moist and well-fed when active, though *semperflorens* is more tolerant to a slight drying out. Indoors, begonias do best when pots are plunged into containers of moist peat or on trays of pebbles over water. The suggested mixture is two parts loam to one of fresh peat. Keep water off the leaves when watering as this will lead to leaf mildew. Another indoor enemy of the begonia is stuffy rooms, see that they are in an airy room. Outdoors, moisture and some sun will help them to look their best. Lift tubers in autumn before they are caught by the frost. The top growth should be allowed to dry off naturally and then the tuber should be stored, preferably in rather dry peat, until the next spring when they can be started into growth again. The *semperflorens* can be overwintered in a greenhouse after cutting back in autumn and, in spring, they will sprout afresh.
PROPAGATION: *Semperflorens* are best when grown from seed though cuttings from low shoots can be taken. Tubers of the tuberous variety should be planted, concave side up, in peat early in the year then potted on in good light under cover till the frost is over. Harden off before setting outdoors in early June.

Bellflower see **Campanula**

Beloperone guttata (Shrimp Plant)
A little gem of a plant that is forever in keen demand. This evergreen can flower almost continuously. Its arching shoots are tipped with cones of white flowers shielded by overlapping, browny-pink bracts. The soft green leaves are on stiff, wiry stems.
LOCATION: Light and airy, shaded from hot spells. It can be moved to a sunny spot outdoors in summer.
CULTIVATION: Set plants in pots of loam-based soil with extra peat. Give ample air in warm weather. Water freely in the growing season but sparingly in autumn and winter. Feed weekly with liquid fertilizer from May to September. Shorten leggy stems by half in February. For larger plants, remove the bracts on the young plants for the first few months. The stems need no support till over 45cm (18in) tall.
PROPAGATION: From cuttings of half-ripe shoots taken in spring and rooted in fresh peat in a propagator.

Browallia
This blue-flowered annual can be sown in March for summer-flowering or in August for winter-flowering. These are excellent flowers for hanging baskets, *B. speciosa major* is a species with trailing stems.

LOCATION: Good light, perhaps in an east window.
CULTIVATION: Set plants in loam- or peat-based mixture. They like plenty of water in spring and summer and feeding every two weeks when growth is vigorous. Sow in gentle heat, plant sturdy seedlings singly in small pots and pot on when roots fill the container. Nip out growing tips for free branching and abundant flowering.
PROPAGATION: From seed.

Busy Lizzie see **Impatiens**
Calamondin Orange see **Citrus mitis**

Calceolaria (Slipper Flower)
This summer-flowering plant usually has soft and slightly hairy leaves with pouch-shaped flowers in shades or red-orange or yellow, marked with contrasting colours. These blooms are borne in large clusters on the top of the plant.
LOCATION: This plant likes a cool, light, well-ventilated room.
CULTIVATION: Must be kept moist at all times and well fed. Small plants will benefit from immediate repotting into loam-based mixture which will reduce the need for feeding and encourage plants to retain the rich green colour of the foliage. Discard when flowering is finished.
PROPAGATION: By seed or cuttings.

Calendula officianalis (Pot Marigold)
This summer-flowering or spring-flowering plant can be seen to flower throughout much of the year with successive sowings in the open. The double-flowered hybrid, 'Geisha Girl' is pure orange with incurved petals like a show chrysanthemum. 'Orange King' and 'Lemon Queen' are a few representatives of a plentiful selection.
LOCATION: Indoors good light and cool atmosphere. The sunnier the position, the shorter and sturdier the plants will be.
CULTIVATION: These should be planted at least 30cm (12in) apart in light soil. Indoors they must be kept constantly moist and airy. Outdoors they need little attention. If the houseplants are planted in the garden after flowering and are stripped of all dead heads they may produce a second show.
PROPAGATION: By seed sown in the open or from cuttings.

Camellia
These winter- and spring-flowering evergreen shrubs have deep glossy green leaves which complement the fragrant single, semi-double, double and anemone-centered blooms in white, pink, red and variegated colours.
LOCATION: Outdoors in shade from strong sunshine or in a cold greenhouse. They can be brought indoors to a cool, airy room while flowering or for protection from severe weather.
CULTIVATION: Shrubs should be set in larger than usually recommended pots or tubs of peaty, lime-free soil. Keep soil moist at all times. Feed with sequestered iron in spring and summer and mulch with peat in summer to keep the soil cool. Spray foliage frequently. Prune after flowering.
PROPAGATION: Raise new plants from stem or leaf and bud cuttings in late summer.

Campanula (Bellflower)
In August and September these small-toothed, heart-shaped leaves are smothered with a profusion of starry blue, lilac or white flowers. They are trailing plants.
LOCATION: Good light, preferably where they can trail and spread freely, in some shelter. Indoors some humidity is essential.

Camellia

CULTIVATION: Water freely in growing season and feed weekly with liquid manure when the buds are forming. Grow in pots of a proprietary potting mixture. They will winter well under cool conditions indoors.

PROPAGATION: Seeds sown October–November or March and April. Cuttings can be taken of non-flowering, low shoots in April and May.

Capsicum (Peppers)

These summer-flowering plants are grown mainly for their attractive, colourful, edible fruits.

LOCATION: Sheltered, sunny position.

CULTIVATION: Seedlings that have grown to reasonable size should be potted into small pots of loam-based mixture and potted on as required. Spray leaves daily during the flowering period to assist fruit-setting. Feed with diluted liquid fertilizer at ten-day intervals when fruits first appear and until they show colour. In summer they can be placed outdoors in a protected position. They are best treated as annuals and discarded when the ripe fruits have been harvested.

PROPAGATION: From seed sown in gentle heat in spring.

Christmas Flower see Euphorbia pulcherrima

Chrysanthemum

This is a flower of autumn and early winter, although now available from cultivators around the year. There are numerous varieties and colours, both with single and double flowers. *C. varinatum* and *C. coronarium* are most dependable for pot culture.

LOCATION: A cool, well-ventilated room with as much light as possible but out of direct sunlight.

CULTIVATION: Because these plants are fairly uninspiring when not in bloom, it is more practical to buy the inexpensive pots of buds and discard them or plant out when flowers have finished. If bought when several flowers are well-opened and lots of buds showing colour promise to follow, they can be expected to give pleasure for a long time. They can be left in their pots or planted in containers or sunk in their pots in mixed containers. The soil should be kept constantly moist. They can be fed weekly.

PROPAGATION: Many varieties can be grown from cuttings.

Chrysanthemum frutuscens (Paris Daisy or Marguerite)

This summer-flowering plant is often sold in pots in bud or in full bloom. The single white daisy has a golden eye.

LOCATION: Out of doors ideally, in a sunny position in summer and indoors in winter although it can be used year round indoors.

CULTIVATION: This plant is usually sold in pots which will bloom throughout the summer and can be cut back again after flowering to bloom in autumn. It does not need a great deal of heat, but must be overwintered under cover. Young plants can be made bushy by pinching out the growing tips to build the required shape. They need regular watering and feeding.

PROPAGATION: Cuttings root easily in peat and sand in August.

Cineraria cruenta (Senecio cruentus)

This plant blooms from December to March, producing masses of richly-coloured, daisy-like flowers from shoots clothed with large heart-shaped, light green leaves. The growth is bushy and compact, usually with many blooms on a stem.

LOCATION: Lightly shaded and airy. This plant is ideal for poorly-lit windows or balconies and doesn't mind draughts.

CULTIVATION: Cinerarias are best treated as annuals and discarded when past their best. Keep in rich, loamy, well-drained mixture always just moist. Feed when flowering and check often for greenfly.

PROPAGATION: Usually from seed, sown from August to December and kept cool.

Citrus mitis (Calamondin Orange)

Usually a summer-flowering plant, the *citrus mitis* is somewhat unpredictable. It has small, glossy-green leaves which are attractive in themselves, and white, heavily-scented flowers. It produces tiny miniature edible oranges.

LOCATION: Cool and light conditions indoors, but plant outside in summer where it will get as much sunlight as possible.

CULTIVATION: Repot the plant almost as soon as purchased, especially if growing in a small pot. A mixture of two parts loam to one of fresh peat is best. Use clay pots to prevent top-heaviness. Careful watering is required but not overwatering as the root system is weak. Equally harmful is too much drying-out. It needs regular feeding with a weak liquid fertilizer. Water must drain freely and not lie on the surface.

PROPAGATION: From seed or cuttings which root readily at any time of the year, especially in a heated propagator.

Clivia (Kaffir Lily)

This spring-to-late-summer-flowering plant has broad, glossy, evergreen, strap-shaped leaves. In the flowering season the attractive plant produces large stems carrying umbrels of funnel-shaped flowers which are usually red or yellow with yellow throats. Under good conditions these are succeeded by scarlet berries.

LOCATION: Good light sheltered from direct sun.

CULTIVATION: Any good mixture is suitable. Water to keep the soil evenly moist in spring and summer. In autumn and winter give just enough to prevent drying out. Feed during the flowering season and move outdoors in summer to semi-shade.

PROPAGATION: By root division. Divide crowded clumps in spring and pot up offsets in small pots of rich, gritty, loamy soil. They can also be grown from seed.

Clog Plant see Hypocyrta glabra

Colchicum (Naked Boys)

These are mostly autumn-flowering, tuberous-rooted plants with showy, goblet-shaped lilac or white flowers. The flowers appear first without leaves which follow with the seed-pods in spring.

LOCATION: Sunny position outdoors or in.

CULTIVATION: They should be planted in late summer in good soil and deep pots. They can be successfully flowered dry without soil or water but naturally deteriorate unless planted soon afterward.

PROPAGATION: By seed or division.

Coleus see Foliage Plants

Columnea

This trailer is a winter- and spring-flowering plant. There are many varieties, among which *C. banksii*, a glossy, green leaved plant with myriad scarlet blooms, is most popular. Other woolly-leaved, purple-leaved or climbing varieties are available.

LOCATION: Good light out of direct sunlight. Ideal for hanging baskets or high boxes or pots.

CULTIVATION: These plants need some care but are highly rewarding if successful. The temperature must be steady and conditions moist and lightly shaded. The mixture should be an open, peaty one with a little

Colchicum

charcoal and fresh spagnum moss added to sweeten the mix. Keep a little on the dry side for several weeks before flowering, this will encourage abundant blooms. Feed weekly with diluted liquid fertilizer if growth is slow during the growing season.

PROPAGATION: From cuttings rooted on peat and sand mixture in warmth.

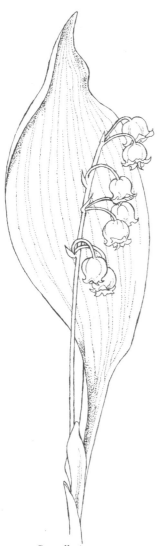
Convallaria

Convallaria (Lily-of-the-Valley)
This spring-flowering plant displays its sweetly-scented, bell-like white flowers on graceful arching stems and deep green leaves. Crowns are available for forcing.

LOCATION: A moist, cool, shady position is essential.

CULTIVATION: A rich moist soil and correct shady position will encourage this plant to increase readily by spreading rhizomes. Retarded crowns, sold in bundles, can be induced to flower out of season. These should be loosely planted together in peat, light soil or vermicilite, kept in a warm, dark place for four to five days then brought into the light and a cooler temperature to flower. The process takes about three weeks. Do not disturb plants until they deteriorate, then replant in October.

PROPAGATION: Plant in early autumn just covering the crowns with soil.

Crocus
These bulbous plants come in many varieties flowering a large part of the year. The most commonly cultivated is the spring-flowering variety, also known as 'Dutch' crocus. They have yellow, purple, white, lavender or striped blooms. The autumn-flowering *C. sativus* and the so-called 'winter flowering' species are often used for forcing indoors.

LOCATION: Full sunshine with some shelter. A light position indoors for flowering.

CULTIVATION: Ordinary well-drained soil in sunlight is best. They can be grown in water and are popularly sold in bulb pots for indoor blooming. Early autumn planting is best for spring- and winter-flowering varieties, late summer for the autumn-flowering. Indoors, crocuses are best kept in a cool place until the flower buds show, when they can be brought into a warm, light room.

PROPAGATION: From seed or by removing and replanting offsets and division of the corms.

Cyclamen
Winter-flowering cyclamen have dark green rounded leaves with small rose-pink, mauve, crimson or white flowers carried high above the foliage. The leaves are often blotched with silver.

LOCATION: These need a cool, light, airy room. In the summer they should be moved to a shady place.

CULTIVATION: These flowers can be bought in bloom when they should be checked for yellow leaves and to see that there are plenty of buds to come. When corms are bought, plant them half-buried as soon as they are received, in good leafy loam. They can be fruitful for years if conditions are maintained, and planted in deep clay pans of their own, corms set with indentations upwards. Always water grown plants from the base, as any droplets wetting the corm may rot it. Allow the mixture to dry out a little between each watering. When flowering is over and foliage turns yellow, they can be put outdoors and pots placed on their sides so that the mixture remains dry. When new growth develops in the centre of the corm, remove the old mixture completely and pot freshly. Water and feed again.

PROPAGATION: Raise new plants from seed in September in gentle heat and humidity. They take 15 months or more to flower.

Daffodil see Narcissus

Eranthis (Winter Aconite)
A winter-flowering, tuberous-rooted member of the buttercup family, this plant has bright golden, chalice-shaped flowers set off by ruffs of pale-green, deeply-cut leafy bracts.

LOCATION: Pans in a cool house or window boxes in light shade.

CULTIVATION: Damp soil is essential. Tubers should be set 5cm (2in) deep.

PROPAGATION: *E. hyemalis* will spread if left undisturbed. Others may be grown from seed or tubers.

Euphorbia pulcherrima (Poinsettia or Christmas Flower)
These winter-flowering plants have bright green leaves surmounted by large, brightly-coloured flower bracts. The most common colour is bright red or scarlet, though pink, white and multicolored forms are available.

LOCATION: These plants should have the lightest possible position, even in full winter sun, though out of direct sunlight in summer.

CULTIVATION: Poinsettias must have reasonable warmth in order to prosper, a temperature of approximately 15°C (60°F) should be maintained. They need careful watering and well-drained soil. A programme that permits the mixture to dry out between each watering so that the soil is kept just moist is ideal, or the pots can be plunged in a large peat-filled container. If plants are expected to flower for the second or third time they must not be exposed to artificial light in evenings from September onwards, as this produces an abundance of leaves but no flowers. A weekly dilute feed during the summer months will also encourage flower production.

PROPAGATION: From tip cuttings inserted in peat and sand mixture. This is easiest in a mist propagating unit. Once rooted, they should be potted on in loam-based mixture with a little extra peat and drainage. Repot as necessary.

Exacum (Persian Violet)
These summer-flowering members of the gentian family have fragrant violet-blue, yellow-centered blooms and small shining oval leaves. A colourful variety is *E. affine*.

LOCATION: Cool position in good light.

CULTIVATION: Plant in small pots of loam- or peat-based soil, water copiously from May to October, shade from hot sunshine and feed every two weeks with dilute liquid manure in flowering periods. Nip out leading shoots occasionally.

PROPAGATION: Raise from seed in gentle heat in March or by sowing in August. Pot on as growth develops.

Fuchsia
These deciduous shrubs have a long flowering period, a wide range of shapes, sizes and colour. The flower is composed of a tube which ends in four sepals and four petals, which are bell-shaped and often in contrasting colours to the tube. Some doubles and semi-doubles are available. They grow exceptionally well in containers, and dwarf and trailing varieties are also easily available. Taller varieties are legion and many are suitable for growing as standards or half-standards, and are very easy to train.

LOCATION: They grow well either in sun or partial shade.

CULTIVATION: The majority of fuchsias will live out of doors throughout the winter in mild climates, provided they are planted a little deeper than normal and banked with soil. The standard and hanging plants will need some cover. If they can be lifted, cut back hard and

place in a cool position under cover. They will then, given a little heat in summer, come into bloom early. Fuchsias enjoy rich soil, regular watering, a moist atmosphere and periodical feeding.
PROPAGATION: By cuttings.

Geranium see **Pelargonium**

Gloxinia
These summer-flowering, tuberous-rooted plants are correctly called *Sinningia speciosa* though most florists would be unlikely to identify them as such. There are many varieties of this green, velvety-leaved plant with trumpet-shaped clusters of red, purple, pink and white flowers.
LOCATION: Good light, but shaded from hot sun in an airy position free from draughts.
CULTIVATION: A moist peaty mixture is needed and potting on as required. Dead flowers should be regularly removed to prevent them rotting the brittle and delicate leaves. Leaves and flowers are formed from a tuber. Feed weekly when buds appear. When flowers and leaves die down in the autumn, allow the mixture to dry out and store the tuber in a dry, warm place until the following spring when it can be started into growth by placing in a box or pot filled with moist peat and maintained at a warm temperature. Watering should be from below.
PROPAGATION: From seed sown in a warm place, preferably in spring. It may be sown in succession to give a long show of flowers. Cuttings from stem or leaves may also be taken.

Goldfish Plant see **Hypocyrta glabra**
Grape Hyacinth see **Muscari**

Hibiscus (Rose Mallow)
These shrubby evergreens bloom from June to September. In most instances the flowers last but a single day, but these are breathtaking in many shades of yellow, red and orange, in both single and double forms. Most varieties have green leaves, though a few are variegated. There should be a continuous succession of bloom on healthy plants.
LOCATION: Light position shaded from intense sun and wind. Best plunged in their pots into a larger peat-filled container to preserve humidity. They can be moved outdoors in summer and taken in in September.
CULTIVATION: These plants like abundant watering in spring and summer. They can be allowed to dry out in winter if temperatures are decreased, so that they shed their leaves and remain dormant. If watered freely and kept moderately warm there will be attractive winter foliage. Regular feeding is essential and a peat-based potting mix. Prune in spring.
PROPAGATION: Usually from softwood cuttings or air layers.

Hippeastrum
Often erroneously known as Amaryllis, this striking winter-flowering plant has huge fragrant funnel-shaped flowers in pink, rose, red, scarlet and white colours, frequently mottled or with petal streaks of white. Up to four long blooms are borne at the top of 60cm (2ft) stems. The flat, strap-shaped leaves are, more or less, evergreen.
LOCATION: A light, warm shelf or window-sill or sheltered from wind outdoors in mild climate.
CULTIVATION: This plant is easy to grow. Start prepared bulb by soaking the lower parts in tepid water for five days, then pot singly in good, well-drained loam and leaf mould mix with enough silver sand to make the

compost friable. Half the bulb should be exposed. Bottom heat encourages growth, so stand on a warm mantlepiece or a shelf over a radiator or in a cupboard in dim light till flower buds show. They should then be placed in good light to develop flowers. Little water should be given for the first two weeks. Do not water too much as the mature plants dislike wet conditions. After flowering, bulbs are usually dried out and stored until next year.
PROPAGATION: By division or by seed.

Hot Water Plant see **Achimenes**

Hoya (Wax Flower)
A summer-flowering plant, the two most popular species are *H. carnosa* and *H. bella*. The first is a vigorous climber, the second a low-growing spreader. Both species have handsome leathery green leaves and umbels of starry flowers of white, crimson or purple centres. Flowers of both are fragrant and leaves can be variegated or silver-spotted.
LOCATION: A light position but shaded from direct bright summer sun. *H. bella* is best in a hanging basket and *H. carnosa* trained over wires or trellis.
CULTIVATION: Use a peat-based mixture when potting and be sure of moderate warmth and ample drainage. Water freely during the growing season. Feed every three weeks from April till September with diluted liquid manure. Overwinter at a minimum temperature of 10°C (50°F). Water sparingly during colder months.
PROPAGATION: From cuttings taken from the firm growth (not from soft stems at the top) almost any time in summer, or with *H. carnosa*, by layering in spring.

Hyacinthus (Hyacinth)
These hardy, spring-flowering bulbs usually produce only one tall flower spike. They have attractive foliage, vivid colours and a delightful fragrance. Roman hyacinths, with slender stems and loose flower spikes in pink, blue and white, bloom earlier than the sturdier Dutch hyacinths, which also have a wide colour range. Multiflora varieties are characterised by several graceful spikes from every bulb. Cynthella or miniature hyacinths are ideal for smaller window-boxes. Most are hybrids of *H. orientalis*. Bulbs for forcing are available.
LOCATION: Sunny.
CULTIVATION: Grow in ordinary potting soil, loamless mix or bulb fibre. Forcing bulbs may be set in water in which a pellet of charcoal has been placed. Leave in the dark to form roots then bring to a sunny spot to flower. In soil, fertilizers are unnecessary, but water regularly to keep the compost moist. Taller varieties may need staking, this is best done in the early stages.
PROPAGATION: Usually increased by division of the bulbs.

Hydrangea
These spring- and summer-flowering shrubs produce many varieties of flower heads in pink, purplish, or purplish to deep blue. *H. macrophylla* 'Hortensis' have domed heads of bloom consisting almost entirely of flamboyant, sterile flowers, while 'Lacecaps' have blooms composed of an outer ring of eye-catching sterile florets that surround a centre of insignificant fertile ones.
LOCATION: Cool, light shade indoors, best with the pot plunged into larger peat-filled container. Transplant in garden in winter when the flowers have finished blooming. Those planted outdoors should be in semi-shade.
CULTIVATION: Indoors, the plant, given the right loca-

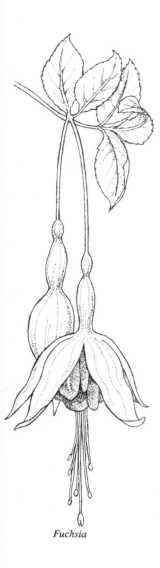
Fuchsia

tion and large pots or tubs, needs an abundant supply of moisture at its roots while in active growth. Cut off spent flower heads when they fade except outdoors in winter. In winter it can be allowed to dry out completely and be placed outside, preferably in a glass frame. Alternatively it may be plunged rim-deep in cool soil indoors or outdoors in mild climates. At this time the spent flower heads can be left as protection for the buds. In early spring they can be taken indoors again and watering begun, or into a cold greenhouse. Once a reasonable amount of growth has developed, plants can be potted on into larger containers using a loam-based mixture (lime-free, for the blue shades of flowers, or limy for pink or purplish). When new shoots develop those that are blind can be used to make cuttings for the following year. Prune in March, removing weak shoots and flowering heads. When buying new plants, a good choice is one no more than 60cm (2ft) tall having stems well furnished with rich green leaves and at least five flower heads—some open, others to follow. Look for those in pots of 13cm (5in) or more, as there is seldom sufficient goodness in small pots to maintain hydrangeas for long.
PROPAGATION: Cuttings rooted in warm propagator in peat and sand mixture.

Ice Plant see Sedum

Impatiens (Busy Lizzie)

These naturally summer-flowering plants can bloom throughout the year in the right conditions. The pansy-like flowers cluster at shoot tips, the leaves are simple heart-shaped which are found in colours from light green to bronze. The hardier varieties are used for container and summer bedding and are grown as annuals.
LOCATION: A warmish, bright room indoors with some shade from hot sun and well-ventilated on warmer days. Outdoors, the hardier varieties will endure either sun or shade as long as they are well-watered.
CULTIVATION: Plants thrive in a peat-based or gritty loamy mixture. They must be kept moist at all times. Feed generously when in small pots and repot when the roots thrust through. Keep house plants warm in winter.
PROPAGATION: Cuttings root easily in water or in soil. Once rooted, pinch the tops to give more bushy growth. If seed is used, sow early in the year with bottom heat. Do not plant outside until any danger of frost is over.

Impatiens

Iris

The large family of the summer-flowering iris includes rhizomatous and bulbous species. The bulbous variety is the best for container gardening. 'Dutch' irises flower from May to June, the 'Spanish' next and the 'English' in July. All come in a variety of colours except the English which has no yellow form. These, however, have the largest flowers. Dwarf varieties are most suitable for window boxes or pots indoors. These include *I. danfoidiae* and *I. reticulata* which can be grown indoors.
LOCATION: Full sun outdoors; light indoors.
CULTIVATION: Plant in October in light soil for the Dutch and Spanish types, which should be lifted after flowering to allow bulbs to dry off before replanting in October. The English irises do not need lifting and do best in a richer, more moist soil. Dwarf irises for growing indoors or in alpine houses will not tolerate hard forcing, so keep them cool—in a cold frame, cellar or shed for about eight weeks, then bring into warmer temperatures to flower.
PROPAGATION: By division.

Kaffir Lily see Clivia
Lady's Mantle see Alchemilla mollis

Lilium (Lily)

The hybrid lilies which are late-winter-flowering, make welcome houseplants. Many varieties are available including 'Brandywine', an apricot-yellow; 'Cinnabar', maroon-red; 'Enchantment', orange-red; 'Paprika', deep crimson and 'Prosperity', a lemon-yellow. Many other lilies make good pot plants for summer-flowering, especially *L. regale* and its hybrids, *L. longiflorum* and *L. auratum*.
LOCATION: Bulbs must be kept in a cool place shaded from direct sunlight until the buds appear, then they can be placed in a warm room to flower. All need some sunshine outdoors when mature.
CULTIVATION: Winter-flowering bulbs should be planted in equal parts of leafmould, loam and coarse sand with a little crushed charcoal. Allow three bulbs to a 15cm (6in) pot and cover with 5–8cm (2–3in) of soil. Keep them warm. Hybrids for summer-flowering will demand rich soil and good drainage. Pots should be quite deep and, if large enough, the bulbs can be left undisturbed for several years, merely being top-dressed with fresh soil. Water only moderately until growth is well-established and then allow to dry out before rewatering during the growing season.

Lily of the Valley see Convallaria majalis

Lobelia

A large genus of hardy and half-hardy summer-flowering annuals and perennials, the lobelia is usually grown as an annual in hanging baskets and window boxes. *L. crinus* is the blue dwarf lobelia most often seen. It is a low-growing type of which some varieties (the Pendulas) trail and others are quite squat. There are white forms and all shades of blue. *L. cardinalis* is a red-leaved upright lobelia. Its dark crimson foliage is arranged in low-growing rosettes. A tall flower spike is capped by brilliant scarlet flowers.
LOCATION: Tolerant of bright sun or shade outdoors.
CULTIVATION: These are ideal for the container gardener as they take up very little space. In shade they become a little looser in form than in bright sun. Average soil kept moist suits *L. crinus*, while *L. cardinalis* likes a richer soil.
PROPAGATION: By seed sown in heat in February. *L. cardinalis* can be propagated by division of the rosette in spring and layering after flowering is over.

Marguerite see Chrysanthemum frutescens
Marigold see Calendula officianalis

Muscari (Grape Hyacinth)

Many types of these winter- and spring-flowering bulbs are easy to grow indoors. *M. botryoides var album* has compact cones of small grape-like, fragrant, white flowers and *M. armeniacum*, also fragrant, is a brilliant blue.
LOCATION: Good light and warmth to flower.
CULTIVATION: Plant 2.5cm (1in) deep in pots of good soil mixture. Keep in a cool place for six to eight weeks, then bring them into higher temperatures to flower.
PROPAGATION: From bulbs.

Naked Boys see Colchicum

Narcissus (Daffodil)

These spring-flowering bulbs with their prominent, often scented, trumpet-shaped flowers are among the most widely grown of all bulbs. There are several thousand registered varieties, but for containers the best seem to be the strong-growing older strains such as 'Golden Harvest'; 'Carlton'; 'Mount Hood'; 'Glacier'; and Cantatrice'. There are also jonquil hybrids which are scented and have several blooms on each stem. Some of the miniature varieties—*N. asturiensis*, *N. bulbocodium*, *N. cyclamineus* and *N. triandrus albus*—are excellent in small window boxes and trough gardens. They flower from February on. Certain of the 'Tazetta' varieties can be flowered on pebbles. There is also a number of varieties that are prepared for Christmas or early year flowering.

LOCATION: Tolerant of full sun, an open situation or semi-shade.

CULTIVATION: Narcissus will tolerate most soils as long as they are kept moist. Early autumn planting is best for spring-flowering varieties, setting bulbs with their tips at least 8cm (3in) below the surface of the soil. All containers should be quite deep as rooting is vigorous. Set bulbs close together on a layer of soil mix, work more soil between them and leave with the nose of the bulbs just exposed, except in window boxes where they must be covered. Prepared bulbs for Christmas should be planted in October with 8–9 weeks in a cool, dark frost-free place indoors. Unprepared bulbs should have 10–12 weeks in cool darkness. At the end of these periods, take into a good light and warmer temperature for flowering. Water freely.

PROPAGATION: By offsets at time of lifting.

Orchid

As there are 20,000 species of wild orchids and 100,000 hybrids, it would be most difficult to give a useful guide to care and growing in this limited space. A few general comments may be instructive, however, for anyone considering buying an orchid for the home. It is entirely possible to grow many varieties in one's living room, but as they are jungle natives and used to high humidity and warm climates they do require special care. With the general use of central heating, the control of temperatures in the home has become more precise and generally temperatures are lowered at night for the sake of economy. This lower night temperature is exactly what most orchids require. The problem of humidity can be solved by one of several methods. The easiest, for a single or a few small plants, is to spread a layer of gravel, sand or some other substance that will retain moisture 2.5–5cm (1–2in) deep in a large shallow container. An inverted flower pot is put in this, the orchid set on the pot and the bowl situated in a warm position near a radiator or heater. This warmth will evaporate the water, creating the vapour so essential for the orchid. A north-facing window in summer and south-facing winter window-sill would be the ideal position for these sun-loving plants which, nevertheless, could not tolerate the full summer sun. On cold winter nights move the orchid into the room if there is risk of chilly draughts.

At least ten hours of daylight are necessary for these plants. In winter the daylight hours can be extended by a mixture of fluorescent and incandescent bulbs—nine watts of fluorescent to every one of incandescent. A special orchid soil mix will be necessary. This is obtainable from the supplier of the plant, who will know the exact requirements of the species purchased. Each species has a different flowering time—some will take as long as eight to ten years before they ever produce a flower from the seed. Orchids should be chosen to flower when they will be most appreciated. Nurseries are usually most helpful with advice as to care and feeding, but this short entry should give you an idea

as to the possibility of growing orchids in your home. They require extra time and attention and are more expensive to buy than most plants, but they are a most rewarding addition to a living-room garden.

Pansy see **Viola**
Paris Daisy see **Chrysanthemum frutescens**

Passiflora (Passion-Flower)

Vigorous summer-flowering climbers with five-lobed dull green leaves and exotic flowers. These plants have been religious and esoteric symbols for centuries. The ten petals, five anthers, three stigmas of various hues, and the purple rays with curly tendrils make a stunning and complex bloom.

LOCATION: Light airy window indoors and a sheltered position, perhaps against a wall in the garden outdoors.

CULTIVATION: Gritty, loamy soil, reasonable watering and light feeding. These are fairly easy plants to care for.

PROPAGATION: From cuttings.

Pelargonium (Geranium)

These plants can flower almost any time of year although they are popularly used as summer-flowering plants. They fall—not too neatly—into several groups. These are the Martha (or Lady) Washingtons, zonals, ivy-leaved, miniature, variegated and scented-leafs, all of which are tender and half-hardy perennials. The Martha Washingtons, *P. domesticum* are shrubby plants with large floppy flowers, most of which are blotched with a stronger colour. They range from white to burgundy but are mostly seen in rich salmon or bright red. They flower in April and May, followed by a long flowerless period. The zonals, *P. hortorum,* have a dark green zonal patch on their leaves and form the biggest group. Flower colour ranges from white to deep red with a wide variety of shapes and sizes. The ivy-leaved varieties, *P. peltatum* and hybrids, are also known as trailing geraniums and are invaluable for hanging baskets and window-boxes. They are mostly found in mauve and pink. The scented-leaved pelargoniums are more usually grown as houseplants, especially the small-growing *P. fragrans*, which has a nutmeg scent, and *P. crispin*, a lemon-scented foliage plant with quilted leaves. The flowers of all scented varieties are insignificant. They are used for balconies, steps and fronts of mixed plants, as the scent is released when touched.

LOCATION: All like full sun.

CULTIVATION: Rich moist soil containing a high proportion of loam with occasional feeding. Starved plants will flower more freely but blooms will be smaller. Set out after frost is over in May. Martha Washingtons should be cut hard back after flowering.

PROPAGATION: Tip cuttings of all will root easily in peat and sand mix in August and September.

Pepper see **Capsicum**
Persian violet see **Exacum**
Poinsettia see **Euphorbia pulcherrima**
Polyanthus see **Primula**
Primrose see **Streptocarpus** and **Primula**

Primula (Primrose, Auricula, Polyanthus, Cowslip)

The large primula family includes many types of shape, hardiness and flower types. Most are winter- and spring-flowering plants. *P. vulgaris*, the early-flowering primrose, is like a small polyanthus. Its compact habit and the ease with which it is grown makes it an ideal plant for container and indoor gardens. The auriculas, which have been developed from *P. auricula*, are beautifully coloured. The 'Dusty Miller' ranges have

Passiflora

flowers in soft, often bizarre colours—usually muted purples, yellow, mahogany and greenish-yellow. A number have soft green foliage dusted by a powdery white farina. *P. kewensis* is easily grown indoors, it bears its scented yellow blooms from December until April. *P. obconica* is another indoor favourite. *P. malacoides* (fairy primrose) has whorls of pink, red or white starry flowers appearing in winter. Polyanthus is a cross between the primrose and the cowslip and is available in all shades. There are countless varieties of this family. Most have large heads of bloom rising on sturdy stems above a rosette of rounded leaves.

LOCATION: All types enjoy light shade and cool, airy conditions if grown indoors. A window-sill screened from direct sun would be ideal. When the plant has finished blooming it can be planted in a moist, shaded part of the garden.

CULTIVATION: All enjoy a loam-based soil. Stimulate growth as blooms develop by weekly liquid feeding. Water freely and maintain a moist atmosphere. Pots can be plunged outdoors in light shade, in a frame for the summer, and potted on in autumn for the winter-flowering varieties.

PROPAGATION: By division after flowering and from seed sown in gentle heat in July.

Streptocarpus

Rhododendron

This family includes a large number of varieties which are suitable for small gardens and containers. The variety should be chosen carefully as most rhododendrons are tall. A few of the best container rhododendrons are the hybrid *R. 'Praecox'* which grows to 1.2m (4ft) tall. It begins to flower in mid-January in mild areas, with rose-purple flowers on a bushy shrub. A red hybrid 'Elizabeth' grows to 60cm (2ft) and has attractive foliage and trumpet-shaped blooms in April and May. *R. willianisianum* grows to 1.2m (4ft) with infolding bronze leaves, changing to green and blue-grey and with reddish-pink flowers in April. Its hybrids, particularly 'Mystic' which is pale pink and grows to 1.2m (4ft) in height over a period of 25 years, are also most excellent choices for gardens limited in space. Two other recommended hybrids are the small-growing blues, R. 'Blue Diamond' and R. 'Blue-Tit'.

LOCATION: Semi-shade.

CULTIVATION: Rhododendrons must have an acid, or at least a neutral soil free from lime. Top dressings of well-rotted leafmould or peat will keep the varieties mentioned here healthy for a number of years. Overhead watering will help in the development of flower buds and a constantly moist soil will also prove beneficial. Remove flowers as they fade by twisting, not cutting them off.

PROPAGATION: By layering or cuttings.

Rhododendron simsii see Azalea japonica

Rosa (Rose)

There is a number of varieties of rose which can be successfully grown in containers out of doors. Strong-growing kinds—hybrid tea or floribunda—are the most popular. Some miniature varieties will survive as houseplants for a few seasons. Roses are not ideal for the beginner.

LOCATION: Some sun is essential but roses can be grown in partly shaded positions. Miniature roses prefer a cool, sunny position for blooming.

CULTIVATION: Pots of at least 20cm (8in) in diameter must be provided and it may be necessary to pot on into 25cm (10in) pots after one year's growth. Any all-purpose potting soil rich in fertilizer is suitable. Planting can be done at any time from October to April. Pots should be well-crocked and, if available, a 5cm (2in) layer of leafmould should be put over the crocks. When planting, fill the soil gradually around the roots, firming well. Some pruning of the roots and shortening of the top growth can be done at planting time. Regular watering and mild feeding throughout growing season will ensure healthy plants. Established shrubs should be top-dressed with fresh soil early in the year when hard pruning should normally be undertaken. Remove all suckers by twisting them off. Remove faded blooms and attend carefully to all pests and diseases such as aphids, blackspot and mildew. Miniature roses used as houseplants are best planted in the garden after one season's flowering.

PROPAGATION: By budding, cuttings or layering.

Rose Mallow see Hibiscus

Saintpaulia (African Violet)

Flowering from June to October, and under favorable conditions all year, these are among the most popular of house plants. Violet-shaped blooms in single- or double-flowered forms in colours ranging from white through shades of pink, red, purple and blue form freely on short, branched heads. Rosettes of rounded hairy leaves of light or dark green provide an attractive contrast.

LOCATION: Good light protected from sun scorch. If possible these plants enjoy a few hours of light of some kind in evenings.

CULTIVATION: Set plants in peat-based soil. Do not water the leaves as the hairs capture the beads of water and may encourage disease. Repot every two years or sooner. They must have clean air and humidity. Feed whenever in active growth.

PROPAGATION: From leaf cuttings or from seed sown in gentle heat in spring.

Scilla (Squill)

These hardy bulbs can be seen flowering from February into the spring. The miniature scillas are most suitable for window boxes and pot cultivation. *S. bifolia* has star-shaped turquoise flowers, sometimes white or pink, on long stems. *S. sibirica* has brilliant Prussian-blue bells on short stems.

LOCATION: Sun or partial shade.

CULTIVATION: All can be grown in bulb fibre or bowls of light soil mix. Keep them cool for 6–8 weeks before bringing into warm rooms to flower. They show colour within a day or two of coming through the soil.

PROPAGATION: Bulbs planted 8cm (3in) deep.

Sedum (Ice Plant)

This autumn-flowering hardy perennial has pale green, succulent, spoon-shaped leaves and flat pink or purple flower heads.

LOCATION: Full sun.

CULTIVATION: Moist rich loam. As flower stems die down in the fall they should be snapped off. New shoots emerge early in the year. These plants will withstand both cool conditions and a little drying out.

PROPAGATION: Division of clumps.

Senecio see **Cineraria cruenta**
Sensitive Plant see **Mimosa pudica** in *Foliage Plants*
Shrimp Plant see **Beloperone guttata**
Sinningia speciosa see **Gloxinia**
Slipper Flower see **Calceolaria**

Solanum capsicastrum (Winter Cherry)

These cheerful plants, though flowering in summer, are usually chosen for their colourful winter fruits. When

bought in pots they are usually showing green berries which slowly ripen to red or bright orange.
LOCATION: An airy window sill with good light in winter. Young plants can be moved outside for the summer where they will flower and be pollinated.
CULTIVATION: Keep plants well watered at all times, spray the foliage regularly once the flowers appear in summer in order to improve pollination and help berries to set. Raised from seed in early spring these plants should be grown on into small pots of loam-based mix before being transferred outdoors in shelter for summer. Bring them into the home or greenhouse when nights become colder.
PROPAGATION: Can be grown from cuttings. These are usually best treated as annuals.

Streptocarpus (Cape Primrose)
These plants flower from late spring to autumn. A most popular variety, *S. hybridus*, 'Constant Nymph', has attractive blue flowers that bloom from May until October or later.
LOCATION: Good light and cool conditions in the home.
CULTIVATION: A loam-based mixture with a little added peat should be used for potting. Neither watering nor feeding should be excessive. Humidity is essential.
PROPAGATION: From seed or cuttings.

Tulipa (Tulip)
These are excellent spring-flowering bulbs for indoor cultivation. Specially prepared bulbs for Christmas flowering are sometimes available. The early singles and doubles are ideal for window-boxes and higher positions as they are unaffected by wind. These come in pinks, yellows, mauves, and orange-flushed. The taller and later cottage and parrot tulips are more suitable for large tubs or deep containers. Dwarf tulips are ideal for raised beds—varieties like *T. greigii* flower in April. Good forcing kinds are available in singles and doubles in all colours.
LOCATION: A light living room to flower, sheltered light shade outdoors.
CULTIVATION: Outdoors, tulips should be planted deep in October and November in rich soil and some sun, preferably sheltered. Indoors ordinary unprepared bulbs should be planted in a good potting mix and kept cool and dark for 10–12 weeks. A cold frame out of doors is best for this, but a frost-free shed, cellar or room in darkness would suffice. They should then be brought into warm darkness for two to three weeks and then taken into the light to flower. Prepared bulbs for Christmas flowering are planted earlier.
PROPAGATION: By division of the bulbs but not especially successful in our climate.

Viola (Viola and Pansy)
Varieties of this family bloom much of the year if kept cool. *V. cornuta* lives for years. It has either lavender-blue flowers or is available in white. *V. Wittrockiana*, the big, floppy-flowered pansies, are shorter-lived. Some of the larger pansies have huge, scented, velvety flowers with 'faces' of a different colour.
LOCATION: Moderate sunlight.
CULTIVATION: Sow under glass in early spring or outdoors in May and June. Late blooming of most varieties can be obtained by midsummer sowing. Young plantlets will normally overwinter successfully. Good rich soil and careful dead-heading will ensure long and rich blooming seasons.
PROPAGATION: Cuttings taken in August.

Wax Flower see **Hoya**
Winter Aconite see **Eranthis**

Viola

Foliage plants

Adiantum (Maidenhair Fern)
Many species of maidenhair are similar in appearance, having wiry black leaf stalks growing from a quickly spreading horizontal rhizome. Some species grow to a height of 45cm (18in), though most types are under 30cm (12in) high. The leaf stalks carry many-branched fronds of delicate fan-shaped pinnae which are pale green in colour. In mature plants the undersides of the pinnae are edged with brown sori (clusters of sporangia), giving extra colour to the fern. There is a reddish-brown variety, *A. hispidulum*, which is not as branched as the other maidenhairs and with longer pinnae.
LOCATION: A north- or east-facing window sill is ideal. Direct sunlight and dark corners should be equally avoided.
CULTIVATION: This is a fairly easy fern to grow when a humid atmosphere is provided. A daily fine spray with tepid water is desirable, or plunge the pot in a peat-filled container. The best mixture is well-drained leaf mould or a peat-moss base.
PROPAGATION: Easily divided by cutting the rhizome into pieces, each with a few fronds and roots.

Aralia see **Fatsia**
Artillery Plant see **Pilea**

Asparagus plumosus (Asparagus Fern)
These delicate fern-like plants make very effective pot plants and with their finely divided lacy foliage are most welcome additions to mixed containers. A trailing variety is also available, *A. sprengeri*; it is excellent for hanging baskets.
LOCATION: Warm conservatory in a light position but shaded from direct sunlight.
CULTIVATION: A well-drained loam-based mixture fed every two weeks, and well-watered in spring and summer and kept just moist in winter.
PROPAGATION: From seed or by root division in spring.

Aspidistra elatior (Cast Iron Plant)
Long lanceolate leaves up to 50cm (20in) in length produced on short stalks emerging from the soil are the signature of this favourite houseplant of the Victorians. The leaves are green and coarse in appearance; there is a rarer variegated form.
LOCATION: In shade.
CULTIVATION: This plant is very easy to care for but the loam-based mixture must not become soggy, and leaves should be cleaned occasionally with a sponge moistened in water.
PROPAGATION: By division of older clumps, potting into a rich loam-based mixture at almost any time.

Baby's Tears see **Helxine**

Begonia rex
A kaleidoscope of colours can be found blended in the green wrinkled leaves—red, pink, silver, cream, grey, lavender and maroon may all appear.
LOCATION: Window ledges and in mixed arrangements in reasonably light position avoiding strong sunlight.
CULTIVATION: A peaty, open, soil is essential which must be kept moist but never soggy. Mildew on leaves is one of the most troublesome problems of this plant and usually occurs in dark and airless conditions. A buoyant humid atmosphere is needed. Do not drop water on the leaves.
PROPAGATION: By rooting leaves in sand and peat mixture.

Burning Bush see **Kochia scoparia tricophylia**
Button Fern see **Pellaea**

Calathea (Peacock Plant)
Exotically-coloured and patterned leaves in many shades of green and brown make this a most striking plant. Many species are available.
LOCATION: Moist and shaded conditions in temperatures of at least 13°C (55°F).
CULTIVATION: Water and spray often, ideally with rainwater. These are fairly difficult plants to raise in the home as the minimum temperature must be maintained. An open, peaty soil must be used and the mixture must be neither too moist nor too damp.
PROPAGATION: By division of rhizomes in summer.

Cast Iron Plant see **Aspidistra elatior**
Castor Oil Plant see **Ricinus**

Chamaedorea elegans (Parlour Palm or Neanthe bella)
These small palms are extremely easy to grow. With light feathery foliage they are natural miniature palms ideal for smaller rooms, bottle and dish gardens.
LOCATION: Light shade.
CULTIVATION: Small pots of open mixture are ideal in reasonable warmth.
PROPAGATION. By seed sown in peat beds and kept at temperatures of no less than 21°C (70°F), then potted on into individual small pots when formed.

Chlorophytum elatum (Spider Plant)
A colourful green and cream-striped plant which is very easy to grow in the home. It is grass-like in appearance with long spikes of leaves and attractive formation of small plantlets formed on stalks.
LOCATION: Light window sill.
CULTIVATION: Ample watering in spring and summer, a weekly feed in summer and annual potting-on in March and April using a loam-based soil.
PROPAGATION: By pegging plantlets in pots of soil until they root, at which time the stalk can be severed.

Cissus (Kangaroo Vine)
A natural climber or trailer, *C. antarctica,* the Kangaroo vine has shining green leaves with markedly toothed edges. Stems are stiff and green. *C. rhombifolia*, the grape ivy, is reddish with leaves that are silvery-pink at first, changing to green.
LOCATION: Cool, light shade.
CULTIVATION: Keep the roots moist in good loamy soil and position where it will be able to climb. Feed weekly in summer but keep on dry side in winter.
PROPAGATION: From cuttings.

Cocos nucifera (Coconut Palm)
These plants grow to 27–30m (90–100ft) tall in their natural habitat but can be restricted in containers to reasonable size. They are very slow-growing. Foliage has quite an erect habit, with dark green arching leaves, silvery-grey beneath.
LOCATION: Light shade.
CULTIVATION: Pot in a well-drained soil and avoid cold temperatures. Leaves will enjoy an occasional sponging. Feed moderately in growing season.
PROPAGATION: By division, suckers or seed.

Codiaeum (Croton, or Joseph's Coat)
These are challenging plants to grow. They are available in many shades of orange, red, yellow, white, cream and purple-black. Some plants have all these colours in a single shiny leaf. New leaves are green and turn different colours as they grow older.
LOCATION: Maximum sunlight with care against scorching. A warm room with good filtered light and care against draughts should be ideal.
CULTIVATION: These plants should have a constantly moist, loamy mixture. They are best plunged in their pots into peat-filled or sandy containers to maintain humidity. Feed once every week during summer, established plants should have at least double the manufacturer's recommended dosage. Do not allow temperature to drop below 15°C (60°F). Sponge leaves every two weeks.
PROPAGATION: By cuttings from top growth.

Coleus (Variegated Dead-Nettle or Painted Leaf)
These brilliantly-coloured plants appear in an almost infinite variety of combinations of purple, red, bronze, yellow and white.
LOCATION: Good light and reasonable warmth indoors or shelter outdoors in mild climate for the hardier varieties. East or west windows are ideal indoors in autumn and winter.
CULTIVATION: Pinch out the insignificant flowers for bushy growth. Do not allow them to dry out completely. They should be planted in good rich loamy soil and fed weekly.
PROPAGATION: From August cuttings, or seed sown in early spring.

Cordyline
These palm-like shrubs, often confused with dracaenas, appear in many varieties. The durable *C. indivisa* has long narrow leaves, green with red or yellow midribs, arising from a single unbranched trunk up to 1.2m (4ft) tall. More ornamental and more tender is *C. terminalis* which has sword-shaped leaves that are deep green in young plants but which mature to brilliant red, purple, cream, bronze or pink according to variety.
LOCATION: Good light will preserve the colouration.
CULTIVATION: Loam or proprietary peat mixture kept moist but avoiding extremes of wet and dry is best. Soft rainwater is advisable for watering. *C. indivisa* will endure cool temperatures, but *C. terminalis* must have at least 13°C (55°F) in winter.
PROPAGATION: Cuttings of the thicker fleshy roots in May and June.

Creeping Fig see **Ficus**
Croton see **Codiaeum**

Cyperus (Umbrella Grass)
The cyperus develops a grass-like growth at the top of long slender stems, giving it an umbrella-like appearance. Stalks of some species grow to 2–2.4m (6–8ft) tall. A compact variety, *C. diffusus* will not exceed 25cm (10in) in height.
LOCATION: Light shade or light avoiding direct sunlight.

Cyperus

Dieffenbachia

CULTIVATION: The loamy mixture must be kept permanently wet, it is usually advisable to allow the pot to stand in water. Maintain a moderate temperature at all times.

PROPAGATION: By dividing mature clumps or from seed.

Dieffenbachia (Dumb Cane)
Few species of this family are suited to other than warm greenhouse conditions. Among those that will survive in the home is *D. picta* 'Exotica', an impressive plant which has a compact habit and variegated leaves. As plants age, typical arum inflorescences are produced from the topmost leaf axils, but these should be removed. The sap of the dieffenbachia contains a poison that could render one speechless if enough of it were to find its way to the tongue. Wash hands carefully after cutting. There are varieties ranging from white-spotted yellow leaves edged with green, to green leaves with white spots. Size ranges from dwarf to 1.5m (5ft) or more.

LOCATION: Warm and moist shaded positions protected from draughts.

CULTIVATION: Warmth is essential and moderate watering. It is advisable to water these thoroughly by plunging and then allow them to almost dry out before the next watering. They grow best in rich, loamy soil.

PROPAGATION: By removing young plants from around the base of the stem or by cutting the main stem into 5cm (2in) sections and then partly burying them in moist peat in a warm propagator.

Dracaena
With the exception of the lower-growing *D. godseffiana* 'Florida Beauty' these are erect plants of superb and varied appearance. *D. marginata* has green, narrow, rigid leaves with a faint red margin and is one of the easiest varieties to care for. There are many forms of *D. deremensis*, all with boldly striped leaves on stems that attain a height of 2.4m (8ft) in ideal conditions. Forms of *D. fragrans* have broader leaves that become longer and more curved as the plant develops.

LOCATION: Light shade and reasonable warmth.

CULTIVATION: Rich loam, warmth and watering very sparingly will be ideal for this plant.

PROPAGATION: Simplest is to cut stems into sections and partially bury them horizontally in peat and sand mixture. *D. godseffiana* is propagated from top cuttings with three of four leaves attached.

Dumb Cane see Dieffenbachia

Euonymus (Spindle Tree)
The golden form of this hardy plant will flourish indoors in proper conditions. The best variety is *E. japonica* 'Aurea' with golden-yellow glossy ovate leaves. There are also silver and gold-bordered varieties.

LOCATION: Light window sill and in a cool, well-ventilated room. Avoid direct sunlight.

CULTIVATION: Water carefully and avoid excess. Feed moderately. To retain variegation, all green growth must be removed as it appears. Most good soil mixes will support this plant.

PROPAGATION: Cuttings taken in spring or summer.

Fatshedera
Attractive, five-lobed, green leaves are borne on erect stems that become woody with age. These plants will climb and wander in any direction towards which they are trained. They can reach heights of 2.4m (8ft).

LOCATION: Cool, lightly shaded positions. These are perfect plants for staircases and balconies where they can wander.

CULTIVATION: Grow in a rich, loam-based mixture. Pot on annually in March. A stake for support is essential and leading growth can be tied to point in the desired direction. Keep moist.

PROPAGATION: From cuttings taken in July and August of either the top section or from single leaves with some stem attached.

Fatsia
Large palmate leaves of this plant are glossy green in colour and form compact, quick-growing plants. These are extremely attractive additions to mixed arrangements. Plants can reach a height of 2.4m (8ft).

LOCATION: Cool and light indoors, or in window boxes or containers, in shade, outdoors.

CULTIVATION: Avoid dark and stuffy conditions. Ordinary soil mix will suffice with ample watering and humidity.

PROPAGATION: Raised from seed sown in spring, or by removing rooted suckers.

Ficus (Fig)
The many species of this large genus are extremely varied and require somewhat different conditions. *F. benjamina*, the 'Weeping Fig', is a graceful indoor tree with glossy green leaves that grow into architectural shapes. *F. lyrata*, the 'Fiddle-back Fig' also develops into tree size in time. It has glossy leaves that are shaped like a body of the violin. These are somewhat difficult to raise in the home. *F. diversifolia* is slower growing. It takes years to grow into a smallish bush. Small berries, however, appear on even the smallest of these attractive plants. *F. pumila*, commonly called the 'Creeping Fig', has a prostrate habit and small green oval leaves on thin, wiry, trailing stems. *F. radicans* 'Variegata' is similar in habit, with slightly more pointed leaves that are white and green variegated.

LOCATION: All figs enjoy moist and shaded conditions.

CULTIVATION: Watering and feeding must be regular but moderate, keeping the mixture slightly moist. A winter night temperature of approximately 13°C (55°F) is necessary for best results.

PROPAGATION: Some can be raised from seed, but most varieties will grow from cuttings taken between April and June, either from the top of the plant or from leaf with some stem.

Ficus elastica (Rubber Plant)
This is the most common member of the fig genus appearing in the home. *F. elastica* has the large glossy leaves growing from tall erect stems which are such a familiar sight.

LOCATION: Light, warm position.

CULTIVATION: Keep warm in winter, especially at night. Water moderately, allowing a slight drying out before the next application. Feeding must also be moderate. When potting on the plants, the new pot should be only slightly larger than the old one, and the need to repot should only arise every second year, unless growth is uncommonly vigorous. Clean leaves with a soft damp cloth occasionally.

PROPAGATION: Cuttings taken between April and June from leaves with a little stem attached.

Fittonia (Snakeskin Plant)
Both *F. verschaffeltii*, with red-veined oval leaves and a creeping habit, and *F. argyroneura* with ivory-veined leaves of similar shape, are difficult plants to care for. A miniature variety of the latter, however, is much more tolerant. It has silvery leaves.

LOCATION: Out of direct sunlight in moderate warmth.

CULTIVATION: The miniature variety is fairly tolerant

of room temperatures. All varieties must have constant warmth and high humidity if they are to be happy. A peaty mixture should be used.

PROPAGATION: The simplest method is to place a small plant in the centre of a pot of moist peat and to allow the plant to grow over the peat and root into the medium as it does so. When rooted, the pieces can be snipped off and potted up individually in peaty mixture.

Geraniums see **Pelargonium** (Flowering Plants)
Goose-Foot Plant see **Syngonium**
Grape Ivy see **Cissus**
Hare's Foot Fern see **Polypodium aureum**

Hedera (Ivy)

There are countless varieties to choose from in shades ranging from glossy dark green to almost white. *H. canariensis* 'Variegata' has white and green variegation. There is a mottle-leaved 'Maculata' and a large green-leaved variety with pale yellow centres, 'Gold Leaf'. *H. helix* is a smaller leaved ivy much in demand for mixed arrangements. All are naturally trailing or climbing.

LOCATION: All varieties will tolerate lightly shaded conditions. Most enjoy moist and cool atmosphere. In all cases avoid hot and stuffy rooms. Outdoors, either sun or shade is suitable depending on type. In dense shade the colour is usually lost in variegated varieties.

CULTIVATION: A peaty mixture kept reasonably moist and cool is the most desirable although many ivies will be happy in full sun. All will train to trail or climb.

PROPAGATION: Cuttings will root easily in a peaty mixture.

Helxine (Mind Your Own Business or Baby's Tears)

The tiny leaves of helxine will spread quickly and form neat mounds of brilliant green that can be used to carpet large pots or to provide a low splash of colour on a window sill.

LOCATION. Good light.

CULTIVATION: Tolerant of most conditions other than dark, excessively hot positions. Keep moist and make new plants periodically, disposing of the old ones.

PROPAGATION: Root minute pieces broken from clumps.

Howea see **Kentia**
Ivy see **Hedera**
Kangaroo Vine see **Cissus**

Kentia (Howea)

This palm is found in two main species. *K. forsteriana* has leaves of a rich dark green. It has a more erect habit than *K. belmoreana* which, as it ages, adopts an attractive drooping appearance as the midriff of the leaf arches. *K. forsteriana* is more suitable for indoor growth.

LOCATION: Light shade.

CULTIVATION: Reasonable warmth, moisture and firm potting in a well-drained soil are necessary. The addition of coarse leafmould to standard potting mixture will help plants grow more freely indoors.

PROPAGATION: From seed.

Laurus (Green Bay or Sweet Bay)

This evergreen is both a culinary herb and a very decorative shrub with glossy green lance-shaped leaves. It is extremely tolerant and can be clipped to a pyramid shape or as a mop-headed standard.

LOCATION: Plenty of sunshine is best although it will survive in some shade. It should be moved outdoors in summer. Avoid stuffy rooms.

CULTIVATION: Never allow these shrubs to dry out completely in containers. If grown in large tubs they

Laurus

may grow quite quickly and need periodical snipping back. They are subject to frost damage in cold districts and so if grown in a patio they should be taken indoors in the North and kept in a cool place. Trim to shape during summer.

PROPAGATION: By cuttings.

Maidenhair Fern see **Adiantum**

Maranta (Prayer Plant)

The most striking variety of this plant is *M. leuconeura* 'Kerchoveana'. Its grey-green leaves have dark blotches. The broad oval leaves close as darkness falls and open at first sign of morning light. 'Erythrophylla' has reddish-brown colouring and intricately marked leaves in a herringbone design.

LOCATION: These plants need warm, moist and shaded positions.

CULTIVATION: All marantas require a peaty soil and do best in shallow pots plunged to their rims in moist peat. They are rapid growers and need regular potting on. The 'Erythrophylla' variety is the more tolerant of indoor conditions. Pruning to shape is best done in summer months. Regular spraying of leaves is advisable.

PROPAGATION: From cuttings or division.

Mimosa pudica (Sensitive Plant)

This summer-flowering, sub-shrub is grown for its acutely sensitive ferny leaves and pink blooms. When the midrib of the leaves is touched in daytime they react by drooping, recovering after a few minutes.

LOCATION: Good light and moist atmosphere shaded from hot sun.

CULTIVATION: These plants need a loam-based soil, free watering and weekly feeding during the growing season. Give them plenty of air if temperatures are too warm and syringe pots to provide humidity.

PROPAGATION: By seed sown in February and March.

Mind Your Own Business see **Helxine**

Monstera (Swiss Cheese Plant)

M. deliciosa has rich, green, glossy leaves that grow to enormous size. They are deeply serrated along their margins and have natural perforations. Aerial roots grow from the main stem. Inflorescences are creamy and the spadix develops into an edible fruit.

LOCATION: Shaded from the sun and reasonably warm.

CULTIVATION: Monsteras like moisture and a potting mixture composed of equal parts loam and sphagnum peat or clean leafmould. Aerial roots can be directed back into the pot or into a container of water from which it will draw, reducing the need for too-frequent watering of the root pot. Mature leaves should be cleaned occasionally.

PROPAGATION: By removing the growing tip with one mature leaf and rooting it, or from seed.

Mother-in-Law's Tongue see **Sansevieria**
Neanthe Bella see **Chamaedorea elegans**
Parlour Palm see **Chamaedorea elegans**
Peacock Plant see **Calathea**

Pellaea (Button Fern)

The brown hairy scales of *P. rotundifolia* cover a wiry petiole and rachis which has about 20 pairs of alternately spaced dark green, leathery leaves. Fronds up to 10cm (4in) long form a low-spreading mat. *P. viridis* is more upright and bushy with fronds growing to 75cm (2½ft). Rachises are green when young, changing to shiny black with age. Leaves are bright green and spear-shaped.

LOCATION: Fairly tolerant, the pellaea does well under the lower intensities of fluorescent lighting. A window sill facing north or east is the perfect position in the home.
CULTIVATION: This plant is able to utilise any humidity available from surrounding peat-based potting mixes. Useful as temporary ground covering, these plants are excellent spreaders. They need a fairly warm minimum temperature.
PROPAGATION: By spores or by division.

Pellionia
These are prostrate, creeping plants with small and multicoloured leaves in unusual combinations of shades of edging and veining.
LOCATION: Light shade.
CULTIVATION: A minimum amount of fertilizer will give the leaves even brighter colours. Plants root easily into peat, gravel or any other loose surface over which they can wander. They need warmth and careful watering.
PROPAGATION: Rooted pieces cut from the parent plant.

Peperomia
The most popular peperomias are varieties of *P. magnoliaefolia* which has a compact habit and thick, fleshy leaves of attractive cream and green in the variegated form. Similar in colour is the trailer, *P. glabella* 'Variegata' which has small, light green and white leaves. The larger *P. obtusifolia*, has purplish-green leaves. Many combinations of colour and leaf-shape are available.
LOCATION: Reasonably light position out of direct sunlight.
CULTIVATION: Keep the mixture towards the dry side. Provide a humid atmosphere from April to September, syringing the leaves twice a day when the weather is hot. All perperomias do well in a soilless or very peaty mixture.
PROPAGATION: From top cuttings with two or three leaves attached, or from leaf with stem attached taken in April to August.

Philodendron scandens (Sweetheart Plant)
This favourite houseplant has small heart-shaped leaves which can be trained to climb or to trail. They are light green when young and darker when mature. All are glossy.
LOCATION: Warm, light, moist conditions, shaded from hot sun.
CULTIVATION: All philodendrons will appreciate the maximum humidity and thrive with pots plunged into peat-filled containers. Regular syringing would also be beneficial. If trained as climbers, a thick layer of sphagnum moss can be wired to the supporting stake to provide additional moisture through aerial roots. Pot soil should never be allowed to remain too wet, it is best composed of a peaty mixture.
PROPAGATION: From individual leaves with some stem attached.

Phoenix Palm
P. canariensis and *P. robelenii* (the most popular type for growing indoors) are members of this family which includes the commercial date palm of North Africa. These are slow-growing plants with stiff leaves and robust appearance.
LOCATION: Light but sheltered.
CULTIVATION: Avoid saturating the potting mixture. Good drainage is the principal requirement and a rich potting mix is necessary.
PROPAGATION: From seed.

Pilea (Artillery Plant or Aluminium Plant)
P. muscosa has pale to mid-green leaves and inconspicuous tufts of yellow-green flowers. It has a bushy growth to 28cm (11in) tall. *P. cadierei* (the Aluminium Plant) is the most popular and easiest to care for of pileas. It has dark green, oblong leaves with silvery markings. It grows to a bushy 23cm (9in) tall.
LOCATION: Out of direct sunlight.
CULTIVATION: Regular feeding and pinching out of leading shoots will keep these plants colourful and compact. Replace old, overgrown plants with freshly-rooted ones occasionally. Keep moderately warm and humid. Water regularly.
PROPAGATION: Easily from cuttings. Some varieties will seed themselves.

Pittosporum
Many types of pittosporum are available, most with glossy green foliage. There are some variegated forms and others with undulating leaf margins. All form into small, slow-growing shrubs.
LOCATION: Tolerant of position but best in a light location out of direct sunlight.
CULTIVATION: Pots of good loam in moderate temperatures will give best results. Spray leaves occasionally.
PROPAGATION: Cuttings taken in July from half-ripe lateral shoots inserted in a propagating frame.

Platycerium (Stag Horn Fern)
These are unlike any other fern in appearance. Sterile fronds are wavy-edged, fan-shaped, pale-green in colour and grow from a very short rhizome. With age they enlarge and, in nature, grip a tree trunk or branch, making a firm anchor for the fern, growing frond over frond so that the originals rot to provide food for the successors. The fertile fronds are a darker green but appear greyish because they are covered by fine white hairs. Sori form large brown patches on the underside of the antler-like tips.
LOCATION: A window sill facing north or east.
CULTIVATION: A stag horn may be grown in a pot or attached to bark padded with sphagnum moss. In either case the sterile fronds will cover the holder in time. It should be watered by immersing the pot or bark periodically, preferably in rainwater. Do not handle, or the beautiful velvety appearance of the fronds will be spoilt.
PROPAGATION: By spores.

Polypodium aureum (Rabbit's or Hare's Foot Fern)
Good specimens grow to 1m (3¼ft) tall. The frond has a light green petiole turning brown with age, a blue- to yellow-green blade made of single and opposite pinnae, each up to 13cm (5in) long, some having wavy edges. Each frond arises from a thick silver-to-brown, furry rhizome that will creep over the surface and follow the contour of a container. Dead fronds drop away, leaving a scar on the rhizome shaped rather like a small footprint.
LOCATION: A window sill facing north or east.
CULTIVATION: Daily spraying, moist but well-drained soil. A potting mixture of one part sterilized leaf mould to one part sterilized loam and one part gritty sand plus small pieces of charcoal will keep this plant healthy. Regular weak liquid feeding every two weeks during the growing season will also be helpful.
PROPAGATION: By division of the rhizome or by spores.

Prayer plant see **Maranta**
Rhoicissus rhomboidea see **Cissus**

Phoenix palm

Sansevieria (Mother-in-law's Tongue)

Erect, sword-like leaves of dark green with mottled grey bands make these a startling addition to mixed arrangements or very sculptural shapes when used alone. The leaves of *S. trifasciata* grow to 45cm (18in) high. *S.t.* 'Laurentii' has creamy margins to the leaves.

LOCATION: Full sun.

CULTIVATION: Sansevierias need a loam-based soil mixture which should be allowed to dry out completely between waterings. Keep them dry in winter. Feed established plants every three or four months during the growing season.

PROPAGATION: By leaf cuttings or by dividing the rhizome.

Scindapsus

These plants have heart-shaped leaves attractively variegated with green and cream.

LOCATION: Shaded in summer, well-lit in winter.

CULTIVATION: Warmth and moisture are essential. A peaty mixture is preferred. A mossy support for the climbers will also be beneficial.

PROPAGATION: From individual leaves with some stem attached.

Snakeskin Plant see **Fittonia**
Spider Plant see **Chlorophytum elatum**
Spindle Tree see **Euonymus**
Stag Horn Fern see **Platycerium**
Summer Cypress see **Kochia**
Sweetheart Plant see **Philodendron**
Swiss Cheese Plant see **Monstera deliciosa**

Syngonium (Goose Foot Plant)

These plants have large, glossy green leaves resembling in shape the imprint of a goose foot. Young plants have single, dark green leaves with silvery markings. These later develop into three unequal lobes and then eventually up to eleven, entirely green leaflets appear in a fan-shape.

LOCATION: Bright but indirect light is preferable although can also flourish in shade.

CULTIVATION: These are best grown in a loam-based mixture kept barely moist. Keep leaves clean and give support if necessary. Avoid fluctuating temperatures.

PROPAGATION: From stem cuttings with two leaves attached rooted in a warm propagator.

Syngonium

Tradescantia (Wandering Jew)

Most varieties of this popular trailer are extremely easy to care for. The ovate leaves, closely set on the trailing stems, are striped in various colours. The flowers are three-petalled and basically triangular in shape.

LOCATION: Best in hanging baskets in light and airy conditions. Avoid blazing sun.

CULTIVATION: Moderate temperatures are best. These trailers will prefer a pebbly mixture and will need generous watering. They can also be grown in water.

PROPAGATION: Put several pieces in a small pot and remove growing tips to encourage bushy growth.

Umbrella Grass see **Cyperus**
Wandering Jew see **Tradescantia** and **Zebrina pendula**

Zebrina pendula (Wandering Jew)

The zebrina is a superbly-coloured plant with vivid purple on the underside of the leaves and a rich green, purple or silvery colouring on the upper surface.

LOCATION: As in tradescantia.

CULTIVATION: As in tradescantia.

PROPAGATION: As in tradescantia.

Bromeliads

As most bromeliads share the same needs and require similar location and cultivation, the following information about growth and care of these indoor plants will be suitable for all bromeliads described in this section except where specifically indicated.

LOCATION: All bromeliads will need good light positions, although direct sunlight should be avoided. They are generally best positioned where sun shines through curtains or through the leaves of other plants.

CULTIVATION: Bromeliads need a good deal of heat—up to 29°C (85°F) to bring young plants to flower, but after this they may be maintained at a normal living room temperature. In the winter temperatures may be allowed to drop to 10°C (50°F) for short times, providing that the soil is kept just moist, but they survive better in the regions of 15°C (60°F). Keep the central vase that is typical of all bromeliads topped up with tepid water. Pots should be smallish for the size of the plant and just enough to balance them. The root system is very small. Occasional feeding during late summer will be beneficial. They need a light soil.

PROPAGATION: From offsets detatched from the parent plant when they are at least 15cm (6in) high, or if they have been growing for several months. Remove, with roots, from the parent plant and pot, keeping them warm, until they establish. When potting, do not bury the crown but cover the roots. Keep the mixture moist and shaded until well-established.

Aechmea (Urn Plant)

The aechmea most commonly grown as a houseplant is *A. fasciata*, a handsome variety with narrow, silvery grey-green leaves cross-banded with white. It has a bright, rose-pink, cone-shaped flowerhead whose flowers, blue at first, appear in summer. The flowerhead lasts for several months, though each flower dies after a few days. The plant may be as high as 60cm (2ft) and at least 30cm (1ft) wide.

Ananas (Pineapple)

A. comosus, the pineapple, is a terrestrial bromeliad which is a most attractive foliage houseplant. The 'Variegatus' variety has narrow, prickly-edged leaves formed into a rosette and striped longitudinally in creamy white, flushed pink. The centre turns rose-pink at flowering time in the summer. The whole plant grows to 1m (1yd) wide and high.

Cryptanthus (Earth Star or Starfish Bromeliad)

The cryptanthus are mostly rather low-growing and their central vase is almost none existent. They make excellent foliage houseplants and, because of their dwarf habits, are also suitable for bottle gardens. The colour alters according to the intensity of the light in which they are grown. One variety with two, cream-coloured, longitudinal stripes on an olive-green background will flush with deep pink in strong light. Another variety with horizontal banding of whitish-grey and copper-brown will appear only dark and light green in dull light. The 'Tricolour' variety has light green leaves broadly edged with cream, flushing to pink and is a more upright variety than the other two, about 30cm (1ft) wide and high.

Neoregelia

These bromeliads are found in the rain forests, but because of the leathery nature of their leaves they will stand a dry atmosphere. The 'Tricolour' variety, *N. carolinae*, is one of the most popular, with outer green leaves centred with yellow or white, the inner pink leaves with pinkish red. The flower-head is bright red with violet flowers, but it stays within the rosette which can be as much as 40cm (16in) wide. The flower does not grow on a stem. Flowering is in late spring and summer. *N. concentrica* has broader leaves 10cm (4in) wide and 30cm (12in) long. They are purple-blotched. The bracts are purple and blue flowers appear in the centre on a kind of pincushion.

Nidularium

These are very like the neoregelias in appearance, but their cultural treatment is different. They need more shade and humidity and higher temperatures to produce flowers. The flower heads do not emerge from the rosette but remain compact so that the flowers appear on a mound in the water in the vase. *N. innocenta* has dark red to almost purple-black leaves with flower bracts in autumn of orange to copper-coloured with white flowers sitting on top.

Pineapple see **Ananas**
Starfish Bromeliad see **Cryptanthus**
Urn Plant see **Aechmea**

Vriesia

The leaves of these plants are thick and shining green, often cross-banded in a darker colour. *V. splendens* (Flaming Sword) has a long, flattened, bright red flower spike about 60cm (2ft) high with yellow flowers. The dark green leaves have purple bands. *V. gigantea* has 45cm (18in) long leaves with yellowish-green tessellated markings on the upper side, dark on the under-surface. The whole plant can be 2m (6ft) tall. *V. psittacina* is small with yellowish-green leaves 20cm (8in) long and a feathery flowerhead with red bracts and yellow flowers in July. These plants grow best in a steamy atmosphere of 18–21°C (64–70°F).

Cacti and succulents

CACTI

Chamaecereus (Peanut Cactus)
C. silvestrii is very easily grown, with finger-like curving stems 2.5–8cm (1–3in) long., lying flat on the soil. Bright red, open flowers of about 2.5cm (1in) in diameter appear in May, sitting directly on the stem.
LOCATION: Full sun.
CULTIVATION: Rest this cactus in winter and keep cold without watering for profuse flowering in spring. Start watering in March.
PROPAGATION: Stems will root readily as long as the base is in contact with the soil mix.

Epiphyllum (Orchid or Water-lily Cactus)
This family produces beautiful flowers in late spring or early summer. Some hybrids also flower in autumn. These blooms can be 15cm (6in) long and as much wide, in open trumpet-shape, mostly in shades of red or pink but magenta, purple, white and yellow are also seen. The centre consists of long cream-coloured stamens and some flowers, especially the yellow and white hybrids, are also fragrant. The stalkless flower buds are produced directly from the edges of the leaf-like stems. Each flower lasts three or four days. Epiphyllum can grow to 1m (3ft) tall and need support. The flattened stems are about 5cm (2in) wide with pronounced dark green segments or pads. Stems will carry flowerbuds when two years old.
LOCATION. This cactus will need some shade and fresh air.
CULTIVATION: Rest these plants in winter, after the second flush of bloom and for a short time in early summer after the first flush. Potting mix should be rich in humus. Keep out of intense heat in summer. Water frequently, preferably with rainwater or soft water in the growing season. A little humidity should be provided.
PROPAGATION: From seed or from cuttings 15–30cm (6–12in) long.

Orchid Cactus see **Epiphyllum**

Parodia
These globular cacti are small and slow growing reaching 5cm (2in) tall. The parodias are usually grown for their spines, which appear in a number of colours— yellow, white and brown, and their small funnel-shaped flowers in yellow, brown red and apricot.
LOCATION: Full sun.
CULTIVATION: Parodias are very prone to root rot, so water very carefully.
PROPAGATION: From seeds or offsets.

Peanut Cactus see **Chamaecereus**

Rebutia
These are marvellous flowering cacti, freely producing their trumpet-shaped blooms when only a few years old. Flowers appear near the base of the plant, almost covering it in spring with yellow, red, lilac, salmon pink, orange or white blooms. Rebutia are small, rounded plants producing many offsets. It is not ribbed and has few spines.
LOCATION: Good direct light in summer.
CULTIVATION: These plants should be given virtually no heat or water in winter.
PROPAGATION: Offsets or seed.

Rhipsalidopsis (Easter Cactus)
This may be sold under former names of *Schlumbergera gaertneri* or *Zygocactus gaertneri*. This is one of the hanging cacti with flattened leaf stems about 1cm (½in) wide, segmented into dull green pads. New growth appears from the tips of the end pad, as do the flower buds. A well-grown plant may be 45cm (18in) high and just as wide. Flowers are trumpet-shaped and pendant with narrow, pointed red and purple petals appearing in April and May.
LOCATION: Light or sunny position to flower.
CULTIVATION: The Easter cactus rests from autumn to late winter then begins to push out new flower buds; after flowering it grows new pads during summer on which next year's flowers will appear.
PROPAGATION: From seed or stem cuttings.

Neoregelia

Schlumbergera (Christmas Cactus)

This may be sold under the former name of *Zygocactus truncatus*. Flowering can be between October and late January but it will only form buds if subjected to short days. The drooping, narrow, trumpet-shaped flowers grow up to 8cm (3in) long in magenta or rose pink.

LOCATION: Full sun in flowering season.

CULTIVATION: Do not subject this plant to artificial light in autumn and early winter. Keep it in warm darkness during the evenings. This plant rests from late winter until late spring then starts to grow again. Do not water from September until November except for a light spray every two weeks. Warmth will encourage flowering.

PROPAGATION: From cuttings taken just below a joint which should be allowed to dry and form a callus at the cut end before placing in damp, sandy potting mix to a depth of 1cm (½in).

OTHER SUCCULENTS

Agave (Century Plant)

This succulent is a rosette of fleshy, pointed leaves sitting close against the soil. From its centre it produces a flowering stem when the plant reaches maturity. This can be at the age of 500. The stem grows up to 7.5m (25ft) tall as in the *A. americana* whose spiny leaves can be as long as 2m (6ft). In a container, however, these plants do not grow so tall, usually about 1.2m (4ft) tall, and are unlikely to flower. *A. victoriae reginae* is easier to grow in the home, reaching a width of 50cm (20in) and height of 15cm (6in). Its fleshy leaves are edged with dull green.

LOCATION: Light and airy.

CULTIVATION: This plant requires a minimum temperature of 10°C (50°F). They need more water than most succulents in the summer, but require little watering in winter.

PROPAGATION: From offsets or seed.

Aloe

Of the many species in this large genus, the 'Partridge-Breasted Aloe', *A. variegata*, is the most popular. It has a dark green rosette of leaves arranged in overlapping ranks, variegated with white horizontal bands with light red flowers in a loose spike 30cm (12in) tall in spring. The plant is usually about 10cm (4in) wide.

LOCATION: Light and airy.

CULTIVATION: This plant is best kept dry in winter.

PROPAGATION: From seed or offsets.

Crassula

This large succulent family contains shrubs and herbaceous plants. The leaves of many are extremely attractive, and some have lovely flowers as well. *C. falcata* has grey-blue leaves in layers on a stem which grows to 60cm (2ft) tall, with a cluster of bright red flowers on the top in summer. *C. arborescens* grows to 1m (3ft) tall and has spoon-shaped, fleshy, grey-green leaves with red margins. Clusters of white starry flowers appear in May. *C. lactea* is shrubby with dark green leaves and white flowers in mid-winter.

LOCATION: Light position, outdoors in summer.

CULTIVATION: They need heat, sun and water.

PROPAGATION: By sprouting the leaves.

Echeveria

E. elegans has almost white translucent leaves on stems eventually 30cm (1ft) tall with pink flowers. *E. gibbiflora* is shrubby with blue-green leaves up to 20cm (8in) long in rosettes flushed with pink or purple. Red flowers appear in autumn. The variety *E.g. metallica* has pink-bronze leaves with a pink or red edge. *E.g. cristata* has frilled leaf margins. *E. setosa* has a flat and silvery rosette with red flowers throughout the summer. *E. secunda* and *E. glauca* are ideal, low-growing, grey-blue rosettes for bowls, shallow pans and window boxes.

LOCATION: Full sun, they can be summered outdoors.

CULTIVATION: Give a richer potting mix than usual for succulents. Keep cool, water moderately throughout the year, but keep it off the leaves. Allow the mixture to dry out slightly between watering.

PROPAGATION: From offshoots.

Kalanchoe

K. blossfeldiana 'Tom Thumb' is a small succulent with rounded fleshy leaves and clusters of bright red or yellow flowers. *K. tomentosa* has thick, furry silvery leaves edged with chocolate brown hair, growing to 75cm (2½ft) tall and producing flowers on silvery stems. Many other varieties are available.

LOCATION: Light position.

CULTIVATION: Kalanchoes are easily grown, needing a little more water in summer and more food than most succulents. They also like humidity. Feed in spring and keep dry in autumn.

PROPAGATION: From plantlets sprouted from leaf tips.

Rochea

Best known species is *R. coccinea*, a shrubby plant which grows to about 60cm (2ft) tall, with small fleshy leaves arranged in regular ranks up the stem and a head of red fragrant flowers at the top from May or June onwards. *R. jasminea* has prostrate stems and white flowers in spring.

LOCATION: Shade in summer.

CULTIVATION: Remove dead flower stems to make room for new shoots flowering later in the season. Rochea needs water all the year and a little shade in summer.

PROPAGATION: From cuttings.

Sedum

S. sieboldii has fleshy, blue-green leaves with a pale yellow or white stripe in the centre and red edges. In September it produces clusters of pink flowers but then dies down completely for the winter. *S. pachyphyllum* (Jelly Beans) grows to 30cm (12in) tall, has blue-green fleshy leaves, clubbed and red at the tips and red and yellow flowers in spring. *S. robrotinctum* is small 20cm (8in) and has small, thick, berry-like leaves which turn coppery in the sun. The yellow flowers are seldom seen.

LOCATION: Sunny, outdoors in summer.

CULTIVATION: Feeding is not required. Shallow containers and a dry potting mix are best.

PROPAGATION: From cuttings.

Stapelia

A fleshy plant with bizarre and spectacular colouring. All flowers are also fleshy. Some species are foul-smelling. Most, however, have no odour at all. *S. grandiflora* has starfish-shaped blooms 2.5cm (1in) wide, dark brown with fringed and hairy petals. *S. revoluta* can reach a height of 38cm (15in) and has purple flowers. Tiny *S. verrucosa* has saucer-shaped flowers, yellow with red spots.

LOCATION: Warm, sheltered position.

CULTIVATION: All stapelias flower in summer and rest in winter. An ordinary potting mix with extra grit is fine. A larger pot than usual will be needed, as these must have plenty of root room.

PROPAGATION: From cuttings of side shoots.

House Plants

Understanding plants

If our plants are to remain decorative for as long as possible we have to get to know and understand them. First of all we should realise that a house plant is not really any different from a garden or wild plant except in as much as we have brought it into the home. It is special because it is attractive and adaptable. A house plant is one that is grown indoors under normal living conditions.

Yet often our living conditions are not those of the plant if it were growing naturally. House plants have become such because of their adaptability—we really should call them home plants. How marvellous it is that a plant which comes from the dim, steamy jungle, can live cosily inside four walls in different climate and soil and that next to it a cactus from the hot, arid desert will bloom on a sunny kitchen windowsill.

Indoor plants vary just as much as those which grow out of doors for there are herbaceous kinds, shrubs, trees, climbers and creepers, bulbs, tubers, corms and rhizomes. There are perennials, biennials and annuals. There are evergreen and deciduous plants. There are those we prize for their foliage and others which we admire for their flowers. There are even some indoor plants we grow for their fruits. There are plants to suit us all and the different ways in which we live.

For the sake of convenience house plants are divided into two groups, temporary and permanent plants. The terms speak for themselves although one should realise that permanent needs to be taken at its hairdresser's value. Generally speaking, the temporary plants may be considered to have a life, once brought into the home, which is measured in weeks while that of the permanent plants may be measured in months or even years. We should aim for years. Fortunately many are both agreeable and adaptable.

The temporary plants are more familiar to more people than the permanent kinds. They include such flowering kinds as azaleas, cyclamen, heaths, primulas, cinerarias, the berried solanums and capsicums and the ornamental leaved coleus, the scented exacum and bromeliads. All of which have been grown with one aim; that they should be at their best when they reach the customer. It is only natural that one should want the flowers to go on as long as possible. Yet what so often happens is that from the moment the plant is brought into the home its flowers slowly but steadily decline in beauty and life. This need not happen. If we can learn

Right
Many new species of cacti are constantly being introduced, and those already familiar to cacti-lovers have become great favourites. *Parodia microsperma* shown here comes from Argentina, and is a member of a large family of cacti many of which are easy to cultivate.

Below
Cryptanthus zonatus. This is an agreeable cryptanthus (known as the Zebra plant) which lends itself to all kinds of decorative schemes. It can be grown in a pot, in mixed arrangements, used in pot-et-fleur or even fixed with other small bromeliads to a mossed branch. The leaves can grow up to 9 inches in length.

to appreciate the plant's needs we ought to be able to enjoy it to the full. Fortunately, it does not take long to get to know plants.

The four things that plants get in their early days that help them to grow and give them a good start in life are: warmth, light and humidity, steady temperature and freedom from draughts. Of these basic requirements of a healthy plant, we are normally able to supply only warmth and light. For in our homes temperatures tend to fluctuate, usually they rise to a peak in the evening and then swiftly drop during the night. We may pride ourselves on the air in our rooms being nice and dry, yet our plants need humidity. It is really surprising what plants will put up with. It is also surprising how easy it is to give them what they need. It so happens, as we shall see, that in making a plant comfortable, in ensuring that it shall live as long as possible, we also make it more decorative. It settles in more attractively. It becomes part of the environment.

As you would expect, those plants which are most popular, most often seen, are the toughest. The same goes for those which have been around for a long time such as aspidistras, palms of many kinds, rubber plants and ivies. If you see the same kind of plant growing well under many different conditions it follows that this is an easy type and if you are new to house plants you would do well to get one like it.

Indoor plants are rather like pets. They have different habits, different needs, according to their kind. You will get to know a plant as you would get to know a pet. For instance, one kind of plant may need watering just

The sansevieria, tough and
adaptable, will live for years. It
is highly decorative and
provides splendid contrasts of
colour, texture and shape to
groups and arrangements,
demonstrated here in a group
which includes a scindapsus,
Pelargonium crispum and
peperomias.

once a week, but should it stand in a very sunny, well ventilated yet warm room, it may sometimes need watering every day. It is important for the new indoor gardener to realize that he or she is very much in command. Mostly, someone who cannot see either the plant or its setting can do no more than generalize.

Fortunately, there are a few plants which are so tough, so house or home-hardy, that it is possible to give fairly precise directions for certain aspects of their care. These ensure that the plants live. Whether they thrive, flourish and even flower is in the hands of the plant owner.

Among these easy-going types are some in a family known as bromeliads. The pineapple is a typical, though tall, member and because a bromeliad other plants belonging to this family are known as room pines. While it is possible to grow an ordinary pine-apple indoors and even to have it bear fruit, it is the lovely variegated forms which are most often seen.

Possibly the best known of the family is *Aechmea fasciata* the Greek vase or urn plant. The vernacular name comes from the shape of the plant, the bases of its leaves overlap and form a vase in which water will remain. This reservoir is a characteristic of bromeliads. Some have a more pronounced vessel than others but it is effective all the same. In the wild state and growing on trees, the plants trap their water this way. In the home, where they are mostly grown in pots of soil they can still take their water this way though it is also possible to grow them on wood. It is comforting to know that all you have to do is to keep the centres filled with water.

There are several species and varieties of bromeliads on sale and it is possible gradually to make a collection. Cryptanthus species are flatter and more star-like than the tall aechmeas. Vriesia and neoregelia come between the two. All have strange, handsome markings and some are vividly coloured with brilliant reds and coral pinks. They produce odd, and tiny or conspicuous and strangely beautiful flowers. They look so wonderfully exotic that it is hard to believe that they really are easy – but they are. They live for years and after flower-ing they send up new shoots or offsets from which you can propagate more plants. They will grow in many places in a home, from a fireplace to a sunny window. Some of them are delightful subjects in mixed arrange-ments of plants or plants and flowers which are known as pot-et-fleur.

Resembling the taller bromeliads in some ways with its long pointed leaves and handsome leaf markings, the sansevieria, a member of the lily family, shares their agreeable toughness and adaptability. It too will live for years and will grow so large in time, widthways not in height, that you can either divide it into several smaller plants or repot it into containers of ever-increasing girth and so allow both it and your reputa-tion as an indoor gardener to grow to a great size.

Its right to be included in the easy plant group is due to the fact that you can water it in the same way as you water cacti, once a month from October to March and then once a week. During summer a little soluble plant food will be welcome.

The sansevierias have thick chunky leaves. They are semi- or sub-succulent and as such are able to store water. This is the reason why they can be left unwatered for so long. Too much water poured into the pot soil will cause the leaves to rot at their bases.

They also are plants which will grow almost any-where, even tolerating low temperatures from time to time. They tend to remain static where conditions are not really to their liking and often you will find that if a plant is moved to some more agreeable situation it

Right
Rebutia kupperiana. Many of the species are easily raised from seed. Not only do the plants themselves produce this freely but it germinates quickly. Sometimes you will find seedlings growing round the parent plant. The flowers remain for about a week and close at night.

Below left
Vriesia splendens and *Aloe aristata.* Many plants grown for the beauty, shape and texture of their foliage also produce attractive flowers. Here, the spikey inflorescence of the vriesia is seen contrasting with the pendent flowers of the aloe. Vriesias are bromeliads, and aloes are leaf succulents which often produce growth in winter and should also produce frequent offsets.

Below right
Epiphyllum ackermannii. This particular plant which itself produces gorgeous showy flowers is the parent of many other handsome hybrids. These have a delightful colour range and beautiful blooms. See also pages 19 and 48.

Far right
Chamaecereus silvestrii is known also as the pea-nut cactus and the prostrate cereus. It is usually happy in a sunny position where it will produce two-inch-long flowers from May to July.

30

will produce several new shoots quite quickly. If this happens, take the hint and let it remain in its new home. Because of their tall, spiky outlines, sansevierias look well in arrangements.

Another member of the same family, *Aloe variegata*, sometimes called the partridge plant because of its bird-like bars and dots, is also easy. It is often to be seen in windows and although it will grow in sunshine it will also flourish in a shady window, if this is not a contradiction in terms. This aloe also is succulent.

This term – succulent – is used to describe a plant and it is also the term for particular types of plants. Cacti are succulent by nature and also botanically. These are very easy plants to grow and once you have coaxed a cactus into flower it will continue to bloom each year. Some have some very gorgeous blooms, others are small and even dowdy but what they lack in flower power they tend to make up for in plant form and texture. Cacti do not produce leaves. They have plant bodies. Unless they are very fine specimens, cacti do not create a striking decorative effect if they are just stood about in little pots. On the other hand, they do lend themselves well to all kinds of massing and grouping, as we shall see. They are not suitable for mixing with other plants since their water requirements differ.

There are three distinct tribes of cacti. Those in Tribe 1, the pereskieae, are not usually of interest to the house plant collector. Tribe 2 contains most of those we see on sale and which are so good for grouping and for filling bowls and dish gardens. Tribe 3 contains the cereus or night-blooming cacti. Among the loveliest of all, and certainly the most decorative for indoors, are the epiphytic species known loosely as epiphyllums or leaf-flowering cacti. The latter name is really a misnomer because the flowers are not produced on leaves but on flattened stems or plant bodies which somewhat resemble leaves. Most people know the vividly coloured, prettily pendent Christmas cactus, which is just one of the many lovely plants in this group. These can be very decorative and well grown they will make really large plants which become smothered with dozens of blooms.

Often cacti and succulents, from several different plant families, are grouped together under the 'Cactus' heading. It is important to understand that not all succulents are cacti.

One non-cactus family, crassulaceae, contains so many lovely succulent plants which are a delight to the

indoor gardener. Their great appeal is that they are beautiful, even when not in bloom. Unlike most cacti, they have no spines. Their leaves are thick, chunky, sometimes wavy-edged, prettily shaped and sometimes gorgeously coloured or perhaps covered with a blue-grey bloom like a grape. Individual plants are often flower-like in form, reminding one of great, thick-petalled roses. Often they are sessile (stemless) and their great rosettes spread out over the soil and out beyond the pot rim. *Aeonium tabulaeforme* is a handsome example. Others in this family carry their plant rosettes on thick, stout trunks and sometimes there will be several rosettes to one stalk. This, like so many in this family, is a good plant for the beginner who will be enchanted with the long well branching flower stem which supports a mass of dainty primrose-coloured flowers.

Many of these succulents produce spectacular flowers, the coral coloured echeveria and the bell-shaped oliveranthus, really an echeveria, are examples. Among this group are the dainty species of crassulas and the fragrant rochea. Some of these closely resemble a kalanchoe and you are likely to find them in bowls of mixed plants which have been assembled and marketed by the florist or nurseryman.

So long as all of these are kept in a temperature of round about 10°C. or 50°F., they will prove to be both easy and rewarding. If you are short of house room they, like cacti, can be stood outdoors for the summer.

Even with the few types we have already discussed, the bromeliads, the lily family succulents, cacti and the crassulas, we have the beginnings of an attractive collection in which there are contrasts of shape, texture, colour and size.

A group of plants which have been standing around indoors, in many countries, for a very long time are the so-called potted palms. These really are tolerant. They will flourish under the most difficult conditions, or so it seems. They must surely be the most undemanding of all of the plants we grow. The palms you are most likely to find on sale are the *Chamaedorea elegans*, a graceful, slow-growing little beauty which is just the right size for many arrangements although it looks very well on its

Right
Unlike most other cacti that can be grown at home, *Aporocactus flagelliformis* has drooping stems, sometimes as long as two feet. As a result it is known as the Rat's tail cactus and it looks well placed on a pedestal or in a hanging basket.

Far right
Rhipsalidopsis gaertneri syn. *Schlumbergera gaertneri.* Revelling in good light, this particular leaf-flowering cactus blooms in spring, hence its popular name, the Easter cactus.

own, especially if it can be silhouetted in some way (this goes for all palms) – you may find this on sale under its synonyms, *Neanthe elegans* or *N. bella* and *Collinia elegans*; *Phoenix dactylifera*, the date palm, sometimes sold as cocos (which it is not, that name belongs to the coconut palm) and perhaps other phoenix species such as *P. roebelinii* and *P. canariensis*, *Butis capitata* whose synonym is *Cocos capitata*; *Howea belmoreana* (synonym *Kentia belmoreana*) the curly palm and *H. fosteriana, (K. fosteriana)* the flat or thatch leaf palm, and *Livistone chinensis*, the Chinese fan palm.

So often, when one buys a palm, it seems much too large for its pot and one's first impulse is to repot it to give its roots more living room. However, this would be a mistake, for palms appear to grow best where their roots are restricted. It is possible to keep a plant for as long as two or three years in a 60 pot (3 inch), but plants in such small pots are difficult to deal with and become top heavy. As a temporary expedient plants in too small a pot may be placed, small pot included, in a larger and heavier pot. Pot-bound plants, the term for those whose roots really fill the pots, will require more frequent watering than those with plenty of soil between their roots, which holds more water. For this reason palms and many other plants, as we shall learn, are best plunged, but more of that later.

Palms were at the height of their popularity during the last century during which time two other deep green plants were also much sought after and cherished. One of these was the aspidistra, now rare enough in some countries to be a collector's item. Known then as the parlour plant and as the cast iron plant it flourished in dim, smoky rooms as well as well-lit surroundings. In summer it was stood outdoors so that its leaves could become cleansed by the summer rains and in winter it went back to its place not so very far from the coal fire. It is a plant which is most difficult to kill. It will send up new leaves in spite of bad treatment, yet if you were to treat it as lovingly as the most precious new plant in your care you would find that it is the ugly duckling among house plants. Grown in good mixture, repotted from time to time, given regular watering and feeding, it gradually turns into a lovely green swan! A good specimen is among the most handsome of all house plants. It will grow high, wide and handsome. A good plant could fill a wide fireplace.

There is a variegated form, *A. elatior* 'Variegata' which, though not quite so robust as the green type, is very attractive. If you find one, keep it in a slightly warmer temperature and in stronger light than the green species but keep it out of direct sunlight.

Probably one of the best known of all our house plants is the so-called rubber plant, *Ficus elastica*, 'Decora', yet it too was a favourite Victorian 'green'. In its natural state this ficus becomes a very tall branching tree but the potted plants are usually grown single-stemmed. The plant grows slowly, a quality, really, in some house plants for once they are in place in the home it is usually most convenient to have them stay in the same position. A good plant should be well clothed with leaves right down to the base of its stem.

It is a jungle plant which means that it can tolerate a

Below
Those who enjoy collecting strange plants often keep a *Stapelia variegata* or some other species of this family of strange succulents which produce fantastic and enormous blooms. Unfortunately some of these have a carrion odour and so the plants cannot always be kept in a much used room.

Far right
Epiphyllum hybrid. One of the many lovely epiphyllums which can be grown indoors. Their colour range is good, from near white through yellow, orange, red, crimson and rose. Their usual height is one to two feet and there are no true leaves – the stems are flattened and look like thick leaves.

good deal of shade—its dark leathery leaves are an indication of this. Plants grown towards the back of the room have better-looking foliage than those which are grown in a sunny place.

There are other species and varieties of ficus which make good house plants although most of them differ in appearance from the rubber plant. Some, like *F. pumila*, are trailers which will cling to a wall if they get the chance and if conditions are right. For instance, if you wished to clothe a wall, stand or plant this ficus near it and keep the wall surface sprayed from time to time. Other ficus have smaller leaves and are more branching in habit than *F. elastica*. *F. benjamina* much resembles a neat citrus tree except, of course, that it does not bear coloured fruits. Mature plants of some of the ficus species do produce little green fruits and you may find them familiar in appearance because ficus is the fig genus or family.

A tall fig is extremely striking in appearance and well deserves the term architectural which is often applied to it. This term is also sometimes used to describe another jungle plant with tough, leathery, deep green leaves, the monstera. While the figs' leaves are simple, those of the monstera are irregular in outline with great slashes and even holes through the leaves. The latter have caused it to be known to some people as the Gruyère cheese plant.

So long as one observes a few simple rules, this handsome plant is easy to grow. It likes a shady position and

Left
Howea belmoreana (syn. *Kentia*). Palms are both decorative and very long-lived. They appear to grow best when their roots are restricted and so they should not be repotted frequently. However, pot bound palms need more water than those which still have plenty of soil between their roots.

Above
Ficus benjamina is just the plant for those who admire the qualities of *F. elastica* (see following page) but not its size or form. Neat, evergreen and prettily branching, it is happiest in rooms where the temperature is never below 50°F (10°C).

Right
The indomitable aspidistra, once so common, is now a rarity in some countries. It will struggle to live in bad conditions, but fed and well cared for it will make a handsome and decorative plant.

it likes to be left to grow in the one place. It likes plenty of pot room and you can always tell when it should be repotted because the leaves become less and less slashed and holed. It is a plant for spacious interiors or for some place where it can roam a wall.

The monstera is botanically allied to philodendron and, as we shall see, there are very many of the arcid family (the Araceae) that make attractive house plants, especially those which like the monstera are climbers. The arum lily is probably the most easily recognised of these. There are several good house plants in this group but not all of them are easy. Many of them flower and some, like the spathiphyllum have white arum-like blooms. Others have green 'arums'. One of the easy and agreeable species is *Syngonium podophyllum* which continues to flourish even under what might be considered to be poor conditions. Like many philodendrons it can be persuaded to grow in water or in sand and water or pebbles and water. As one can appreciate, this facility opens the way to different methods of displaying plants–think, for instance, of the variety of vessels which can then become plant containers. This method of growing will be discussed more fully later on.

Like the bromeliads and the epiphyllums already discussed, philodendrons are also tree growing–epiphytes. Often a new indoor gardener is puzzled by the strange thong-like growths which appear on the stems of some of these plants. These are aerial roots through which the plant takes in moisture from the air, its other kind of roots being used to anchor it to the ground and clinging to the tree on which it grows. When they appear on house plants these roots are best trained down into the soil of the pot.

Of all the philodendrons, *P. scandens*, with deep green heart shaped leaves (because of these it is sometimes called sweetheart plant), is possibly the easiest of all to grow. It is also tolerant and can be moved around more than most. Although a climber when given support, it is also a pretty trailer and so is useful in plant arrangements.

Equally tough, in my experience, is a species with much larger leaves, *P. erubescens*, of which there is a form with coppery young leaves known as 'Burgundy'. It is a climber but it grows very slowly and what might appear to be a bushy plant when bought might stay that way for a very long time and then gradually begin to extend its stem and climb.

Also tough is *P. bipinnatifidum*, a non-climbing plant with large feathered leaves of deep, glossy green. These three and others which are on sale, can be grown well back in a room if required.

Where house plants are grown for their decorative qualities, climbing kinds are an essential. Monsteras and certain philodendrons will play this role but there are a few other tough and agreeable plants which also should be considered. Among these are two close relatives to the grape vine, *Cissus antarctica*, which has simple tooth-edged leaves and *Rhoicissus rhomboidea*, which has prettily divided leaves. We shall be meeting these two again.

As one would expect, climbers which also trail are useful to the decorator and if they are also varied in colouration with many hues of green, with white, grey and yellows, they become even more so. The ubiquitous ivies are such plants. The simple, small-leaved green species *Hedera helix* has been a treasured house plant for a long time and it has repaid our love and interest by sporting and producing a remarkable range of different ivies which for convenience sake are known as varieties. So far as easy plants are concerned, here again the old rule proves sound, that the greener the leaf the more tolerant the plant. However, leaf texture also

Above left
Philodendron scandens and *Scindapsus aureus*. Of all the philodendrons, *P. scandens* is possibly the easiest to grow. It trails as prettily as it climbs. The same can be said of scindapsus, although it is a more tender plant which does not tolerate direct sunshine and needs to be kept moist.

Right
Monstera deliciosa in the foreground with a howea by the windows. A large specimen like this will grow in a comparatively small pot for three or four years before needing repotting. When mature, it will produce creamy-coloured spikes which are followed by cone-shaped edible fruits.

Left
Known popularly as the rubber plant, *Ficus elastica* has been a valued house plant for many decades. 'Decora' is an improved cultivar of the original and there are other varieties to be found as well. *F. elastica* can easily grow up to ten feet in a tub if you allow it to.

Following page
Philodendron bipinnatifidum. This particular plant has lived for five years in a room where it receives no direct light. As you can see, its leaves turn towards the main light source. Philodendrons generally are tolerant plants. Keep them warm, fairly humid, but never in bright sunshine.

seems to be of some influence so far as the ivy is concerned and those varieties such as *H. h.* 'Glacier', with small leaves charmingly coloured in grey and white, which have tough textured leaves, as opposed to silky, will tolerate the same dim or away-from-light situations as *H. helix*. On the other hand, large silky-leaved plants such as the cream and green *H. canariensis*, another species altogether, needs a different situation, in good light but not in direct sunlight.

Anyone who hopes to make many plant arrangements throughout the year would do well to build up a stock of varied ivies. These are both cheap to buy and easy to propagate. No other plant, except perhaps the pretty little tradescantia, scrambles so attractively over the edge of a bowl or some other container.

If ivies are given support they will climb. They will also cling, to ceiling or wall should you wish them to do so. If the plants are grown in a tall container or raised from the floor level by some other means, they will also send some of their trails down over the rim and so furnish the lower levels of the container easily and attractively.

As you can see from these few descriptions, house plants vary considerably. As a general rule, the more highly coloured the foliage the more difficult the plant. For example, crotons are perhaps the most gorgeous of all house plants but unless they are grown inside a Wardian glass case or some other enclosed container, a carboy for instance, these will not last for long. Some of the dracaenas have lovely colouration and these also are a little on the temperamental side. Often such plants will grow quite well during the summer months and it is a good plan to introduce them into the home at that time so that they can gradually adapt themselves to their surroundings.

On the other hand, there are some almost hardy garden plants which make good house plants. These could be so useful for those who want some plants for a situation in which it is not possible to provide much warmth, an outer landing to a flat for instance. Ivies, which might take a few weeks to become adjusted if they have been brought from a warm greenhouse, *Araucaria excelsa* or Norfolk Island Pine, fatsia and fatshedera and forms of euonymus are examples.

Far right
Cissus antarctica, popularly called the kangaroo vine, can be grown as a pillar or with its long trails divided to cover a wall. As its specific name indicates, it prefers a cool situation to one which is warm and arid.

Right and Below right
Rhoicissus rhomboidea (the grape ivy) will fit into many places in the home. Here it is climbing well and being encouraged to frame an archway leading from kitchen to dining room. If required, it can be kept neat and bushy by pinching out the tips of its growing stems. It looks attractive placed at the edges of a group or arrangement so that some of its trails can cascade prettily, and will grow well away from direct light.

Flowering plants

Most flowering plants have to be regarded as temporary decorations. Fortunately, they are so extremely beautiful that what they lack in staying power they make up for in colour and general beauty. It is quite natural that most of us should wish to keep them for as long as possible, perhaps to bloom another year, but this is seldom possible.

So many of our flowering plants are annuals, examples are cineraria, exacum, browallia, and once these have flowered they die. There are some flowering kinds which are perennials treated as annuals, which means that they can be brought quickly into bloom but this causes them to expend their energies so freely that they are soon spent once they have flowered.

Other perennials and some shrubs, azaleas and

Left
A November display of cyclamen, begonias and cinerarias. All these plants need careful watering if they are to live any length of time.

Below
Anthurium scherzerianum.
Known as the Piggy-tail plant, because of their curly spadices, these anthuriums are really quite tough house plants. They grow best in good light, without this they will not flower. They dislike draughts and dry conditions.

Right
Caladium with Hippeastrum,
which is popularly though
wrongly called amaryllis, has
such spectacular flowers that
it is hard to believe that the
bulbs are easily grown. It is
sometimes possible to buy
prepared, ready-potted bulbs
which will flower very quickly.
Plant the bulbs singly in a
loam based compost leaving
the top of the bulb exposed
and keep moist until the
leaves die down.

Opposite page top
A west-facing window is an
ideal spot in which to grow an
assortment of plants. Among
these flowering here are an
epiphyllum hybrid, an Easter
cactus and the dark-leaved
*Impatiens walleriana
petersiana*. Impatiens are
shrubby semi-succulent plants
which have clusters of bright
flowers. Some of them are
perennials and tip cuttings can
be taken at any time.

Below right
Hyacinths will grow in water
alone with a nugget of charcoal
put at the bottom to keep the
water sweet. There are special
glasses made to hold the bulbs.
A little grass sprinkled over the
soil surface furnishes a simple
flower pot. Crocuses, scillas
and most small-flowering
bulbs should not be brought
indoors until the buds are
ready to open.

Below far right
Many lilies can be grown
quite well in pots of soil like
any other bulbs. There are
some, like this midcentury
hybrid, 'Enchantment' which
may be sold ready potted and
prepared to flower quickly
with the minimum of attention.

daily. If there are still many buds to open it is also wise to feed them weekly because the plant foods become leached out by so much water.

Hydrangeas need much the same treatment. These are among the few flowering plants which do best away from strong light.

Solanum capsicastrum the winter cherry and the kinds of pot peppers, capsicum, need very careful watering if they are not to drop their buds and leaves. These grow best when they also can be sprayed daily. Like cyclamen, they prefer a cool atmosphere and good light. While they are in bud, bloom and fruit, they should be fed weekly.

Cyclamen should be watered from the base—the water should be poured into the saucer or whatever other vessel the pot stands in. Better still, they should be plunged. Always avoid pouring water over the corm because droplets tend to rest between the bases of the stems and these cause the corm to rot. One great cause of cyclamen dying apart from incorrect watering are fumes of gas, oil, smoke, paint and others in the atmosphere. Keep them cool, never in a warm room.

Many plants appreciate a little moisture sprinkled or sprayed over their foliage and this is best done in the early morning but not when the sun is shining on the leaves, the reason for this being that droplets can cause diseases to take hold.

Primula obconica and *P. sinensis* seem to do best when they are moistened in this way and I think that it helps any type of these of plants grown indoors, especially any lifted from the garden.

It is not generally known that the garden primroses and polyanthus can be grown in pots on a windowsill in good light. These should be potted in a potting mixture in autumn or at any time during winter. If you have no garden, buy garden plants and pot them yourself if they are not being sold already potted.

Most primulas will grow indoors but some are better than others as house plants. *P. kewensis* has fragrant yellow flowers in clusters on tall stems.

Speaking generally, those just mentioned can be grouped as temporary plants and with them the many others that I may not yet have mentioned simply because there is always a continually changing supply of annual flowering plants on the market which may include exacum and browallia, besides some which have vivid foliage such as coleus.

So far as the perennials are concerned, there are people who manage to keep these from one year to the next—an operation which is simplified if one has a greenhouse or conservatory. Azaleas, cyclamen and solanums, for instance, can be kept outdoors, the pots sunk or plunged in garden soil in some partially shaded place. Those who have no gardens sometimes keep the plants on a shady outer windowsill or even indoors in a cool shaded window. At the end of summer the plants are brought indoors or, in the case of those already there, given a little more attention, extra food and water. The azaleas should be repotted in pure peat, well rammed down, after flowering, solanums when they are brought in for the winter and cyclamen corms when they have died down.

Among those flowering plants which are temporary or semi-permanent, according to the skill of the gardeners, are some which are grown from tubers, for example, achimenes, begonias, gloxinias (*sinningia* botanically) and the handsome caladiums which are grown for their colourful leaves and are gorgeous enough to be classed as flowers in this case.

Some begonias do not make tubers and are fibrous-rooted and some of these are also known as winter-flowering begonias.

Many of the flowering plants we shall discuss more fully when we deal with plant arrangements and pot-et-fleur, but just a few words about a special few.

Most columnea species available are beautiful trailing plants with long green-leaved stems which become studded with scarlet-orange flowers.

Euphorbias are varied and the showy poinsettia is one of this family but there are others which resemble cactus plants. Poinsettias are inclined to be temperamental. They dislike too warm rooms, fumes of any sort, draughts either hot or cold and direct sunshine. Their roots should be kept constantly moist and the plant is best plunged. Gardenias, again, are not easy because they need humidity. In some ways it is more important to spray the foliage than to water the soil. Gloxinias, like cyclamen should be watered from below. They need airy not close surroundings but no draughts. *Hoya carnosa*, a pretty little thick-leaved climber is most often sold with its trails trained round in a hoop resting on the rim of the pot. You can unwind these stems and treat the plant like any other climber if you wish but it will go on round and round the hoop if you prefer it that way. This plant must have warmth. Hypocyrta, known as the goldfish plant because of the shape and colour of its little flowers is quite tough and can be grown in a not-so-warm room.

Impatiens or busy lizzie, a great favourite, often appears to thrive in spite of its owners and its surroundings. A well-grown plant should be smothered in flowers. Keep the tips of the shoots pinched out to keep the plant bushy. Feed it when it is in bloom. Keep it warm in winter. Saintpaulia or African violet often fails because of bad light, polluted atmosphere and low temperatures. It grows best when plunged and a bowl or trough of mixed varieties can look very attractive indeed.

Among the bulbous plants you can expect to grow all year round, as opposed to those which have to be planted in the autumn and forced into bloom are the following: clivia with handsome strap-like leaves, haemanthus or blood lily, hippeastrum or amaryllis, hymenocallis, nerine, oxalis, vallota and velthemia.

Below
Euphorbia pulcherrima. Known universally as the poinsettia, this is the most flamboyant member of the spurge family. The vividly coloured bracts surround the tiny berry-like flowers. To keep the colour (red, pink or cream), give the plants plenty of light at all times, but not direct sunlight.

Right
Saintpaulia ionantha 'Diana Blue'. There are many named varieties and some good strains of African violets now available. If you are successful in growing them you will find that they are also easy plants to propagate. They like good light, clean air, humidity and feeding when in flower.

heaths (*Erica*), are subjected to even more severe methods of cultivation and by various means are forced into bloom completely out of their natural season. It is not the purpose of this book to explain these processes but it is important that I should point out that should such a plant continue to live after it has finished flowering it is most unlikely to produce flowers again in the following year in the same season. Usually, such plants take two or three years to become adjusted. Poinsettias are the best known examples.

On the other hand there are many other much more permanent plants which flower prettily and for more than one year at a time. Some, like saintpaulia or African violets may flower more than once a year.

Some of these may be grown for their flowers alone, their leaves being unremarkable and the plants themselves not highly decorative except when in bloom. There are also many foliage plants which reward one with the odd flower or two. As I described earlier, aechmeas and some other bromeliads produce unusual flowers which are extremely decorative and long lasting, others are more interesting than decorative. The same applies to aroids: anthurium and spathiphyllum produce showy blooms but others may be green and leaf-like.

Lovely flowering plants which present few problems are those which are grown from bulbs. These can be bought in pots and bowls already planted and in bud or bloom. Alternatively, the indoor gardener can grow them from the very beginning. The bulb is planted in bulb fibre, soil, water or water and pebbles – according to its kind. If the bulb has to be forced into flower out of season, it is usually expendable for it will not flower in the same way nor at the same time the following year. Often forced bulbs of hardy plants, hyacinths, tulips and daffodils, for instance, can be planted in the garden and there they will gradually recuperate and bloom again one day.

Some bulbous plants are perennial indoors in the sense that they can be saved and grown again year after year. Often these have to be rested which means that they remain in their pots but are not watered. When the time comes they are repotted, watered and started into growth again. Hippeastrums, sometimes called amaryllis, hymenocallis, sprekelia, lapeyrousia and nerines are examples and all of these can be bought easily from bulb merchants.

More and more kinds of bulbs are being marketed ready planted but not grown. These bulbs have also

been specially prepared and their cultivation is simplicity itself. The gardener is so well rewarded for the minimum of effort, one simply follows the bulb merchant's instructions. Often there is nothing to do but to water the pot and stand it in good light and soon there are gorgeous hippeastrums, lilies, lilies-of-the-valley, tulips, narcissi, hyacinths or colchicums to admire. All is astonishingly easy. New types of bulbs which can be grown this way are being introduced annually. It is also possible to buy prepared bulbs of certain kinds of flowers and to plant these yourself.

Whatever group flowering plants might fall into generally speaking there are a few rules which apply to all. Except for a very few kinds, spathiphyllum, a shade lover is an example, plants in bloom need good light though not, as has been stressed already, direct sunlight which might scorch them.

If the plant is not highly decorative when not in flower, you might find it convenient to move it around and to keep it in some less obvious place until its flower buds show. However, do choose the new site with care.

You can tell if a plant is not getting enough light because its stems become drawn and floppy and its flowers are not as well coloured as they should be. We shall discuss the influence of light on plants more fully later. Obviously, if you notice signs you should take action. Conversely, if you notice the blooms on a plant have suddenly flopped, even petals clinging together instead of being wide apart, you should move the plant to a less sunny place, for the time being at least. If you have no other site but a sunny windowsill, hang a fine curtain between the glass and the plant.

However, it may not be light alone which is causing the trouble. Water and humidity are also essential to flowering plants and at times, lack of these two may be critical.

One group of flowering plants which seems to do best in a really sunny window and in a dry atmosphere is the pelargonium, popularly called geranium. Although they are more often grown outdoors in windowboxes and hanging baskets than in the home, they are in fact good decorative house plants. They must have good light. Sometimes in summer a plant in a very hot and sunny situation will loose too much water and droop its leaves and should this happen it should either be given a larger pot or moved to some other place. The plants produce flowers intermittently throughout winter, even those which have been grown outdoors and are

This page
The commercial grower can induce chrysanthemums to flower all year round. He can also dwarf them to make compact and floriferous pot plants. Like most flowering plants, and the berried solanums with them here, they need good light.

Right
Some of the most popular gift plants. Of these the azalea and heaths should be kept constantly moist at the roots. Primulas and chrysanthemums need cool situations if they are to last well. *Solanum capsicastrum* and a prettily variegated ivy complete the picture.

brought in for decoration during the winter months.

Azaleas and heathers should never be allowed to dry out and are always best plunged. Feed these fortnightly when they are in bud and water them with rain water.

Cinerarias are among the very few plants which do best if they are watered every day. Certainly, they should never be allowed to become dry at the roots for once these plants wilt they will never properly revive.

Becoming almost dry at the roots does not harm some plants as much as one might expect. Indeed, the aeration caused by the rushing of the water through the dry soil and out through the pot is beneficial to the roots, but this does not apply to many flowering kinds.

Other plants which, like cinerarias need watering and feeding liberally are calceolarias. These need a warmer temperature than the foregoing but like them they need really good light.

The many little pot chrysanthemums now on sale, usually dwarf and very compact and grown under intense scientific cultivation, are often found to have small pots packed full of roots. This being the case, the plants need plenty of water. In a warm room, perhaps

Top right
Vividly coloured cinerarias and calceolarias will last longer and produce more blooms if they are watered liberally and fed whilst in flower. There are many lovely varieties of both kinds of plants in a gorgeous range of colours.

Right
Hydrangeas are an exception to the general rule and are among the few flowering house plants which do best in some shade. If they are stood in full sunlight they are likely to flag too badly ever to be fully revived to their former brilliance.

Left
Primulas are attractive flowering plants and there are a number of different species; the large-flowered *Primula obconica* and the daintier *P. malacoides* are probably the best known. They like plenty of water and light feeding when in flower. Plants may be raised from seed quite easily. Also in the picture is a standard azalea, a sansevieria and a small-leaved ivy.

Right
Hoya carnosa. There is also
a charming variegated variety
of this plant as well as the
green-leaved *H. bella* which
produces even more brilliant
wax-flowers, as they are called.
A climber. the hoya is a little
slow in beginning, but speedy
once established.

Opposite above
A group of three flowering
plants showing greatly differing
'blooms'. The 'rat tails' are
the flowers of *Peperomia
glabella*, on the left are the red
piggy tails of an anthurium,
and behind are the vivid blue
flowers of browallia, which is
an annual and easily raised
from seed. Peperomias like a
humid atmosphere and the pot
soil should be kept fairly dry
in winter.

Opposite below
Some ornamental-leaved
begonias flower prettily, like
this *Begonia haageana*. There
are many species and varieties
which will grow well, even
luxuriantly, indoors so long as
they have warmth and some
humidity.

How to choose your plants

Few of us have an opportunity of buying direct from the nursery. Those who live in cities have to buy from a florist or perhaps a garden centre and this means that the plants have left the nursery, travelled to market and been sold there either by the grower's salesman or by a wholesale florist. The retail florist has to buy the plants from the market, transport them to his own establishment and there, finally, place them on show for your selection. Obviously, there have been several opportunities for some harm to come to the plant and with the best will in the world it is not always possible for the retail florist to keep a close enough eye on each of his many plants to ensure that they are always in the best of condition. Furthermore, not all florists are horticulturists and may not recognise that a plant is suffering or is likely to do so.

So far as flowering plants are concerned, our method of marketing means that there is unlikely to be sufficient time for any of the blooms to have passed their peak and be on the way out. Most have some blooms and plenty of buds still to come which is what you should look for. Should you be offered any plant on which it is obvious that even one flower is fading treat it a little suspiciously and select another if you can. Watch out for fading blooms and for those which are flagging or wilting. This may be caused only by thirst and if the plant has been dry only for a short period no harm is done and the situation is soon rectified, but flagging can also be caused through draughts and severe cold. A good guide is to buy plants and flowers rather in the same way as one chooses salad vegetables. Look primarily for crispness and colour. Whether the plant you seek bears flowers or whether it is grown for the beauty of its foliage, a healthy plant has a certain crisp appearance about it. Stems are turgid, stiff, not limp or drooping, even if it should be a trailing kind. Colour should be deep and glowing, leaves should gleam. Be suspicious of any plant which seems faded in appearance. Certain leaves have a metallic sheen on them which is more intensified when they are in the pink of condition. Hairy leaves should look new-brushed and not shabby.

Accept nothing that has spots on it, that is, unnatural spots which are obviously the result of burning or disease. The tissues of these spots will be drier than the main leaf fabric or blistery in appearance. There may be only one spot on a leaf or there may be several. Test the spot by merely wiping the leaf gently between the finger and thumb. Some green plants have a slight deposit caused by the water with which they have been sprayed, particularly if it is limy, but this is easily smoothed away and does no damage.

Some leaves may appear to have a dried brown edging to them. Do not accept a young plant in a small pot in this condition for this is usually an indication of a damaged or sick leaf. However, should the plant be a handsome specimen with very many leaves, begonias

Left
Beloperone guttata. The brownish-rose flowers give this plant its common name of shrimp plant. Although it grows best with some warmth and humidity, cooler and dryer conditions tend to deepen the colour of the attractive bracts. Feed moderately, particularly when in flower.

are examples, it might be that one or two of the older, that is the first formed leaves, are on their way out, as might be expected. They still have a role to play for leaves are the lungs of a plant, its stomach too for that matter, and it is unwise to cut away any leaf while it still has life for it continues to contribute to the well being of the plant and is part of its metabolic system.

A plant should fill its pot. Be suspicious of a plant whose pot looks too large for it. Ailing leaves may have been cut away.

Always examine the growing tips or shoots to make sure that they are sturdy, plump, healthy and capable of further growth. Buds should be succulent. Pointed tips as in philodendrons should be well filled. If they are papery they probably do not contain a living shoot and this indicates that the plant was neglected at some time. There might be future trouble in store. Papery buds do not contain flowers. See that buds are all alike. If you are examining a flowering plant check that there are many more buds to come. If you buy a plant with all its blooms open wide then expect it to be at its best for a short period only.

Whether the plant is a temporary or permanent kind always treat yellowing leaves with suspicion, unless, of course, they are supposed to have some yellow variation in them. Usually, the leaf of a green plant yellows because of ill health and there is a change of texture too. The leaf becomes less tough, sometimes even pappy to the touch. Several yellowing leaves on ivy, cyclamen, from bulbs and others, usually indicate that either the plants are older than they ought to be or very sick, though one leaf may, as has already been suggested, merely be a spent leaf and is no cause for worry.

As I said earlier, a pot should be well filled. Unless stems are naturally leafless, such as those of cyperus which produces little umbrella like topknots, the foliage should always persist to the base. This need not necessarily be thick and bushy but it should be healthy. Plants without tall main stems, such as saintpaulias and begonias should have full crowns. They should fill the pot so well that they cover its rim.

Plants like solanums or winter cherries, heaths and azaleas, all entirely different kinds of plants, show distress by shedding their leaves. One or two only may drop but sometimes these one or two are the beginning of a real fall. If when you are choosing a plant, on the soil surface you see a leaf, or in the case of heaths, some needles do not buy the plant, unless its length of life is really of no consequence. This leaf drop can be caused by more than one factor, drought, draught or insect pests.

So far as size is concerned, all tastes are catered for. Small pots are useful for making plant arrangements and pot-et-fleur. Climbers and plants which are required to stand in a certain place in the home and to act rather as a piece of furniture are best bought in a large pot so that they need never be repotted. The most popular size of pot plant is a 60 or 3 inch, measured across the rim, but there is a large 60 and a small 60. Take care when buying containers that size is taken into account or you will be left with a misfit. It is surprising to discover, as one does, that most 'cover' pots have been designed and made without reference to flower pot sizes. Unless they are arranged and plunged into some moisture retentive medium, small pots are apt to dry out rather quickly once they carry a lot of growth. However, as we shall learn, there are ways of avoiding this. A plant in a 48, the 5 inch pot, is usually about twice the price of the same plant in a 60. Incidentally, pots came by these odd terms because of the way clay pots were made, so many in a cast.

Many flowering plants are sold in 60s and these are

Above right
Calathea zebrina. Closely related to the marantas, calatheas like warmth and humidity. Plants grow best plunged in moist peat inside a larger waterproof pot. They should be kept out of direct sunlight.

Above centre
Crocus chrysanthus 'Princess Beatrix'. All bulbs are safe buys and their successful flowering depends on the conditions and treatment. Crocuses are more difficult than some other bulbs to grow indoors – hyacinths are the easiest for the beginner (see pages 102, 106 for planting instructions).

Far right
Citrus mitis is a rewarding plant to keep at home since it will flower and fruit when young and nearly all the year round. The leathery green leaves quickly indicate if the plant is not healthy by turning yellow.

Right
Gloxinia. With a little planning these flowers can be enjoyed during many months of the year. They can be raised from seed and from cuttings of stem or leaves. The plants form tubers which can be saved from year to year.

African violets, *Saintpaulia
ionantha*, are very varied and
come in colours ranging from
white through pink, rose,
purple, violet and blue. These
are beautiful flowers from a
healthy plant: their colour is
good, there are plenty of buds,
the hairy leaves and stems are
stiff and well brushed.

Left
Philodendron scandens and
Philodendron ilsemanii. The
many pointed tips of
Philodendron scandens are
well filled and the leaves
glossy and healthy. Leaves of
all plants should be kept free
of dust if they are to remain
healthy and attractive.
Regular sponging with clean
luke-warm water keeps them
shiny.

Right
Nidularium fulgens. This is a
useful plant to have around
because it is tolerant and can
be moved to fill any odd corner
or to make a glowing focal
point to an arrangement or
group of plants. It is a
bromeliad and so easy to
water – simply keep the central
zone always filled. The leaves
should be dark and glossy and
they grow up to 12 inches long.

Right
Rhododendron simsii. Among the most popular of all flowering house plants, and better known as azaleas, they should be regarded as temporary tenants. More azaleas die of drought than from any other cause, since the root ball must never become dry.

Below
Cyclamen are such popular house plants and there are so many in all florists, particularly around Christmas, that it is important to choose these plants with great care. Check that no leaves show signs of being at all unhealthy and that there are flower buds to come. Many plants are brought on too quickly before they are sold and are consequently difficult to keep.

Far right
Primula obconica is a winter blooming primrose which you can keep from year to year. The colour range is very wide, and again when choosing a plant check that there are plenty of buds to come and that the leaves are a fresh green in colour with their stems firm and upstanding.

Centre right
A really healthy African violet produces flowers which glow strongly with colour.

Below right
Aphelandra squarrosa is a most attractive plant to have in the home. The flowers provide a striking contrast to the dark green banded leaves. Keep the atmosphere moist in summer.

very useful for plant arrangements for they can be treated a little like a bunch of flowers and replaced when they have passed their best.

Azaleas and ericas or heaths are peat-loving and so are potted in peat. This can create problems. If the peat, which is very porous, is allowed to become dry, it shrinks. If the root ball is allowed to remain dry it shrinks and pulls away from the sides of the pot. It is possible to soak the plant and so recharge it but sometimes the drying has gone so far that the re-soaked plant is never the same again. Look at the lower portion of the stalk or little trunk. This should always be moist and darker than the wood above it. When you have the plant at home, keep it this way and then you will know that the roots are moist enough.

If you buy plants for gifts, do not collect them too much in advance of the date when you want to give them. Certainly order these well in advance. If you take the plants home too soon, they will begin to adjust to your own home conditions and then when you pass them on to another home they will have to begin all over again and they may sulk. Your gift will then not be as acceptable as you had hoped.

Never leave plants wrapped. Wrap the plants at the last moment if you must. If you are going by car and the weather is fine you can take plants unwrapped. Otherwise, the best thing is to slip each plant inside a large clear plastic bag so that it is entirely enveloped. Blow into the bag to inflate it so that the plastic stands well away from the leaves and flowers and fasten the top securely. Be generous and use a large bag so that when it is pulled off it does not brush against the plant itself.

Guard against the plant falling over or about. Quite often the best way to secure it is to take a cardboard box, turn it upside down and pierce the centre. From this hole make a few incisions, short or long according to the size of the container and press the pot down into the space thus made open. Allow about two thirds of the pot to go down into the box. The plant will then be elevated and out of harm's way and it will then be possible to push heavy objects against the sides of the box to prevent it moving. Another method, and this is good for small plants, is to fit a box or tray with a block of Oasis foam and to press the pot into this.

If the weather is really cold when you buy plants, avoid street stalls and ignore any plants put on show in the open air. They are likely to succumb later. Always insist on having the whole plant you buy covered and not just the pot. If you can have it slipped into a plastic bag so much the better.

Nurserymen tend to concentrate on those plants which are good do-ers, as you can appreciate. Not only must they grow well but travel well also. A plant must look as well on sale as it did in the nursery. This means that some plants are hard to find, the easy-going plectranthus which is somewhat too brittle to market, is an example. Such plants can often be found at small nurseries, market stalls and horticultural societies' stalls.

Growing hints

Most plants that the nurserymen send out are in soil that will provide sufficient nourishment for plants for a while though it will probably be necessary to feed the plants during their growing season. If a plant fails to thrive one can be almost certain that it is due to the conditions under which it is grown or to the lack of skill on the part of the gardener which are to blame and not the soil in which the plant is growing. Soil mixtures or composts as they are often called are carefully prepared. Mixtures vary sometimes for different plants yet there is a standard soil mixture or compost which suits the majority of plants. It is possible for the indoor gardener to mix his or her own composts and it is possible to buy these from a garden shop or centre.

Many plants die because they have been given too much water and this means that they, or part of them, drown. When there is too much water in the soil, roots die because they cannot breathe. Roots need air as well as moisture. Unless a plant's roots are happy and

growing well it will not be able to function properly above soil level. It is always best to err on keeping a plant a little on the dry side than to allow the soil to remain constantly moist–unless the plant is one which likes a boggy condition, a cyperus is an example.

Roughly speaking, most plants have a root system equal in size to the portion above soil. Of course, in a pot, the roots cannot spread as they would in the open ground. So instead they reach out while the plant is very young and after a time they come to the side of the pot. They then begin to curl around this and in time a plant might form a thick root layer around the sides of a pot. And curiously enough, when a plant has grown in its original pot like this for some time, you will find that there is very little soil left among the roots. When

this happens, the plant needs repotting. Where it is no convenient to repot a plant it is possible to keep i growing in its crowded container simply by feeding i regularly with soluble plant food. Usually plants a root-bound as this need watering more frequently tha they would if there was more soil in the pot. If you fin that a plant is wilting frequently and that you have t give it more and more water, this is most likely to be a indication that it is root-bound.

As soon as a plant comes into your hands see if i needs water. The simplest test of all is to take a scra of newspaper and with the thumb press it on the soi surface. If the soil is moist enough the paper wil immediately become damp. Another method is t weigh the pot in your hand. A pot filled with damp soi is heavier than one in which there is dry soil. If the po is made of clay and not plastic you can rap it with pencil or some other object. A pot of dry soil will ring a pot of moist or wet soil will give a dull sound. You wil get to know simply by looking at the plant whether o not it is needing a drink.

Once the plant is truly under your care it is likely tha you will get to know simply by looking at it whethe or not it is needing a drink.

If you find that the plant is dry, take a bucket or bowl or if you have several plants use the sink, but se that the water level will come above the rim of the po Plunge carefully and watch for a stream of bubble which should rise from the soil to the surface of th water. Wait until the stream of bubbles stops. Take ou the pot plant and stand it on the draining board or i the sink and clean the outside of the pot. Leave th plant to drain.

From this time on, how often any plant will nee watering will depend entirely upon the plant itself an its surroundings. Usually a flowering plant will nee more than one which has large leaves only. Test, a suggested, by pressing with newspaper.

Although most house plants need a certain amount o warmth, central heating is not good for them unles this can be tempered by humidity. It helps tremendous ly if you can spray the air round a plant and sometime its foliage also with clean water from an atomiser. Us rain water both for watering and spraying if possibl This is essential if the house water contains lime an you are growing azaleas and other lime haters.

Fortunately, there is a method of providing humidit which also improves the general appearance and conse quently the decorative value of the pot plant as wel This involves plunging the plant pot inside a large cover pot. All kinds of vessels can be used for this pur pose. Flower vases, especially those with a stem or sho pedestal base are ideal because they lift and display th plants so attractively. Most bromeliads, which are in clined to be top heavy sometimes, look well in the urn type, classic flower vase. Pedestal vases are invaluabl where a spreading plant is growing in a small flower po Unprotected or un-anchored it is likely to become easil knocked over.

But to return to the actual plunging. In any of thes cover pots–and the term extends to troughs and othe large containers, you should pack well-moistened pea bulb-fibre, sand, moss, old crumbled Oasis which yo have used for flower arrangements, vermiculite or an clean water-retentive material you can find, including if all else fails, shredded kitchen paper. This packin should go under and around the pot plant, reachin right up to the rim which should be well below th edge of the outer pot, to make watering clean and eas

The packing or plunge material should be kept mois but not sodden. If you use this method you will find tha plants grow better, even though you do not have t

Right
Plants sometimes need to be – and can be – kept under control. The Hoya at the back of the group, instead of being allowed to climb, has been trained round a hoop. The trailing plectranthus has been kept in a small pot to constrict its growth and the striped cryptanthus has been left to grow into a cluster.

Far right
Caladium hybrids. Caladiums are among the few foliage plants that are very difficult to grow. They rarely survive the winter outside a green-house. They grow from tubers and require plenty of warmth and water while they are growing freely.

Right
Epiphyllum hybrid. One of the many lovely flowering cacti known as leaf-flowering—a misnomer because the flowers are really produced on the flattened stems or plant bodies. The main flowering period is from May to June.

Opposite page top
Dieffenbachia picta. There are several species of this plant. They like warm, humid, light conditions but will become adapted to cooler, dryer environments. Stem portions and sap are highly poisonous to humans causing swollen mouth membranes, hence the popular name Dumb Cane.

Opposite page bottom
Watering bromeliads is quite a different operation from caring for other plants. In their case it is important that the little well, vase or reservoir at the heart of the plant and made by the overlapping leaves is always kept filled with water.

water them so frequently, than if they are simply stood on a saucer with the surface of the pot exposed to the drying air. Cacti should not be in a moist plunge but some succulents, especially the epiphytic kinds, benefit from it. Several different kinds of plants can be mixed together in a plunge medium but we will discuss this more fully when we come to the subject of plant arrangement generally.

Although plants help to cleanse our atmosphere for us, taking in the gases we cannot use and expelling precious oxygen, they or at least some of them can become badly affected by some atmospheric conditions. Fumes from oil lamps and heaters, from manufactured gas appliances, from paint, cleaning fluids, even tobacco can affect some so much that they become ill or even die. Saintpaulias, pelargoniums and cyclamen are examples. Generally speaking, once again, the dark green tough-leaved kinds are best able to tolerate pollution and those with thick chunky leaves or plant bodies such as sansevierias and cacti seldom show signs of distress.

Unfortunately, we find that just as plants become over-watered so do many of them become over-fed. One should certainly feed plants from time to time but never too generously. Too much plant food can kill so never be tempted to give just a little more. Plants producing flower buds, or those which have been rested and are coming into growth again, usually need feeding but generally speaking they need only sufficient food to keep them healthy and of good appearance. As a rule, it is much more convenient for a permanent plant to grow slowly. Plants which grow too fast and consequently too large, can be a nuisance. You have to find new homes for them. By feeding a plant very lightly we can keep it growing in proportion with its environment and to the purpose for which we chose it. It will thrive— but slowly.

We should always remember that plants in our homes are influenced by the amount of artificial light and extra warmth around them and so they cannot be expected to behave as they would if they were growing naturally. All plants rest at some time of the year but this period of rest may not necessarily be in winter or, if this is the proper time for the plant to take its rest, growth might continue because artificial light extends the length of the plant's day.

It is not difficult to tell whether or not a plant is making new growth. If it is winter and you see no signs of this, do not feed the plant but allow it to rest instead. Usually, during these rest periods, you will find that plants need less water also. As soon as you see signs of new growth you will find that a little more water is needed and once this happens you can give the plant a little help by feeding it with a very little soluble plant food. It is best to start very gently by putting just a little in the regular water and then you can lead up to maximum amounts should these be necessary, tapering off again when you feel that the plant is slowing down.

Plant care

Plants that are unhealthy cannot remain decorative for long and so it follows that if we want them to give us full value we should learn how to care for them when they are healthy and how to tend them when they are ailing in some way or other.

First of all let us make quite sure that we all know what is meant by watering a plant. This does not mean pouring a tablespoonful over the surface each morning nor does it mean allowing a pot to stand in several inches of water for some hours.

In every pot, bowl or other container, there should be a free area between the top soil or soil surface and the brim, rim or edge. Thinking in terms of the flower pots themselves, this space should be between a ½–1 inch for a 60, and for a 48 more, because more water is needed for a larger plant. Bear these points in mind when you repot plants or make dish gardens or plant other types of containers – you need room to water.

When the plant is watered this area should be filled. If the soil compost is properly mixed and well-drained or open as it should be, and certainly if the soil is dry, the water will be quickly sucked through and, if the plant should be standing in a saucer, you will notice that this quickly fills. This water should not be tipped away but should be left so that the soil and roots can slowly absorb it. If the pot soil is already wet enough the water takes longer to drain through. This may be an indication that you are watering too much or too often. Should this be the case, you can apply a little first aid by standing the pot on some absorbent material, several folds of newspaper for example, so that moisture is drawn out. Allow the soil to become almost quite dry before you water the plant again. Plants which are plunged lose their water into the plunge material and are able to re-absorb it slowly.

Plants in flower are at their peak and usually they need more water at this time. If they are in bud when you buy them, or if you have them young and so watch them come into bud, they should be fed. As we have already learned, plants need humidity and one should remember that a plant in flower has an even greater surface through which precious moisture will be lost if the atmosphere is too dry. If your plants are plunged you may have to water them a little more often than usual, so it is wise to check. Use an atomiser on the plants but keep the spray off the actual flowers in case these are the kind that become discoloured. If your plants are newly bought and are labelled, you may be advised to water freely. It is difficult for me to say just how often this might be necessary because this depends upon the size of the plant, the number of its blooms and where it stands. It might need no more than a weekly watering, on the other hand, some flowering plants in

Left
Aphelandra, begonia and variegated hibiscus. These and rex begonias need a high degree of humidity in the home. They are best grown with their pots plunged inside another filled with some moisture-retentive material such as peat. The aphelandra is a beautiful plant; the leaves can be up to ten inches long and it has large yellow flowers set in vase shaped bracts.

Below
Maranta leuconeura. 'Erythrophylla'. Marantas need a warm, moist atmosphere or they will not produce a succession of new leaves. A gentle spray of clean water on the foliage from time to time will help to keep them happy.

hot sunny weather, need watering every day.

Some people let the plant pot stand in a puddle of water in a saucer and although this might work sometimes it is not really to be recommended. The soil seldom becomes aerated this way and it is possible for it to become so water-logged that the plant finally dies. Plants should 'paddle' only when directions for their culture include the advice, 'keep the soil constantly moist'. An example is the little flowering rush-like *Cyperus*.

It is important to clean plants so that their leaf pores do not become clogged with dust. If it is convenient, stand plants outdoors in a gentle summer shower but guard against wind and torrential rains because these could damage the leaves. If you can spray climbing and large leaved plants in situ, so much the better. To avoid making the soil too wet if you do this, spread a little plastic or a dust sheet over the pot surface.

If leaves have become very dusty one must guard against scratching them with any grit particles which might be in the dust. The best way to clean a really dusty plant is to syringe it so that the dust is washed away. It is possible sometimes to blow the dust by using a vacuum cleaner in reverse, in which case one has to work quickly to suck the dust in from the air immediately after this. Alternatively, carefully sponge the leaves with a sponge, soft cloth or tissue. Use tepid water, try to wash the whole of one surface with one gentle stroke, wipe off the moisture with another drier cloth. If the dust is grimy or greasy as it is sometimes in cities, squeeze a few drops of detergent into the water, use this water and then rinse with untreated water.

Do not smear the leaves with oils or any substance other than water unless this be an insecticide. Pores can so easily be clogged with oils and once this happens the leaf cannot breathe nor work properly and it dies.

House plants sometimes become infested with insects as do garden plants. Quite often these will spread from one plant to the others. Some plants are notoriously dirty, cinerarias for instance. These seem to draw aphis to them. Inspect the undersides of their leaves every day.

Before you decide to buy insecticides and a syringe or atomiser with which to apply them, ask yourself if this is economic – sometimes the cure costs more than a new plant.

Do remember that insecticides are poisons and do not use the spray in the home. The only exceptions are fly-killers designed specifically for domestic use. Incidentally, these are often effective against a mild attack of aphis or greenfly. Otherwise take plants outdoors, out of the wind, spray them and allow them to become dry before you bring them back indoors. Read the labels and follow the directions carefully. Systemic insecticides can save some bother if you add a small dose to the water once a month because this will prevent serious infestations. Certainly use this method once you have sprayed a plant.

The aphis usually cluster first on young shoots of the plants. This weakens the plant and it also can spread diseases. Systemic insecticides work through the system of the plant. If these are watered into the soil they can be taken up through the roots and then spread through the plant. Their action is not immediate, it might take two or three days before the poison reaches the pest.

If you are not squeamish, often the most effective means of ridding a plant of a pest is to squash it between thumb and finger.

Greenfly usually cluster first on young shoots of plants. You may be first aware of them either because the surface of a windowsill is sticky from their exudations or because spent insect bodies lie like dust under a plant. It is advisable to keep a magnifying glass handy

and to inspect soft-leaved plants frequently. If you notice that a leaf has become distorted this also might be a sign of greenfly or some other aphis colony starting up. Instant action is often effective and the plant does not suffer a great deal.

Another reason why humidity is essential in the cultivation of happy house plants is that it deters the infestations of an unpleasant little mite known as red spider. Some house plant owners have never seen this little creature for it occurs only when the atmosphere is too dry. A badly affected plant will look rusty and this will be because of the thousands of tiny red mites, not really spiders, encased in webs which cover leaves and growing tips.

Apart from a plant not looking well, signs that red spider is present are brown even brittle leaves and many shed leaves. The mites usually collect first of all on the underside of the leaves and they are almost impossible to see with the naked eye. In certain lights it is easy to see the web but not always. The standard way of detecting this is to drop a little cigarette ash or to blow a little powder onto the underside of a leaf. If this clings you will know that the web is there.

Red spider is difficult to eliminate without total wetting with some proprietary insecticide. It might be best to discard the plant. If you do this be sure to clean wall surfaces, sills, flower pots or containers and to throw away soil or plunge materials used for the affected plant.

To prevent your plants from becoming infested make sure that humidity is provided. Spray with clean water wherever possible.

Mealy bug is another, milder, nuisance but it often attacks those plants which are difficult to treat, for instance, it will cluster down between the spines of a cactus. It is white or greyish and mealy, looking like a tiny piece of cotton wool which has become caught in the plant. This meal hides a nasty little sucking bug, a relation, I believe, of the cochineal bug. A spray of insecticide will not always reach the cracks and crevices in which these insects lurk and the best way to remove them is to take some denatured alcohol and a matchstick and with lots of patience, scrape away at each little tuft.

Incidentally, I find that I can keep large spiny cacti fairly clean by passing the dusting brush of the vacuum cleaner over them each week. By the same method I suck out dead leaves caught up in the spines of euphorbias. Dead leaves often harbour mealy bugs. From time to time, gently shake climbing plants such as rhoicissus to release any leaves which may be caught up in the trails.

The most frequent disease seems to be mildew and the various kinds of mildews are caused by overwatering and sometimes a combination of too much water and too little heat. Some mildews affect the soils, some the leaf surfaces which become covered. Overwatering also causes wilts and root rots. Plants thus affected are really best discarded.

Fortunately, in spite of these awful descriptions house plant pests and diseases are relatively few and are not, or need not be, troublesome in most homes. The important thing is to keep watch on the plants and to keep them clean. Sponging and syringing leaves deter insects almost as much as more drastic measures do.

Increasing plants

There are some house plants which lose much of their appeal as they grow older, especially if they have to be confined to small pots. Some, like tradescantia become straggly and lose colour, plectranthus can grow too rampant and take over a shelf or some corner of a room, *Begonia rex* varieties can grow much too large for their pots and present an unattractive root portion in the centre of the plant, an aechmea after it has flowered may develop so many offsets or daughter plants round the main vase that it becomes top-heavy. All of these and others like them are best replaced by younger, neater and more vigorous specimens.

Many house plants can be very easily increased by some means or another. Stem cuttings can be taken from tradescantia and plectranthus and others and these will root in moist sand, in cutting mixtures and even in plain water. Large begonia plants and many others can be divided into several smaller ones. The best of the mature begonia leaves can be used as leaf cuttings and will produce plants. Offsets from aechmea and many other plants can be detached from the parent plant and grown on individually. There are also other means of propagation, all simple, and within the scope of the most amateur gardener.

Those who hope to make many plant arrangements or pot-et-fleur arrangements will find that a stock of small plants will prove invaluable. Sometimes, you can use cuttings in the place of plants and these can be growing roots while they are part of an arrangement.

Cuttings are the easiest form of propagation. Often all you have to do is to nip off a growing shoot and simply push into another pot or into water, it is that easy. Cuttings vary considerably; they can be a shoot from the growing tip of a plant, a section of stem, a portion of root, a snip of a leaf or a full leaf.

The tips of some plants, such as tradescantia, plectranthus, rhoicissus, philodendron, impatiens and hedera are among the easiest of all. As a rule, the shoot is cut or nipped out about a quarter-inch below a leaf. The lower leaves or leaf are trimmed off, with scissors or a sharp knife to avoid peeling the stem, in case they lie in soil or water and so create a source of infection. The bare portion of stem is then inserted into whatever rooting medium is chosen. Usually one should aim to have at least one third the length of the cutting as a rooting portion. Hormone rooting powders can be used to accelerate the formation of roots. If you use these, follow the directions carefully.

The plants mentioned above can be rooted in plain water. Later when puddle-pots are being described, more names will be added to the list. Rooting mixes cannot be bought but most cuttings root extremely well in a simple home-made mixture of half sand and half soil mix with a little extra sand as a top layer. Put a few stones or pebbles in the bottom of the pot first.

If you wish to save space you can plant several cuttings to a pot, inserted round near the rim in a ring. When they are rooted, tip out the root ball very gently and just as gently tease them apart and pot them separately.

Fill the pot, ram the mixture down a little because cuttings root better in a firm medium, make a little hole to take the stem with a pencil or skewer. Take it to the required depth, remove and insert the trimmed stem. Push the dibber down at an angle at the side of the cutting so that it is firmed and the hole in which it is set filled at the same time. Give the pot a sharp tap to settle the soil and then water the cuttings.

Rooting mediums should be damp and they should not be allowed to dry out. To keep moisture in you can cover the cuttings in some way, with a jamjar or with a transparent plastic bag for instance. If possible let these covers stay on until the cuttings root. If excessive moisture forms inside the cover, remove it and wipe it dry. A plastic bag needs only to be turned inside out and the dry side is then inside. Should you see mildew forming on any of the leaves, pick them off and give the cuttings more ventilation by taking the cover off for a while each day.

If you strike cuttings in water you can easily see when the roots have formed. If the cuttings are in pots give them a gentle tug at any time after two or three weeks to see if they are anchored or not.

For those who enjoy indoor gardening, taking leaf cuttings can be rewarding in more ways than one. Actually, a great many house plants can be propagated this way but not in the casual manner I am about to describe. Most will need the warm, close, humid atmosphere of a special propagating frame, most practical to run in a greenhouse although it is possible to buy small electrically heated frames for use in a home.

Begonia rex leaves, or those of other types are extremely easy and the satisfying thing about these is that you can use them first in flower arrangements and then as cuttings. Insert the leaf with its entire stem under the water into a little vessel. This can be glass or opaque, it does not seem to matter. After some days roots will emerge from the stem base and then a little later a tiny cluster of miniature leaf buds will begin to develop at

Left
Fibrous-rooted begonias and some of the new tuberous-rooted varieties are easily raised from seed in a warm place. They are all very free-flowering and bloom for months on end.

Above
Chlorophytum elatum 'Variegatum'. The little plantlets produced at the tips of the arching flowering stems can be encouraged to make individual mature plants. These can each be directed into a pot of soil. When it has grown into this the plantlet can be detached from its parent plant. Plantlets can also be detached and rooted in water.

the junction of stem and leaf. Soon these grow into leaves and eventually you have a beautiful new young plant which often retains its mother leaf for a long time.

Peperomias, saintpaulias or African violets and gloxinias will root easily this way in the home. If you want to try others, take them and keep the cutting inside a glass storage jar or a transparent plastic bag in good light and in a warm place – even on a shelf over a radiator which is not a place I would usually recommend for plants. All of these can also be rooted in compost.

Another method of taking begonia cuttings is to divide the leaf in such a way that the leaf bud clusters are formed in several places on its surface. Lay the leaf face downwards on the table and cut through the thickest veins with a sharp knife making cuts of about a $\frac{1}{2}$ inch from one side to the other. The cuts should be

made at the point where the veins divide and on the side nearest the stem. Retain the stem – or at least about an inch of it.

Have ready a 50–50 mixture of peat and sand in a seed pan, flower pot saucer, special little propagating tray with plastic lid which you can buy for this purpose and for raising seeds or, and this I use, a shallow plastic food container with a transparent lid.

Holding the slashed leaf carefully in the palm of your hand, turn it the right way up. Gauge its length and make a hole for the short stem. Insert this as you lay the leaf flat. See that the leaf lies flat on the moist medium, weight it down here and there if necessary with a little more, just a pinch will do.

Plantlets should spring from the cut areas. Cover the box or pan with glass or transparent plastic. When the plantlets are well formed pot them up.

Some plants produce plantlets without being goaded into action this way. Some ferns form plantlets on fronds, some succulents on their leaves or like the bryophyllum in a delightful fringe round the margin of a leaf. These plantlets may be potted and will grow into large plants.

Other plants send out plantlets on the ends of runners or stolons. These remain on the parent plant until the little plantlet finds a home for itself and then the runner gradually rots away. In the home, we can direct these

stolons to drop their plantlets on a pot of soil ready waiting. Here the little plantlet will soon grow into the soil and all you have to do is to snip the umbilical cord. Chlorophytums send out a number of these stolons which add to the attractiveness of the plant. Often you will see the thick thong-like roots forming while they dangle in the air.

A similar method may be used for layering plants. In this case, one leads a good trail of any climber to a pot of soil, or even to a vessel of water. The stem is held down on the soil or in the water – a stone is usually the best means, just lay this over the stem so that it stays in place, and roots should grow from the part of stem which comes in contact with the rooting medium. Often roots grow quicker into soil if the skin of the stem is scraped away at this point.

Air-layering is a means of renewing, even tidying some plants. As varieties of *Ficus decora*, dieffenbachias and dracaenas grow older often the tuft of leaves is borne higher and higher on the tip of a stem which has become a trunk. As a rule the plants are not attractive so unless there is a special reason for keeping a tall plant it is best to air-layer the portion of plant at the top of the trunk.

At a point a few inches below the lowest leaf and with a sharp knife, mark a circle round the stem by cutting through the skin. Mark another circle about a $\frac{1}{4}$ inch. lower down. It should now be possible to peel the skin away from this area. This should now be covered with some material into which roots, which should spring from the cut portion, will grow. Traditionally, moist sphagnum moss is used, a handful say about the size of a tennis ball, spread round the stem and then tied to it and finally covered with plastic to cut down loss by evaporation. Should you find it difficult to buy the moss, use a small cylinder of Oasis, cut down the centre. Soak this in water and then take the two halves and place them on each side of the stem. Press them against the stem and bind them in place and cover them the same way as you would cover the moss.

The piece of plastic – sheeting or even a clear bag will do – should be tied firmly both above and below the rooting medium. It is prudent to examine it after a few days to ensure that all is keeping moist.

Once you can see the roots through the plastic, the new plant can be severed from its parent stem. Rather than damage the new roots, pot the whole mass, i.e. moss or plastic and roots together.

You can see when a plant needs repotting often without knocking it from its pot. Turn it upside down and see if any roots are roaming through the drainage holes. With other plants, it is quite obvious that they are bursting their bonds and that not even a move into a larger pot will really benefit them. Primulas, some ferns, chlorophytums, aspidistras, begonias, impatiens are a few examples which come quickly to mind. Sometimes, and this is expecially the case with ferns and with large epiphyllums and aechmeas, the roots are so massed, that one can do no more than to cut the root mass into great chunks each with its own topknot of leaves. Others can be tipped out and sections simply teased out from the mass. Keep the new pots on the small side, just large enough to take the new root portion comfortably.

After dividing or repotting plants treat them a little tenderly. Water them in, as this settles the soil round their roots, but avoid giving them too much water, give them time to make new roots first. Spray them overhead so that their leaves are kept moist instead if this is practicable. Keep them in good light but out of the sun, even if they are sun lovers.

Left
Red Edge, *(D. marginata)* a delightful dracaena variety. These plants will grow for years, but as they age and lengthen their stems may become bare, something which can be masked when they are used in arrangements or in groups. Otherwise one can make 'new' plants of them by the technique of air layering.

Home Produce

Home produce is relatively inexpensive, seeds or plants costing about the same as a loaf of bread. In addition, there is a great deal of enjoyment and pleasure to be gained, even while watching the plants grow and develop. The final product will be really fresh and firm, with a vastly superior taste to that of the tired fruit and vegetables which are so often all that can be obtained in the supermarkets. The choice of vegetables, fruit and herbs open for cultivation is wide, although dependant on the climate and available space for root-run. The less usual cultivars can be selected—especially those with exceptional flavour—as well as the less common crops such as kohlrabi and figs.

Before growing crops indoors, it must be remembered that plants require light, moisture, an adequate root-run, and nutrients. Space is also critical, and this means that apple trees, for instance are not very suitable. A special 'growing' room can be made, with fans and supplementary lighting installed, but this is impractical in most homes where lack of space simply does not permit this. In the home, excessive draughts and sudden temperature changes must be avoided and the growing media kept moist, never too wet nor too dry.

SITING

Having decided to grow crops, the next consideration is where they are to be grown. Obviously larger crops cannot be grown indoors, but many can be grown successfully on a patio. Indoors, large pots and troughs can be used as containers for plants in living rooms; and window boxes, troughs and pots may be used on window-sills both inside and outside, while on the patio, tubs and containers of all kinds can be utilised.

If there is a border of soil in the growing area, the soil may well be impoverished, and in this case it may easily be improved by incorporating organic matter such as garden compost. It is also advantageous to raise beds above ground level, thus giving a greater depth of soil. Some homes, however may only have a concrete backyard, or a balcony, but using some ingenuity and imagination, a 'growing area' can easily be made and the same advice adopted. A raised bed can be constructed from railway ties or planks and the space filled up with top soil or good, loam-based mixture obtainable from garden centres, into which plenty of organic matter such as vegetable compost should be incorporated.

Another type of 'bed' can be made from a series of boxes, which can be arranged in steps against a wall, and not much knowledge of carpentry is required to construct a simple frame with secure ends. The length of the 'steps' can be adapted to the space available, with at least a 15cm (6in) width and depth for the plants to have sufficient root-run. When using boxes of similar size, they can be mounted like a flight of steps, leaving sufficient space for air circulation on the wall side. The same principle can be adopted to make a free standing 'bed' of double size, which, for the best results should be orientated north/south in order to get maximum sun.

Very large seed boxes can be made from good sound timber easily available from sawmills, or even from refuse dumps, and these trays can be raised on legs or even mounted on wheels where space allows, so that they may be moved around to catch sunshine at all hours of the day.

There is a wide variety of containers suitable for patio gardening—barrels, wheelbarrows, old, hollowed-out tree stumps—indeed anything that will hold earth. A Scottish horticultural adviser has a patio garden made from kipper boxes collected from neighbouring beaches—a true Scottish idea! Half barrels or tubs may be regarded as the most attractive to look at, but anything goes in a patio.

An herb garden can be made from any suitable sized container, and by using different species, an attractive display can be achieved. Likewise a half barrel can be utilised for making a salad garden with an eggplant, pepper or tomato as a central feature. Growing strawberries in barrels is an old idea, utilising both top and sides for the crop, but why not plant a melon or gourd on the top surface and grow it up a trellis while using the holes in the side for strawberries.

For window-sills, unfortunately, it is now usually only possible to buy plastic boxes, but an enterprising person can easily put a wooden cover in front, or construct his own box. Window boxes should be fastened by means of half angle irons to the window sills to stop them from sliding away.

All forms of containers must have drainage holes, and the base must be lined inside with about an inch of drainage 'crocks' (broken flowerpots, clinker or gravel). Drainage holes should be made 2.5cm (1in) square at 25cm (10in) intervals.

Within the home the same type of containers can be used. Kipper boxes should of course be washed well and all wooden containers should be treated with a wood preservative such as cuprinol but, on no account, use creosote. Large plastic trays should be placed under them to hold excess water; and to provide light, spot lamps can be erected. There are various suitable light fittings that can be adopted from fluorescent tubes to the artistic 'Artemide' type lamps.

The utilisation of space is a personal choice, but any room can be enhanced by an attractive display of plants, ornamental and edible, suitably illuminated.

Vegetables

The choice of vegetables that can be grown indoors in the home is naturally limited. However, near windows, on window-sills, or otherwise near light and sunshine most of the fruiting vegetables can be grown; and by using window boxes the range widens to include rows of carrots, radishes, lettuce or peas, with parsley or chives as edging, or even a tomato, pepper or aubergine at each end.

Outdoors, in raised beds or containers, the range of vegetables that can be grown is wide, so much so that a system of rotation can be practised. In market gardens, a four crop rotation is practised, with potatoes as the first crop followed by roots, peas, and finally greens. Potatoes are too large for a patio garden, and so a three year rotation is adopted—greens, roots, and legumes (peas and beans), while if a fourth year crop is desired onions might be grown. Crops are rotated so that build ups of nutrients, pests and diseases are avoided, since each crop has different needs—greens

require plenty of nitrogen, while root crops need phosphates. Legumes have the property of being able to 'fix' nitrogen in the soil, and therefore are crops to grow before greens, or to follow roots. Although rotation is important it is often impractical especially with window boxes or just a few tubs, and in this case the soil can easily be renewed. When using raised beds and 'flats' the garden can be divided into sections and a simple rotation adopted.

Tubs make ideal containers for a variety of vegetables, and they can look very attractive. Plant a pepper or eggplant in the centre, and then grow concentric rings of other crops such as carrots, radishes, parsley and lettuce, or alternatively the tub can be devoted to a single crop. Pole beans make an attractive feature in a tub, and so it is easy to see the variety of ideas possible. The soil in the tub must be rich enough to feed the crops throughout the growing season, and so prior to sowing or planting, incorporate plenty of organic matter such as peat or garden compost plus a general purpose fertilizer at the rate of 225g per sq in (8oz per sq yd). Suitable loam based potting soil can always be obtained from garden centres.

It is important to stress that only certain cultivars are suitable for container gardening, and so careful selection is necessary to choose those that are compact, small to medium in size, and quick to mature. In all containers the root-run is restricted and space at a premium. For window box gardening this is even more important, and there is little point in choosing peas which will be 1.2m (4ft) tall such as pea 'Gradus' when you can choose pea 'Little Marvel'. A small cultivar of carrot is 'Early Gem' and of lettuce 'Tom Thumb', so make a careful study of the seed catalogue.

A patio can make a sheltered spot suitable for growing vegetables. From left to right: courgettes, sweet corn, lettuces, sweet pepper, cucumber (on trellis), carrots (in trough below), tomatoes, radishes (in tomato pot), runner beans (climbing up pole), aubergines, lettuces. The shallow pot in front contains chives (on left) and parsley.

BEANS, PEAS AND SWEETCORN

Beans

Broad Beans
While not ideal for container gardening and having the reputation of attracting aphids, they are very rich in protein and by choosing a cultivar like 'The Midget' a good crop can be obtained.

Dwarf French Beans, Snap, Kidney or Bush Beans
These can be grown easily in a large pot. Sow three seeds in an 18cm (7in) pot containing a loam based potting soil. Seed should be sown in March, and on germination keep the pot in a well lit position. Stake young plants with split canes or small bamboos. Top dress with 50g (2oz) per pot of general purpose fertilizer about six weeks after sowing.

On the patio try to choose a sunny position and a sandy light soil, or loam based mix, never a heavy clay. Seed should either be sown indoors in small pots, or in place after the last frosts. If sown indoors, give the young plants either artificial light or place them near a sunny window, and keep the seedlings moist. Seedlings germinated indoors can be planted out after the last frosts, and after planting water the seedlings to settle the roots. Keep weed free and watered throughout the growing season, and try to avoid the soil becoming compacted—a light hoe or fork will help aerate the soil and assist the crop to grow. A mulch of peat is also beneficial. After the first good picking is over, apply 125g per sq m (4oz per sq yd) of general purpose fertilizer, but avoid getting it actually on the crop. The beans should be harvested when they are still young and tender, and a bean in perfect condition should snap when broken. Cut the bean pods off, don't pull them as this can damage the plant. Cultivars to choose include 'Stringless Greenford', 'Red Kidney', 'Masterpiece', 'Tendercrop' and 'Royalty'.

Runner Beans
Runner and Pole Beans make a pleasant feature on any patio, and in this country the former are grown almost exclusively as ornamental vines. Abroad some cultivars have white flowers and so, with a careful choice, red and white can be intermingled. The pole bean is the 'Jack in the Beanstalk' Bean, and with good cultivation can grow up to 4.5m (15ft) in height. Both beans do best in a freshly manured soil, and so, prior to planting in a tub or raised bed, enrich the soil with any available garden compost, farmyard manure, or other suitable organic matter. A mixture of peat and general purpose fertilizer would suffice. Firm the soil before planting or sowing the seed and make sure that the trellis or strings onto which the plants are to grow are firmly fastened. In full leaf and full pod, the vines are very heavy and so strong supports are necessary. Sow one seed at the bottom of each string, pushing or planting them 5cm (2in) deep, and as a precaution, in case of failures, sow a few extra in small pots for replacements. After germination mulch the plants with 2.5cm (1in) of peat and keep the plants well watered. Fasten in any loose shoots with raffia—beans should twine themselves. As soon as the first beans form, apply 50g per sq m (2oz per sq yd) of a complete fertilizer about 5cm (2in) away from the plants and fork it in lightly. Harvest the pods when they are about 20cm (8in) in length, or three quarters the length claimed in the seed catalogue.

Since tubs are the most useful containers to use on the patio for growing runner beans, a few reminders on how to fill them may be advantageous. Cover the base inside with 'crocks' and half fill with good loam based potting mixture. Mix in some garden compost, or other organic matter. Fill to about 5cm (2in) of the top and mix in 225g (8oz) of a complete fertilizer, and firm well. Fasten the strings with screw eye at about 8cm (3in) intervals around the outside.

The ornamental 'Scarlet Runner' or 'Kentucky Wonder' (green or wax), 'Blue Lake', 'Crusader' and 'Romano' are all suitable cultivars from which to choose.

Peas
Like beans, peas are legumes, and together they are probably the most widely used vegetables, being marketed in numerous packets and tins, of which the average household consumes great quantities during a year.

Peas like a slightly acid soil, as well as a moderate cool climate. They require at least sixty growing days before temperatures reach the 20°C (70°F) mark. To correct excess acidity in the soil, apply lime at the recommended rate to correct the pH. To test the soil, use a soil testing kit. Peas also like plenty of humus, and so peat should be incorporated, or they can be grown in soil manured for a previous crop. Peas are suitable for growing in raised beds or window boxes because a free draining, moisture retentive soil can easily be achieved.

Sow the seed 5cm (2in) deep in early spring, transplanting is not necessary and peas should be grown in place. However, to gain time young plants can be raised in small pots indoors and then planted out. Shelter from cold winds.

After planting keep moist and two weeks later apply a mulch of compost about 10cm (4in) deep. Pea sticks can look very unsightly, and so trellis is the answer. It is just as effective and easily used for several years. Nail plastic mesh on to poles and the peas will quickly scramble up. Throughout the growing season keep them moist but never sodden, and apply a complete fertilizer at the rate of 125g per sq m (4oz per sq yd) about six weeks after germination. Although it has been stated that peas are a cool growing crop, a cold wind can easily cut them back. Peas should be kept growing continuously. They are ready for harvesting when the pods are well filled and seem firm when lightly pressed. Cut the pods off, never pull them or the whole plant may come away in your hand. For a successful crop try 'Alaska', 'Little Marvel', 'Burpee', 'Frezonian', 'Meteor', 'Onward', or for a taller grower, try 'Alderman'.

Sweet Corn
Sweet corn makes an attractive feature on the patio in raised beds, or perhaps in a large tub. One key to success is to grow a block of not less than four plants as this aids pollination. In cooler climates a fast maturing cultivar such as 'Midget' or 'Early Sunglow' should be grown, while in warmer zones most cultivars will succeed.

The site should be a light sandy soil, and so incorporate peat and sand into the chosen bed or tubs in the winter months, as well as plenty of organic matter. Sweet corn is easily grown from seeds sown outdoors in a sunny position in May, but for earlier results, sow indoors on the window sill in full sun in March, using peat pots and a peat based mix. Always place two seeds per pot, and later remove the weaker one. The seedlings will be ready to plant out in late May or early, after all risk of frost. Prior to planting out, enrich the bed by applying a complete fertilizer at the rate of 125g per sq m (4oz per sq yd), forking it lightly into the top soil. Do not let the bed dry out, and

apply a further dressing of complete fertilizer in mid-July. Water and mulch to conserve moisture and weed the bed regularly, drawing a little soil up to the stems.

Pollination is essential and that is why they are planted in blocks. The male flower is a tassel occurring right at the top of the plant, whereas the female flower occurs lower down the stem on the same plant and is known as an ear. The ear is covered by modified leaves which form what is called the husk, and between the ear and husk are some long 'silky' threads on which pollen must alight for any corn to develop. An ear is matured when a milky liquid emerges from a seed if it is punctured by a finger nail or pen knife. Gather the ripe ears by snapping them from the main stem of the plant. Suitable cultivars for warmer climates are 'Golden Beauty' and 'Barbecue', again relatively short plants less subject to winds.

Onions

Onions are the mainstay for flavouring soups and stews, and no cook can decry their value since they can be eaten raw or cooked, in salads, sauces, pickles, soups, stews, or cooked as a vegetable.

Since they like a deep rich soil, they may not be suited for container work, but an adequate yield can be obtained in raised beds that have been properly prepared by incorporating plenty of organic matter and 125g per sq m (4oz per sq yd) of a complete fertilizer. Onions can be grown from either seed or sets, but sets are much less bother, being easier to handle, and requiring neither transplanting nor thinning. (Sets are simply small onions that have been grown in a warm climate, dried and stored.) Plant the sets as early as your season permits at a spacing of 8 × 30cm (3 × 12in) and firm well. The tips should be just clear of the ground. Keep them well watered, and apply a top dressing of a complete fertilizer at a rate of 50g per sq m (2oz per sq yd) every fortnight during May, June and early July.

If one chooses to grow onions from seed, sow indoors in early March and prick out into boxes or individual pots, planting them out in mid-May. Once the crop of onions begins to ripen, that is when the tops start to yellow, bend over all the top growth to assist in ripening. When the tops have shrivelled, lift and dry the onions off thoroughly on the patio. Any remaining tops, or straggly roots should then be removed, prior to storage in net bags. If an onion string or 'rope' is to be made, leave on 15cm (6in) of the top growth for plaiting.

For growing from sets buy whatever is available and for seed choose from 'Sweet Spanish', 'Yellow Utah', 'Yellow Globe', 'Crystal White Wax'.

For salad or spring onions grow bunching onions from a sowing in April for a summer crop, or in September for a spring crop. Use 'Evergreen Long White Bunching'.

Tree Onions

The tree onion is a strangely attractive and unusual plant, and can be useful where space is limited. The plant grows from rooted bulbets, and small onions grow in clusters on top of the stem, from where they may be picked for use, or gathered and when dried off, stored for winter use. If allowed to fall over, the 'onions' will root and begin to grow, and so it may be advisable to grow against a trellis against a wall, as they can grow up to about 1m (3ft) in height. Their requirements for growth are similar to that of ordinary onions, but they should be planted in September and will continue to supply onions for years.

BRASSICAS

Cabbages and allied crops

Cabbage and its close relatives commonly called greens, are easy to grow, but not indoors. They are gross feeders requiring plenty of nitrogen for leaf growth, and so prior to sowing or planting, the bed must be properly prepared by incorporating plenty of organic matter, plus 125g per sq m (4oz per sq yd) of a complete fertilizer. Seed may be sown in place, with first sowing about six weeks before the last frost, sowing at a depth of 1cm (½in), with successional sowings until late May or early June. Use spring or summer cultivars such as 'Earliana', 'Early Jersey Wakefield', or 'Emerald Cross Hybrid'. Further sowings can be made in late August or late September for spring harvest where your climate permits. Alternatively a few seeds can be sprinkled in an 8cm (3in) pot and transplanted out, applying a complete fertilizer in the same proportion as before after four weeks. The plot should be kept weed free using a light hoe between the plants, or by applying a mulch, and never let the crop become too dry.

Brussels sprouts

Brussel Sprouts are closely related to the cabbage, and they can only be grown in raised beds since they need at least 50 × 50cm (20 × 20in) of growing space. A poor soil will result in leggy, loose-leaved sprouts, so the bed must be well prepared, and if acid, lime should be added at the rate of 75g per sq m (3oz per sq yd). Sow the seed in pots in March to April, and transplant when the seedlings are about 13cm (5in) high or buy transplants in May. Water in dry weather, and apply a mulch of peat or similar organic matter plus 125g per sq m (4oz per sq yd) of a complete fertilizer about six weeks after transplanting. In cold areas, pinch out the growing tip, as this will induce the sprouts to mature at roughly the same time. Sprouts are at their best when about 3cm (1¼in) in diameter and they mature from the bottom of the plant upwards. Some proven cultivars are 'Jade Cross Hybrid' and 'Long Island Improved'.

Cauliflower

One of the finest of the cabbage family is cauliflower which is grown for its flower head rather than its leaves. It does, however, require more careful attention than cabbage, and does not stand as much cold, while in hot seasons it can be rather sensitive to 'head up'.

Prepare the soil by working in plenty of organic matter plus 125g per sq m (4oz per sq yd) of a complete fertilizer, and lime at the same proportion and then firm well. Successional sowings should be made to prevent the whole crop maturing at the same time, and seed may be sown in place after the last frost, or up to six weeks earlier indoors and transplants are set at about 45cm (18in) square. Weeds should be kept down by applying a good mulch of compost or peat followed by a dressing of 125g per sq m (4oz per sq yd) of complete fertilizer. Water in dry weather keeping plants moist. Once the heads (curds) become visible, the leaves should be fathered together over the curd, tying them with raffia or a strong rubber band, as this helps to blanch them. After about a week they will be ready to cut and eat. 'Early Snowball', 'Snow King' and 'Purple Head' are all suitable and proven cultivars.

Calabrese and Sprouting Broccoli

Calabrese and sprouting broccoli, like cauliflower, are grown for their edible flowers, but their flowers are produced in a series of loosely formed side shoots. A similar soil type to that required for cabbage is needed and seed is sown in place in April. Keep the weeds down with a mulch of peat or compost and make sure the soil does not dry out. Pick the flower heads when they are small and not too fully developed, and remove the head at the top first, then picking the side shoots. Suitable cultivars are 'Green Sprouting', 'Green Comet' or 'Calabrese'.

ROOTCROPS

When growing root crops in containers it is necessary to remember that the root-run is restricted by the depth of soil in the container, and so globe or stump rooted cultivars must be selected. This is particularly important with carrots, since some of the cultivars, such as 'Imperator', have very long tap roots. A rich soil is to be avoided, and fresh manure or fertilizer must not be added as this will cause the roots to 'fork'. Root crops cannot be transplanted so make sure the soil is right when sowing. A light sandy soil is best for root crops, and they will survive in sand plus peat.

Beets

Sow seeds in place in March to April, or around the last frost date, thin the seedlings to 10cm (4in) apart and keep them well watered. The crop can be harvested as soon as they reach the size of a golf ball, or larger, according to your requirements. Beets can be grown in a large window box, in tubs, or in raised beds, provided correct soil and watering are provided. Some reliable and suitable cultivars are 'Early Wonder', 'Detroit Dark Red', and 'Crosby's Egyptian'.

Carrot

Sow in drifts, or in rows, from March onwards in place. Carrot seed is quite small, and so should only be lightly covered with sand or sifted soil to a depth of 6mm (¼in). For continual supplies of carrots throughout the summer, make successional sowings. When the plants begin to grow, thin to 2.5cm (1in) apart and later to 8cm (3in) apart, using these later thinnings for cooking. Keep the bed moist and free of weeds, and a good crop should result. In friable soils just pull the carrots out of the ground by their tops, but on heavier soils a fork will be necessary to loosen them.

Radish

One of the fastest maturing crops is the radish, taking about one month from seed to table. They are no trouble to grow and do not take up much room. Sow little and often, for successional cropping, as opposed to a glut of radishes. Starting with a light sandy soil, incorporate some *well* rotted (never fresh) manure. Sow 1cm (½in) deep, keep moist and never consider transplanting. When harvesting, simply pull radishes from the ground.

They are suitable for tubs, and window boxes as well as raised beds. Choice can be made from cultivars such as 'French Breakfast', 'Cherry Belle', 'Scarlet Globe', and 'White Icicle', which as its name suggests is a white skinned variety.

Kohlrabi

A more unusual root crop is Kohlrabi, which is a cabbage with a turnip-shaped stem, which grows out of the ground, and it is this part which is eaten. It is an excellent vegetable, with taste something between that of a fresh young turnip and of a cabbage, with a little something extra. Seed can be sown 1cm (½in) deep in March to May, or young seedlings may be raised indoors and planted out 15cm (6in) apart in single rows, taking care not to plant too deeply. Keep weed free and moist and, when the 'swelling' reaches about 10cm (3in) in diameter, harvest by pulling out of the ground.

Turnip

White turnip takes about eight weeks or less to mature from seed to harvest, and is an easy crop to grow. An 'open' soil, well drained yet moisture-retentive is ideal. Broadcast the seeds and keep the germinated seedlings well watered, thinning to about 8cm (3in) apart. When the turnips are about 8cm (3in) in diameter they are ready for harvesting. 'Early Snowball', 'Early Purple Top Milan' and 'Tokyo Cross Hybrid' are all suitable cultivars.

LEAF AND STALK VEGETABLES

Lettuce

Lettuce forms the base of most salads, and without it there are few substitutes other than endive. There are two groups of lettuce, in which there are two further sub-groups. Head forming lettuce, as the name suggests, forms a tight head similar to cabbage—this group is subdivided into crisphead and butterhead. Leaf lettuce, on the other hand does not have a heart, but just a collection of leaves—this group is subdivided into cos and bunching. The bunching lettuce include the cultivar 'Salad Bowl' from which leaves can be pulled as and when required.

It is easy to grow lettuce, but to grow good lettuce plenty of organic matter is required, though because

Head of kohlrabi or turnip-cabbage.

they are shallow rooting this need only be in the top soil. 15cm (6in) of soil is sufficient depth for cultivation of lettuce. Incorporate peat, garden compost, or farmyard manure into the top soil of the patio bed—or into the whole 15cm (6in) of soil if that is all that is available. Prior to sowing rake in 50g per sq m (2oz per sq yd) of a complete fertilizer. Sow the seed as early as the soil can be worked and thin seedlings to 15cm (6in) apart, later thinning to 25cm (10in) apart. The second thinnings can be used for garnishing, but the first thinnings may be transplanted, and the check they receive from transplanting will make them mature 14 days later than the others. Water little but often, never over watering. Successional sowings are recommended to stagger the times of maturity but in mid summer lettuce usually bolts to seed.

Lettuce can be grown successfully in window boxes, or in pots on window sills, but wherever they are grown they must receive sufficient light. Small heading cultivars must be chosen for the smaller containers. Suitable cultivars of different sizes can be picked from:
Butterhead type: 'Bibb', 'Tom Thumb' and 'Minetto'.
Crisphead: 'Great Lakes' and 'Iceberg'.
Cos: 'Paris White'.
Bunching: 'Salad Bowl', 'Black-seeded Simpson' or 'Grand Rapide'.

Endive

Endive makes a good alternative to lettuce for winter cropping but is only suitable for growing in raised beds or possibly the larger type of container. Endives like a cool, moist soil that does not dry out in warm weather, and they also require a good rich organic soil. The bed should be prepared by incorporating peat or garden compost, and thoroughly breaking down any lumps, finally raking it level and making a fine tilth. Sow direct into the permanent bed from July onwards for harvesting from late August into the winter. Thin the seedlings to 15cm (6in) apart at first, and then to 30cm (12in), keeping them weed free, and moist. To protect the young heads maturing from late sowings, cover the plants with glass.

In their green state, the leaves are very bitter and so this crop is blanched. Growth ceases when blancing is begun, so blanch one or two heads at a time. Before starting, make sure the plants are quite dry as otherwise they will rot. Single plants can be covered with a 25–30cm (10–12in) diameter flower pot, making sure to block up the drainage holes with a large stone on top of the pot, in order to exclude the light. Alternatively the head can be tied up with raffia or string. If a group of plants are to be blanched, they can be draped with black polyethylene, or a special black screen erected above the crop. After three to four weeks, the head will be crisp and blanched at the centre—perfect for an autumn salad. The major cultivars are 'Green Curled' and 'Broadleaved Batavian'.

Celery (Self Blanching)

Since the introduction of self-blanching forms of celery, it has become as easy to grow as cabbage, and can be grown in raised beds on the patio. Sow the seeds thinly in pans or boxes, keeping them indoors or transferring to a frame on the patio in cooler areas. Once the ground has warmed up a little, usually about 6 weeks after the last frost, the young seedlings can be planted out. The prepared bed should be of good rich soil, and so, prior to planting, incorporate plenty of organic matter such as peat, garden compost or farmyard manure, working in 125g per sq m (4oz per sq yd) of a complete fertilizer. The soil should never be allowed to dry out, so water in dry weather, as celery must be kept moist. 'Fordhook', 'Giant Pascal' and 'Golden Self Blanching' are all suitable cultivars.

FRUITING VEGETABLES

Tomato

There are three major fruiting vegetables; eggplants, peppers, and tomatoes, and of these the tomato is probably the most important. Indoors, tomatoes can be grown with ease in large pots.

In dry atmospheres, they are inclined to dry out rather quickly, which can cause blossom end rot, in which case a black ring forms where the flower has been, and the fruits become inedible. To counteract this, ensure that the soil never dries out.

When large pots are used, it is best to use a loam based mix and always buy fresh soil each year, as this will reduce the risk of attack by soil born diseases such as verticillium wilt. Peat-based mixes can be used but watering can be tricky, and if they do dry out serious problems can arise. The size of pot required by your tomato plant will eventually be 25cm (10in) in diameter and plastic or clay pots are equally good. Although bitumen-covered paper pots are available these are not recommended for the amateur patio gardener since they start to rot after a few months and tend to look unsightly.

Tomatoes need plenty of light, and cannot be grown in darkness, or in semi-shade. Although they should be kept moist they should not be overwatered. Tomatoes can also be grown on the patio as a central feature in a tub, in a row in troughs, or in a raised bed. A sheltered, warm position should be chosen, and it may also be possible to place the tomatoes next to a wall which will reflect the sun's heat on a cool balcony.

In all cases there is an open choice between buying plants from a garden centre or raising them from seed. There is less choice of cultivar when buying plants, but the plants will have had a good start and should be healthy. When growing from seed, the choice of cultivar is open and much pleasure can be derived from choosing and comparing different ones. Sow the seed indoors

Blanching endives. The covering can be a small flowerpot or black polyethylene.

from February on according to your climate in small pots or pans—utilise margarine cartons—and sow about 10 seeds per pot, using a good seed or potting soil. A temperature of 15°C (60°F) is required for germination, as well as sufficient water, and germination will take about 10 days. When the first seed leaves have fully formed, and there are signs of the first true leaves, prick out into individual 10cm (4in) pots, placing them on a window ledge and keeping them moist.

Pot on into 25cm (10in) pots or containers when the first flower truss is showing, and firm the soil mixture thoroughly with the fingers, watering well to settle it around the roots. Avoid touching the stem of the plant. The seed leaves should be level with the ground. Each plant will require a cane to support it, and so fasten the stem with string, wool or twist tie to a cane—this should not be too tight but just a means of support. Remove the side shoots, and restrict the plant to five trusses. This means removing the growing tip when five trusses are visible. Plants in containers must be watered regularly and never allowed to dry out, as, if this occurs, several nutritional and cultural problems will arise— one of these being blossom end rot. In order to keep the crop growing successfully, apply liquid fertilizer, as per instructions on the bottle, when watering. When the trusses start to form fruit, apply 125g per sq m (4oz per sq yd) of a complete fertilizer, and then mulch with peat.

For outdoor cultivation in cooler areas, sowing can be delayed until late March and then the plants will also be easier to handle. Where there is a frost risk, plant after the last frost date, normally mid to late May, and if the young plants seem pot bound, repot from 10cm (4in) pots into 18cm (7in) diameter pots.

Although it may not sound that way, tomatoes are quite easy to grow provided the important points are remembered—watering, side-shooting and feeding. In addition, if only one plant is being grown it may be necessary to pollinate each flower with a camel hair brush, or the finger.

With cultivars the choice is wide, but from experience 'Pixie' is tiny but one of the best. The fruits have a sweet flavour, are very early in ripening and ideal for indoor cultivation. 'Small Fry Hybrid' is also early, producing a heavy crop of good flavoured tiny fruits. 'Early Girl' produces loads of regular-sized tomatoes with a sweet flavour. Of the regular cultivars, 'Better Boy', 'Big Boy', 'Rutgers' are plants with good sized fruits, fairly early in ripening and easy to 'set'.

Peppers

Both sweet peppers and hot peppers are easy to grow in pots or in containers indoors, and they may also be grown in containers or raised beds outdoors, although, like tomatoes, they should not be planted outdoors until after the last frost date.

There are sweet peppers and hot peppers both of which are half hardy, but hot peppers (chillis or pelepele) require more heat, and although not entirely successful in cooler climates, they will grow happily in a sheltered sunny position under frost free conditions, as well as in southern areas.

In most areas peppers will have to be started indoors, since the seed will not successfully germinate at temperatures lower then 15°C (60°F), and the plants will stop growing and turn yellow if the minimum temperature falls below 13°C (55°F). Blossoms will drop, and this means no fruit, if the temperature falls below 15°C (60°F) or if it stays above 24°C (75°F). In other words, peppers will grow satisfactorily, as long as a maximum day temperature of around 24°C (75°F) and

a night minimum of 15°C (60°F) can be maintained.

Sow the seed from February onwards, according to your climate as for tomatoes, but germination will be slower, and may take up to one month. After germination and the full development of the seed leaves, prick out into 10cm (4in) pots, and then when they are about 25cm (10in) tall, into large containers. Keep weed free and moist, and when the flowers appear start applying liquid feed when watering. Red and green peppers are not different varieties of plant, but merely fruits of the same plant maturing at different times. If left on the plant for a sufficient length of time, a green pepper will redden. Harvest as required.

'Canape' is a good cultivar which matures early with sweet, mild flesh and deep green fruits turning red on maturing.

Eggplants

These have similar temperature dislikes as peppers, but, once more, can be grown successfully on patios or in containers, or they may be grown indoors on window sills. Sow the seed in small pans or pots, and on the appearance of the seed leaves prick out into 10cm (4in) pots. The growing point should be nipped out when the plants are about 15cm (6in) high in order to encourage bushy growth. When the plants are about 20cm (8in) high, repot into 25cm (10in) pots. Eggplants like a sandy soil, and so continue using a light soil, but mix in a handful of complete fertilizer into every pot. To achieve a fruit set, either pollinate with a camel hair brush or your finger. At no stage should the plants lack water or the fruits will crack. When watering, liquid fertilizer should be applied, as per instructions on the bottle or can. The crop takes 80 days to reach maturity, and the fruits should be picked when the skin is glossy and about the size of a large pear or larger.

Suitable cultivars, for all purposes, include 'Black Beauty', an early cropper with oval to round, shiny, almost black fruits; 'Jersey King', a late cropper with round dark purple fruits; and 'Early Beauty', with longish oval dark purple fruits.

Cucumbers

Cucumbers like a rich organic soil, so the best place to grow them is on a mound of garden compost or farmyard manure, or some other nutrient rich material. The traditional spacing for the mounds is 1 × 1.5m (3 × 5ft), but on a patio this is clearly impractical. The solution therefore is to grow them in tubs, pots, boxes, or even hanging baskets.

Cucumbers are a fast growing crop requiring plenty of heat. Sow the seed after the last frost on the mound, sowing about nine seeds, and thinning out the weakest plants after germination to leave six. After a further

Tomatoes cultivated in a growing-bag.

two weeks remove all but two or three of the most vigorous. In cooler areas sow the seeds indoors, or under glass in March for planting out in mid May or whenever safe from frost. These transplants will be tender and may need to be covered on cold nights. Cucumbers need some training or they will get out of control. Fruiting laterals should be pinched out at the second leaf after the first fruit, and pinch out the growing tip when the plant reaches its space limit. Always remember that cucumbers are almost solid water, and so water liberally over the mound ensuring that they *never* dry out. Keep the mounds weed free, and harvest when they are still young and tender—about half the length stated on the seed packet. Suitable cultivars include 'Marketmore', 'Straight Eight', 'Victory Hybrid', 'Burpee Hybrid' and 'Burpless Hybrid'.

Pumpkins and Squashes

Squashes and pumpkins need a lot of space, but by a careful selection of cultivars, a small corner can be utilised for them. Of the two types, bush or trailing, the bush type are the obvious choice for the patio, although they may need hand pollination.

As with cucumbers, a rich organic soil is required. The zucchini group are useful small fruits, and these are harvested when they are about 10cm (4in) long. Frost will destroy them, as, by freezing the water present in them the cells are ruptured, and so, after cutting, they should be stored in a frost free place. They are better harvested while still young and tender unless they are being grown for competition purposes. 'Blowing up' is quite entertaining for children. Remove all young fruits except one or two from the plant and then apply water and more water, using liquid fertilizer as per instructions. A piece of wool can be threaded through the neck of the fruit and placed in a jar of sugar solution.

Squash cultivars can be chosen from summer types like the 'Crooknecks' or the 'winter' types which include 'Table Queen', 'Butternut', 'Buttercup', and the true winter types like the 'Baby Hubbard'; while for the others 'Zucchini', 'Goldzini' and 'Greyzini' are suitable.

The cultivation of pumpkins is the same as that for squashes and for cultivars try select small sorts like 'Jack O'Lantern', 'Small Sugar' or 'Boston Pie Pumpkin' or, if space permits, the giants like 'Connecticut Field' and 'Big Max'.

Cucumber plants can be trained to grow up a wall-trellis.

Herbs

A patio garden composed of herbs has the special attraction of fragrance, and the enthusiastic cook will welcome these additions to her culinary art as fresh herbs are not always easy to find in the shops. By growing them yourself, fresh herbs are at hand, and some may also be dried and stored for winter use.

Many variations in planting patterns can be achieved. One good idea is to plant in the shape of an old cart wheel, making the spokes out of gravel, and planting up the spaces with different herbs. In a large tub, concentric rings of different herbs can be planted, while on the window sill a box can be devoted to three or four of the most popular varieties, and the smaller herbs such as parsley or chives make a good edging to beds or large pots. Indoors, many can be grown in pots on the window sill, suitable ones being chives, marjoram, rosemary, sage, and winter savory, but they will need to be replaced when they grow too large.

Herbs grow well in a sunny position, and preferably a good rich, well drained soil, but they will grow in a poor soil as well. Since the majority of them are perennials, moderately good soil preparation is advisable, and so, in containers use a not-too-rich potting soil and in raised beds incorporate some organic matter. When planting make sure that the taller varieties are at the back so that they do not overshadow the lower growing ones. Mint and tarragon should be grown in large pots, which can be sunk in the growing bed, as otherwise the roots will overrun the entire bed. Raise such herbs as basil, dill, and parsley from seed outdoors on a balcony in late summer and transfer them indoors to pots for overwintering and for use in the kitchen.

When growing indoors, plants must be kept away from draughts, and watered regularly. If the air is dry, stand the pots in gravel on a shallow tray and keep the gravel moist to maintain the humidity around the plants.

Angelica: This herb grows best in rich soil in a shady position. Its stem can be candied and used for decorating iced cakes.

Balm: This is similar to mint in appearance and should be planted 30 × 45cm (12 × 18in) apart in any position on the patio, although it prefers sun. It can also be grown from seed, sown in early summer. The leaves are used for flavouring of soups, stuffings and sauces, and in summer, in cool drinks.

Basil: Seed should be sown thinly in late spring, in fairly dry soil. Water sparingly. The leaves can be picked as needed from July to October, but are difficult to dry successfully. It is used to flavour soups containing tomato, and is particularly good if used to give an extra piquancy to the dressing for tomato salad.

Bay: Grown in a 38–45cm (15–18in) diameter tub, bay makes an attractive feature on the patio. Its leaves are included in a 'bouquet garni', as well as in a wide range of cooked dishes.

Borage: This should be sown in April, in light soil and

later thinned if necessary. The leaves have a flavour very similar to that of cucumber, and make a good addition to salads. The calyx of the flower can be separated from the petals and floated on drinks such as cider or claret cup.

Caraway: Sow thinly in April. By late June the seeds will be ripening. Cut the flower stems then and hang them in bunches in full sun and above a tray into which the ripe seeds may fall. They can be used to flavour bread or seedcake.

Chervil: Unlike most other herbs chervil is an annual. Sow seed in drills 30cm (12in) apart from February to October, making successional sowings, and thinning out to about 10cm (4in) apart. The leaves are ready for cutting six to eight weeks after sowing, and have a wide range of uses, in soups, omelettes, salads, or flavouring of many dishes. Chervil does not grow into a large plant being about 23cm (9in) in height, and has attractive, fern like foliage.

Chives: These are one of the easiest and most useful of herbs to grow, and it makes an ideal edging plant. It may be grown from spring sown seeds, or by root division, dividing into small pieces. The mild onion flavour adds interest to salads, soups and to cream cheese, and it is available throughout the year.

Coriander: Like chervil, coriander is an annual, and seeds are sown in place in Spring, and later thinned to 15cm (6in) apart. Both the leaves and seeds are of culinary use, the leaves being used for flavouring soups, and the seeds, when dried, in stews or in curries. The seeds may be finely ground before use. The plants flower in July and seed heads are cut when thoroughly ripe and dry.

Cumin: A very small delicate plant, growing to not more than about 15cm (6in) high. It should be sown in late spring and the seeds harvested in the same way as caraway seeds. Cumin is an important ingredient in some curries, and can also be used in fish pâtés and fish soufflés. A good pinch of the seed is usually sufficient.

Dill: Sow in April or May, and thin the seedlings to about 7cm (3in) apart. The seeds should be harvested in the same way as caraway seeds. It is used in soups and sauces or cooked with cabbage or cauliflower, and is also an ingredient for pickles of cucumber and other vegetables.

Fennel: The fern-like leaves are attractive foils to other, more colourful herbs; this is a good plant to put at the back of a varied herb container. It is planted in late spring from cuttings, and thrives in fairly dry soil. Dry the seeds as suggested for caraway. The fresh leaves may be cooked with fish, and are particularly good with

mackerel. It has an aroma and flavour reminiscent of liquorice or aniseed, and thus needs to be used in small quantities.

Garlic: Some gardening books describe garlic under vegetables, and others under herbs, but as its use is in flavouring this would seem the better place. It is a member of the onion family, and should be used sparingly and with discretion. For growth it likes full sun, and a finely prepared light soil, and should be planted at a spacing of 15 × 30cm (6 × 12in), in spring or autumn. Lift the bulbs when the leaves die down, dry, and store in a frost free place, as for onions.

Lavender: This is usually grown outdoors, but can be successfully grown indoors in fairly large pots. The flowers should be gathered for drying when they have been exposed to sunshine for a few hours. It can be used as a moth-deterrent among clothes, and is valued for its delicate fragrance.

Lovage: This herb is raised from seed sown in April. It needs fairly rich soil and not too much water to grow successfully. The flavour is similar to that of celery and leaves may be added to soups or stews. It is also particularly good with salads.

Marjoram: Sow indoors in March and plant out after the last frost in rows at a spacing of 30 × 30cm (12 × 12in). The leaves can be used for various culinary purposes from brewing beer to flavouring stews and soups, and dried leaves make a refreshing tea.

Mint: It is best to grow mint in a container of its own, as the frequent watering which it needs in summer may not suit other herbs grown with it. Good drainage is important, as is a sunny position. It can be sown in spring or autumn from stem cuttings with a small piece of root attached, and will grow very luxuriantly if given adequate space. It is especially good for flavouring new potatoes and green peas.

Parsley: Widely used for garnishing hot and cold dishes, parsley has been reputed to be a cure for various different ailments, from indigestion and kidney troubles to rheumatism. It can be grown as a biennial or perennial, but to maintain supplies sow fresh seed every July, thinning to 15cm (6in) apart, remembering that germination of parsley is slow.

Rosemary: Must be planted in a light soil, placed in a sunny position, perhaps a windowsill, and watered sparingly. It is propagated by stem cuttings. It is especially good with lamb and veal dishes.

Sage: Sage is a perennial forming a small shrub, and to keep the plant tidy some of the old wood must be pruned out. Pick the leaves as required for immediate use, and prune in early and late summer, using these for drying and storing.

Savory: There are two kinds of savory, summer savory (*Satureja hortensis*) and winter savory (*S. montana*). Both can be sown in April at a shallow depth, and picked from July onwards. It dries easily if hung or spread out in full sun, and should be stored in a cool, dry place. It enhances the flavour of sausage meat and home-made stuffing.

Tarragon: Chopped leaves of tarragon may be used fresh in salads, in fish sauces or with chicken. Plant young plants, or rooted cuttings 45cm (18in) apart in a sunny position. During summer the plant will have small white flowers, and it will grow in quite a poor but light soil.

Thyme: There are two basic types of thyme, the creeping, which makes excellent ground cover, and the upright (*T. nitidus*) which is the one used along with sage in stuffings. Bees are attracted to thyme and so it is invaluable to the apiarist, and bees are also one of the gardener's best friends, aiding pollination as they go from plant to plant.

Suggestions for a useful, varied herb-garden. Back row, left to right: sage, marjoram, mint. Front row, left to right: parsley, chives, thyme.

Soft fruit

Strawberries

One of the easiest of fruit crops to grow, either indoors or on patios, is the strawberry.

A single plant can be grown very successfully in a 20–23cm (8–9in) pot, and a good rich potting soil. When potting up the young plants, fill up the pots until the plants can be placed with the crown about 2.5cm (1in) below the top. Firm gently with the fingers until the crown of the plant is half covered. When filling the pot always hold on to the plant with one hand. Keep the plants moist and remove any yellowing leaves. Runners which are produced should be allowed to remain as they provide some attractive decoration and young plants can be propagated from them. After fruiting, any dead leaves should be removed and the plant repotted if necessary. Where it is possible to use larger containers there is plenty of variety and scope in the choice of shape and design of container, and indoors, spot lamps can be used to make them a focal point.

Outside, raised beds, stone troughs, hollow tree stumps, barrels and old wheelbarrows are all suitable sites, but it will depend on the location or on what is available. Before starting to plant, all wooden containers should be repaired, replacing any broken sections and treating all wood with a wood preservative such as cuprinol but not creosote.

The most popular container has always been a large, wooden, perforated barrel, which will hold 24 plants in three rows of six on the sides and six on the top surface. Eighteen planting holes must be drilled in the sides of the barrel between the hoops, each hole being 8cm (3in) in diameter, and the top and bottom rows of holes lined up vertically while the middle row is staggered. For drainage, six 2.5cm (1in) holes must be drilled in the base and the barrel stood on bricks so that it is clear of the ground. Grave or 'crocks' are placed inside the base of the barrel to a depth of 15cm (6in) to assist drainage, and a drainpipe filled with sand and rubble is placed vertically in the centre. Fill the barrel with potting soil up to the level of the first row of holes and firm it well. From the inside push a plant through each hole and firm the roots into the soil mix. When every hole in the bottom row has been planted, raise the drainage pipe up a little and repeat the planting process for successive rings, raising the drainage pipe after each ring is completed and finally removing it altogether leaving a drainage channel in the middle of the barrel.

Runners will be produced and these can either be removed or left to root. A top dressing of a general purpose fertilizer will be required every year and 225g (8oz) per barrel is worked into the top 8cm (3in) with a handfork. During winter months any broken sections or holes will need to be repaired. Leaves which turn yellow or start to rot must always be removed as they assist in the spreading of 'grey mould' which is one of the more serious problems affecting strawberries. To prevent the fruits from attack spray with Benomyl (Benlato) or Thiophanate-methyl, repeating this treatment at fourteen day intervals. Always remove diseased fruits which will become covered with a greyish velvety mould.

When growing strawberries in raised beds or troughs, plant the young plants in April in a well prepared site into which 125g per sq m (4oz per sq yd) of a complete vegetable-type fertilizer has been incorporated. A spacing of 45cm (18in) is required between the plants. Place the upper part of the roots level with the soil surface, similar to the technique adopted when growing them in pots. If they are planted too deep the crown bud will rot and if too shallow the roots will dry out. Firm well around the roots using the fingers. In dry weather water regularly and lightly fork in a little peat.

So that the plants can be vigorous and fruit well in following years, remove the flowers until late May. Slugs can damage the fruit, and so scatter a few slug pellets about 15cm (6in) apart around the plants, and at the same time tuck some clean straw, wood shavings, or similar material beneath fruit and around plants. If birds are a menace netting may be necessary—the simplest method is to fix nylon netting over canes inserted in the soil by the plants.

Everbearers will continue fruiting until after the first frost. The plants will need to be replaced after two or three seasons, but utilise runners produced by the parent plants for replanting. A rotation can be adopted where, let us say, a wheelbarrow, trough, and barrel are being used. Choose suitable runners in June or July from healthy plants and root them in small pots adjoining the growing container, keep them well watered.

The choice of cultivars is wide—although the one crop cultivars such as 'Catskill', 'Fairfax', 'Florida Ninety', 'Fresno' or 'Puget Beauty' are reliable for patio use the everbearing cultivars are more suited. They fruit continually from June until heavy frosts, or even November. Such cultivars include 'Ozark Beauty', 'Ogallala', 'Red Rick', 'Streamline' or 'Evermore'. Your local garden centre will advise you on the most suitable cultivar for your area.

Black, White, and Red Currants and Gooseberries

Soft fruits, such as currants and gooseberries, cannot be attempted indoors or in window boxes, but they could be tried on the patio, provided sufficient space and depth of soil is available. Only one, or possibly two bushes, are likely to be really a practical proposition. Blackcurrants (if permitted in your area) like a sunny position and a rich well drained moisture retentive soil. Plant young bushes in spring or fall (according to your climate), spacing them 2m (6ft) apart, and planting them 5cm (2in) deeper in the soil than they were in the nursery, since this will encourage the development of new shoots direct from the soil. After planting, all shoots should be cut to just above the second bud. In March, the bushes should be mulched with peat, or any available organic matter, and apply about 125g per sq m (4oz per sq yd) of general purpose fertilizer. In dry spells ensure that soil is kept moist as blackcurrants are surface rooters.

After fruiting, prune out all crossing branches, and some of the older darker wood—blackcurrants fruit on the previous season's wood, and so never cut out new shoots arising from the base of the bush. Blackcurrants, however, are difficult to obtain in this country.

Red and white currants, likewise may not be grown everywhere because of the white pine blister rust. How-

Clusters of blackcurrants (above) and strawberries (below).

Sprig of blueberries.

ever they are grown on a 'leg' as are gooseberries. Plant in spring or fall, setting the plant with its first bud break about 23cm (9in) clear of the soil level, in good rich moisture retentive soil. Immediately after planting, cut back bushes to four buds. The growth of these currants can easily be manipulated, and they may be trained as cordons, fans, or other shapes against a wall. A mulch and application of general purpose fertilizer is necessary in March, and water in dry weather. When summer pruning, cut the laterals back to about four leaves—just above a leaf joint. With bushes grown as cordons, cut back the leader once it reaches 2m (6ft) in length. Ideally this pruning should be done in late June, when the new growth starts to turn a light brown. Another pruning is done in winter, and in the case of cordons, cut the laterals to one bud, and the leader by about half. With ordinary bushes shorten branch leaders by about a half, always cutting to an outward pointing bud, and cut the laterals to the first bud. Any branches that cross, spoil the bush shape, or are diseased or damaged must also be removed. Suitable cultivars include 'Red Duchess', 'Cherry', 'Red Lake', 'White Dutch', 'White Grape', and 'White Pearl'.

Gooseberries, too may not be grown in white pine regions but where permitted can be grown in any of the ways given for red currants. 'Pixwell', 'Poorman' and 'Oregon Champion' are among the better varieties.

Raspberries, blackberries, and other allied cane fruits are not to be recommended for patio gardening, as they need too much space and attention.

Blueberries

Another soft fruit which can be grown successfully is the blueberry, although for a good crop two different cultivars are necessary. Blueberries are a cultivated form of the wild highbush blueberry, but bear larger fruits of better flavour than those of wild origin. They are lime haters, and so should not be grown in limestone containers, or in any soil mix containing lime. A moisture retentive soil is required, with a high percentage of peat. Plant either spring or fall, the former being preferable in the northernmost areas in containers, or a specially prepared bed in which 1.2m (4ft) spacing is available. Each year, in March, apply 125g per sq m (4oz per sq yd) of a complete fertilizer the nitrogen of which is supplied by sulphate of ammonia and mulch with peat. Water well. Little pruning is required, only the removal of a few of the older shoots after five years.

For a successful crop plant two or three from the following:—'Earliblue', 'Bluecrop', 'Blueray', 'Berkeley' or 'Jersey'.

Tree fruit

On the patio, where space is limited, one method of growing fruit trees is in large pots, or containers. A 30cm (12in) diameter container is the most suitable for young trees, but eventually a 45cm (18in) tub will have to be used. With the correct feeding and pruning, trees can fruit successfully for over twenty years. Alternatively, if space permits, they can be planted in raised beds against a sunny wall.

Apples and Pears

A tree on a dwarf rootstock must be purchased and then apples and pears can be manipulated so that by proper training in fans, cordons, or in a bush tree, an easily managed tree can be derived. Not all cultivars are suitable for restricted cultivation—some are too vigorous in habit, and bear their fruit on the tips of shoots. The most suitable type of cultivar is a short spur fruiting type. It is ideally suited for container work as it flowers late, and fruits early, but for successful pollination of apples, two trees of different cultivars are required. One idea if there is space for only one tree might be to persuade your neighbour to grow a suitable pollinator, or to grow a 'family tree'—a tree which has several different cultivars growing on the same tree such as a '3-in-one' or a '5-in-one'.

A good space saving method, when growing apples against a wall or fence, is to grow cordons. Plant them October or March/April 60cm (2ft) apart, and at an angle of 45° to restrict the plant vigour. The main stem is never pruned until it reaches 2m (6ft), but all laterals are pruned back to within 10cm (4in) of the main stem—this is to assist the formation of fruiting spurs. By spur pruning, successful cropping results, and with established trees, wood formed from the spur in the summer should be cut back to four buds in the winter.

If a fan or espalier form is favoured, just treat each main shoot as a leader, and spur prune the laterals. The same principle is followed when growing in tubs.

Proper soil preparation is essential, and plenty of organic matter must be incorporated as well as bone meal, but an excess of lime is detrimental. Before planting ensure that the hole made is sufficiently large to take the roots without them being bunched in any way. Firm well, filling the hole a spadeful at a time and then firming with the foot around the roots. Always leave about 5cm (2in) clear at the top of a pot or tub for a strawy mulch in the summer months to conserve the moisture.

Pears require more attention and skill than apples, but the principles for successful cultivation are the same. Always choose a tree on a dwarf rootstock, and supply plenty of moisture in dry weather. If in difficulty consult the local garden centre, or nurseryman.

Cherry

There are two kinds of this popular fruit, sweet, which are eaten fresh, and sour, which are used for cooking, bottling, and making jam.

Apple on a twig.

Cherries like a very deep, well drained soil, but they can be grown with moderate success on a patio, or even in a tub. Sweet cherries are very vigorous growers. The sour cherry is less vigorous and can be grown either as a tub specimen, or as a fan. Normally two trees will need to be planted for a crop since cross pollination must take place, but the cultivar 'Morello' will set fruit on its own pollen and it could be grown on its own. Although fan trained specimens have been recommended for sweet cherries, an alternative is to plant two tubs with different sweet cultivars, and by pruning, to keep the trees as dwarf as possible. One easy way of achieving this is to tip back the laterals to five leaves—a form of spur pruning.

Suitable cultivars of sweet cherries are 'Bing', 'Black Tartarian', 'Bigarreau' and 'Napoleon'.

With all these tree fruits, soil preparation is important as well as the erection of some means of support for the young tree. A tub specimen can be free standing although in windy areas a stake on the windward side may be required. With cordons, place wires on the fence or wall at 25cm (10in) intervals, onto which the trees are fastened.

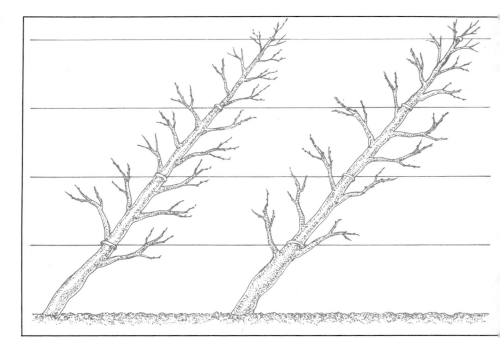

Peaches, Nectarines and Apricots

Peaches, nectarines and apricots can be grown from stones, although there is a risk of failure if the stone is planted during the autumn months due to the stone rotting. Crack the stone carefully with nutcrackers to aid germination, and plant it 8–10cm (3–4in) deep in an 8cm (3in) pot. Nectarines are smooth skinned peaches with a smaller, sweeter and juicier fruit. The same cultivation is used for all three types of fruit, and they can be grown successfully in large pots, or in a raised bed, but in the latter case, sufficient root run must be considered.

The more usual method of growing them is by purchasing a two year old plant of a known cultivar from a garden centre or nurseryman. A good well drained soil is required and so pot up the young trees in John Innes Potting Compost No. 3, sometime in early November, firming the young tree thoroughly and staking it. The pot size should be at least 25cm (10in) and may be up to 38cm (15in) or more in diameter. As such pots are in short supply a wooden tub can be used. Incorporate peat, and about 125g (4oz) per tub of a complete fertilizer.

These fruits can be grown as bush trees or as fans, and both will grow in any position other than in a frost pocket or on a site exposed to cold winds. When grown as fans, they receive more direct sun, and so have a greater chance of success. Support wires should be erected before planting the tree, and wires should be 15cm (6in) apart in the horizontal position.

In late January apply 50g per sq m (2oz per sq yd) of a complete fertilizer—or 50g (2oz) per tub—and mulch the trees with garden compost or similar organic matter. Water in dry weather to ensure that the crop never receives a check. Nectarines need water more often than peaches while the fruits are swelling in order to prevent splitting. All trees are self fertile (do not need another tree for pollination) but it is wise to hand pollinate the flowers when grown under glass or in the home. The pollen is transferred from the male floral parts or stamens to the female parts or style, by gently brushing the centre of the fully open flowers using a fine camel hair brush. This is best done on warm dry days around midday—flowering normally occurs in March or April indoors.

When the fruits have reached the size of marbles the crop must be thinned and all clusters reduced to single fruits. Fruits that have insufficient room in which

to develop should be removed, as should any growing towards the wall. Another thinning should be done when fruits reach roughly the size of a table tennis ball, and to test for ripeness, press gently with the fingers around the stalk end and if the flesh 'gives' slightly the fruit is ready.

Pruning should be done before growth commences. Late summer pruning increases the risk of peach leaf curl. The tree will have been properly trained before purchase, and so the job confronting one is to keep the tree the same shape. With bush trees, remove any crossing, damaged, or diseased branches, cutting crossing branches flush to the parent branch, and damaged or diseased ones to just above a healthy shoot. Any shoots that arise from below the crotch of the tree should be removed, as should any branch that is dying at its tip. When branches become unfruitful through age remove, as this will encourage new wood from the centre.

With fan trained trees, in April remove any buds that are pointing either away from, or towards the wall, and from those remaining, select several good buds at about 15cm (6in) intervals, removing the remainder

except for the growing tips. These selected buds will produce the laterals which will produce fruit in the following summer. In late summer tie in the laterals and leaders to the wires, and remove the tip of any long laterals. Two buds will arise at the base of each lateral, and one of these should be left to grow on as a replacement, while the others are removed when they are 8cm (3in) long. In autumn, cut back each fruiting lateral to its replacement, which is then tied in.

The 'Elberta' peach is probably the best known cultivar. It has a rich flavour and yellow flesh. Alternatives are 'Rochester', with large, yellow fleshed fruits of excellent flavour, or 'Red Haven'. A good nectarine cultivar is 'Golden Prolific' and the fruits are large and of rich flavour.

Figs

Figs can be grown successfully in a warm sheltered position outside and are well suited for patio work in tubs, since when the root run is restricted there is more fruit. It is an unusual fruit for home production, and also has the advantage of being an attractive feature on the patio. They are best grown as fans against a sunny wall, and if planted in a tub or other container, this can be placed in a suitable position near the wall, against which it can be trained. However, if all wall and fence space is already taken up, the fig tree may be grown in bush shape in a free standing container.

If the fig is to be grown in open soil, the soil should be moisture retaining, and not too rich. A hole 1m (3ft) wide and 1m (3ft) deep is dug and lined with drainage materials. A suitable container for patio work would be a large wooden tub, perhaps specially constructed, about 60cm (2ft) in diameter and 1m (3ft) deep, or a box built from strong timber measuring about one cubic metre (one cubic yard). Such containers could be utilised for any tree fruit. Fill the container with a good rich soil and mix in 225g (8oz) of bone meal. Plant the tree firmly and mulch annually with a 2.5–5cm (1–2in) layer of organic matter. Water in dry weather. During the first three years no supplementary feeding is necessary, but from then on, start feeding annually in late spring, and throughout the summer with liquid fertilizer, and apply 25g (1oz) bone meal.

Grown as fans, a 30cm (12in) clearance should be allowed between each lateral, and young shoots spurred back to a lateral—this is done by pinching back laterals to four leaves from their base. The fruit forms in the leaf axils on the new shoots. Select new shoots in July and train them with canes so that they grow parallel to the wall, or naturally follow the canes. Any other shoots should be cut out, removing them flush with the parent stem.

Where the bush shape is adopted, cut back some of the old wood to the parent stem in July to let in light and air.

A lot of young fruit will be produced, and so for steady cropping some thinning is necessary in July. The larger fruits are left to ripen while those of intermediate size are removed and discarded, and the smallest or embryo figs are left on the tree since they make the crop for the following year.

In frosty areas protection is necessary, and in really cold areas they must be brought indoors, in a cold greenhouse or cellar. Protection is not practical however, when the young growth is being produced.

The hardiest cultivar is 'Brown Turkey' which produces large brownish-red fruits with a blue bloom, and they are rich and sugary. It is an excellent cropper, bearing in August. For warmer areas a good cultivar is 'Brunswick', which is one of the largest figs to grow. It also is an excellent cropper, bearing green fruits with dark blue to brown flush and brown spots in August. 'White Marseilles' is an attractive yellow coloured fig of medium size and of very sweet and rich flavour, bearing from mid-August to September.

Fig pruning to allow sufficient space for healthy growth.

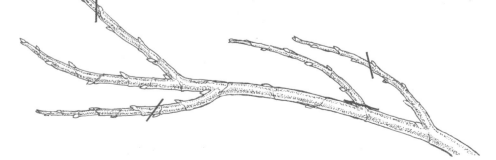

Other fruit

Melons

Melons belong to the same family as cucumbers, but are less hardy, and will only succeed in warm mild areas. Elsewhere they should not be attempted. Like cucumbers, they like a humus-rich soil, and can literally be grown on a heap of compost. On the patio this may not be practical, and so plant them on raised beds into which plenty of organic matter such as farmyard manure has been thoroughly incorporated. When mounds or heaps are used, they should be prepared in the previous autumn, and incorporate 125g per sq m (4oz per sq yd) of general purpose fertilizer two weeks before planting. Raise the seed in 8cm (3in) pots containing a reliable seed compost, and place the pots in a warm, moist place (indoors may be best or necessary). A temperature of 18°C (65°F) is required for germination. After germination pot up into 13cm (5in) pots when plenty of roots have been produced. Once the plants are growing, the temperature can be dropped to 15°C (60°F). Plant out after the last frost, choosing a sunny sheltered position, and allowing 30cm (12in) between the plants. Water is essential for a good crop, and so water slowly and often. Melons root quite deeply so make sure that the ground is thoroughly wet. A surface mulch with garden compost or peat will help to conserve moisture and keep down weeds. About one month after planting, incorporate 125g per sq m (4oz per sq yd) of a complete fertilizer.

The flowers may require hand pollination for best results. This is done by transferring the pollen from a male flower to a female flower by pressing the yellow dusty stamens of the male flower into the central sticky stigma of the female. About four fruits should be allowed to develop per plant. Once the fruit has set, any non-fruiting shoots should be pinched back to the fourth leaf. When fully ripe the melon will come away in the hand in the same way that an apple comes away when lifted.

Melons could easily romp away over a bed, and this would be a waste of space in the patio garden, but they could be grown in a large tub, or on top of a strawberry barrel. In these cases support wires will be necessary at 8cm (3in) intervals around the rim of barrel or tub.

Choose a cultivar or two from 'Ambrosia', 'Honey Rock', 'Haogen' or 'Honey Dew', or ask the local nurseryman for the cultivar suited to your climatic zone. If you wish to try watermelons, try 'Yellow Baby', 'Charlton Gray' or 'New Hampshire Midget'.

Grape Vines

Grape vines are very hardy and can withstand temperatures as low as −20°C (−4°F), but the young growth and flowers may be susceptible to frost and so frost pockets should be avoided. Fruit is produced on the current year's growth which is derived from the previous year's shoots. A rampant uncontrolled vine will produce vegetative growth at the expense of fruit. Wood that has finished fruiting is valueless except for propagation.

The main stem is known as a 'rod' and from it laterals arise on which the bunches of grapes are borne. Purchase a one-year-old vine from a reputable nurseryman in late summer or early autumn, and plant firmly in a rich organic soil which has been specially prepared by incorporating plenty of garden compost or peat. Several vines can be planted, and either one rod trained up, or two or three rods. If single rod vines are grown there will be sufficient room for several cultivars.

Cordon vines are trained against wires that are fixed 30cm (12in) apart and 15cm (6in) clear of a wall or fence. Vines are not as easily grown in tubs because they need good means of support which cannot be as easily provided with a tub. Space the vines 1.2–1.5m (4–5ft) apart, and, after planting, cut back the rod by about one third, and any laterals that develop should be cut back to two buds from the rod.

In the spring, choose the two or four strongest leading shoots from the rod and tie them in to the wires or other supports—all other shoots must be removed, cutting them flush with the stem. The laterals from the rod should be tied in horizontally to the wires. In the first season remove any flower trusses that develop and pinch back the laterals to six leaves from the rod.

Each spring, cut back each lateral's new growth to one or two buds beyond where it started the spring before.

Grapes are self fertile (do not need two vines for pollination), but to aid pollination, tap the rods during flowering. In early summer when the leaves are developed, cut the laterals back to two leaves beyond the fruit truss. In the first year of fruiting only allow one bunch per lateral to develop otherwise the plant growth will deteriorate.

The routine work throughout the season is to water regularly and in March mulch with well rotted compost or manure. Phosphates help fruiting so apply 25g per sq m (1oz per sq yd) of bone meal in early June.

Thinning a bunch does not increase its weight, but it does mean that the remaining berries are larger, so thin to maintain the shape of the bunch, removing berries until none are touching. Use long pointed scissors, such as nail scissors, or special vinery scissors, and never touch the berries as this damages the 'bloom' and spoils their appearance. Cultivar choice is wide— try 'Concord', 'Delaware', 'Niagra' or 'Catawba' in the North and East. In the South muscadines such as 'Scuppernong', 'James' or 'Thomas' may be tried, although they are quite vigorous. On the West Coast try the 'European Muscat', 'Tokay', 'Ribier' or 'Thompson seedless'.

PLANTS FROM PIPS

Many tropical fruits can be grown from pips or seeds with relative ease.

Pineapples do not have stones or pips, but are grown by cutting the top off just beneath the leaves and inserting it in a 15cm (6in) pot to a depth of 10cm (4in) using a soil composed of equal quantities of peat and sand. Slowly the plant will develop. For the first few months cover it with a polyethylene bag to keep the surrounding atmosphere humid but turn the bag outside in daily to avoid a fungal disease known as 'damping off', which is encouraged by lack of fresh air and excessive dampness. Without the bag the plant would dry out too quickly. Within a few months some roots will form as well as some new leaves, and the bag

can be discarded. After four years a pineapple will form, and the process can be repeated.

Another tropical fruit easily grown, although it can take over the whole home, is the avocado pear. However, it does take several years to grow to maturity and makes a very large plant. The hard stone is removed from the middle of a ripe pear, and is suspended, pointed end upwards, in a tumbler full of water so that half of the stone is submerged. The stone may be positioned either by use of a cardboard collar, or by the insertion of matchsticks. The tumbler should either be of darkened glass or else it should be covered on the outside with kitchen foil, since darkness is helpful to germination. Keep the water topped up and when the stone and glass become covered with green slime this should be rinsed off under a running tap. After six weeks or so, a split will occur at the top of the stone from which the root and shoot will appear. When the root and shoot are about 2.5cm (1in) long, pot up the plantlet into a 10cm (4in) pot, using a standard, loam based mix. The top of the stone should be about 2.5cm (1in) clear of the soil level. After potting, place the plant in a warm shady place and keep it moist. When the young shoot starts to grow away, place it in a well lit position and stake the main stem to keep it straight. Prune out any weak side shoots and remove any leaves that turn yellow. Repot when it is pot bound, and always keep it in a well lit position, away from draughts. Eventually it will need a 30cm (12in) diameter pot or larger.

The citrus fruits, oranges, lemons, limes, tangerines and grapefruits, are closely related to *Citrus mitis* (described in an earlier section). They are very easy to grow and after several years will eventually fruit. In

Pollinating melons by hand.

warmer climates they can be grown outside, but require a minimum temperature of 10°C (50°F).

To grow citrus fruits successfully, remove the seeds you require from the appropriate fruit, but do not wash them as this removes some of the enzymes required for germination. Press three each into an 8cm (3in) pot containing a loam based mix. Do not mix three from different fruits in one pot as they germinate at different speeds. The pots should be placed in a warm place to assist germination, which takes about six weeks, after which the pots should be placed in a well lit position such as a window-sill. When the seedlings are about 10cm (4in) high, pot them up taking care not to break the roots. Repotting will be necessary about every two years, or when the plants are pot bound—a useful key as to when a plant is pot bound, is that the top portion should be not more than three times the diameter of the pot. The only routine work necessary will be the removal of weak and crossing shoots.

Date palms are a challenge, and at the Royal Botanic Garden in Edinburgh there is a palm about 200 years old. Date palms can easily outlive their owners. They require a lot of heat, but with suitable care and attention you will succeed. Plant three stones into an 8cm (3in) pot, cover it with a plastic bag and stand near a radiator to assist germination until the shoot appears. As with pineapple, the bag should be turned inside out daily, to avoid damping off. When the plants are about 8cm (3in) high, repot into individual 8cm (3in) pots using a loam based mix.

For lovers of science fiction who wish to grow 'Triffids', the closest the plant kingdom comes to them are mangoes and lychees. Their cultivation is the same as for avocadoes. At first mangoes have fantastic stem contortions which remind one of tropical steamy jungles. Since they are semi-tropical plants keep them moist and warm.

SPROUTING SEEDS

The idea of 'sprouting seeds' can be treated as a gimmick, but by 'sprouting' seeds the food value of the plant is increased by 600 per cent. The seeds that are commonly 'sprouted' are mung beans, oats, fenugreek, pumpkin and alfalfa, and they are very easy to grow. Just soak a handful of seed overnight and then scatter them on a damp piece of flannel, old clean sheet, cotton wool, or any absorbent material. One way of growing them is to place the material on a pie dish or large plate. Put the dish in a dark corner where it is warm, and keep moist, and an almost 'instant' vegetable will be ready within a few days. The temperature should be between 27° and 34°C (80° and 90°F). It is important to buy seeds that are intended for 'sprouting', since many commercial seed firms dress their seeds with fungicides, and such seeds must never be used for this purpose. For the growth of these seeds, in order that they may remain white, tasty and nutritious, darkness is essential. Two tablespoonfuls of seed are sufficient to feed three people.

With mung beans a jam jar is one of the best containers to use for growing. The jam jar should be blackened out by covering the outside with black polyethylene or kitchen foil so that the light does not get in. After soaking seeds overnight, as before, rinse them and place in the jam jar, covering the top with a lid. Each day rinse out the beans, just 'swirling' a little water around in the jar and tipping the water and beans into a strainer through which water is flushed. Frequent washing is important as it keeps the beans fresh—otherwise they will go mouldy. After about six days the seeds are normally ready and should have increased in size by 500 per cent.

Before cooking, it is most important to remove any seed coats that still are attached to the plants. Sprouting seeds, bean shoots, or call them what you will, are at their most nutritious when they are about 5cm (2in) in height.

Another popular idea is the growing of peanuts which are easily obtainable in special packs from seedsmen or garden centres, with self explanatory instructions.

Mustard and Cress

Mustard and Cress are the easiest of crops to grow but if both are to be ready at the same time, sow the cress four days before the mustard. In both cases use thick, wet kitchen paper, or muslin flannel placed on a large plate. After sowing the seed on the paper or flannel, place the plates in a dark place, and keep the paper moist. When germination takes place move to a well lit position, remember to keep the 'paper' moist, and after two weeks it will be ready for cutting and only requires to be washed before using. This crop can be grown on a living room table, or in a child's bedroom, and since it grows quickly and easily it is good for encouraging children to take an interest in growing things.

CONCLUSION

If the enterprising patio gardener attempts to grow every crop that is described there will be no room to sit and enjoy the view of the growing crops—some selection is necessary. Before deciding what to grow, the climatic zone in which the home is situated must be considered, since there is little point in growing Mediterranean crops in cold areas or mundane crops if more exotic crops can succeed. Family interest can be stimulated with, for example, onions for the mother in law, marrows for father, parsley and chives for the lady of the house, and sweet corn for the children. The crops described are only a sample of what can be grown. Experiment with the patio—it is your garden—and remember that variety is the spice of life!

Flower Arranging

Containers

Styles of arrangements for flowers in the home usually are based on the position or place in which the flowers are to stand, though of course, the flowers or plant materials which are used are themselves bound to have a great influence on the patterns into which they are arranged. Obviously, if one wants flowers, heavy stems and wayward leaves to remain in the position and place designated for them, one should employ some means of holding them secure. For this purpose we use stem holders. There are types to suit every purpose, as we shall see. Possibly the easiest to find and certainly the most adaptable and the cheapest is large-mesh wire-netting.

One finds this indispensable not only as a stem holder for flowers, when it can be cut to fit any vase, but also for making cones to be studded with evergreens or flowers, for making pockets or nests to take fruits and gourds which are part of an arrangement but which

should not be in water, and as we have already learned, as a prop, wedge, heightener and support for plant arrangements. In fact, once he or she begins to use wire-netting, the flower arranger will find that it is often the answer to some decorative problem. For instance, certain shapes can be cut out from the netting and then decorated.

Small-mesh wire is not suitable because it is so stiff. Use large-mesh wire: 1½–2 inch mesh is best for flower arrangements because the wire is so pliable and will give as a stem passes through it, yet remain firm enough to hold the stems where you want them. If it is necessary to make an outsize arrangement in which the stems are really tall and tapering, cut a little more netting than usual and after filling the vase take several inches up above the rim of the vase. Place the tallest stem in position wrapping some of the netting, at the back of the container, round the base of its stem until it is secure. One can anchor great boughs of leaves and blossoms or tall stems of such subjects as pampas grass this way.

The usual method is to cut a piece of netting which measures twice the height of the container and a little more than its width. The netting is then crumpled up or bent U-shaped and inserted into the mouth of the container.

Some vases and other containers are so much easier to fill with flowers than others. Waisted vases or those that flute out at the rim and then become very narrow to the base are usually difficult to fill. It is certainly awkward to make some flowers in them fall prettily at a low angle. The way to deal with these is not to attempt to fill the vase with netting from the base to the rim, as is usual, instead, just measure the top width and set the netting in this area only.

This also is the method for using glass containers.

Previous page
Here the soft lines of winter flowering peach, carefully pruned, frame a few early Christmas roses or hellebores, their white petals contrasted against the deep green leaves.

Left
Carnations, roses, chrysanthemums and schizostylis (kaffir lilies) with mixed foliage and honesty. One vase stands inside another to make this deep arrangement. The top pedestal vase is filled with wire-netting and a ring of netting inside the lower vase encircles its foot.

Below left
Ornamental gourds, single chrysanthemums and elaeagnus foliage. Full of colour and exciting texture, a group of flowers, fruit and foliage makes an attractive decoration. Large fruits can be stood, like eggs in a cup, in jars which are easily hidden by the other components.

Below
'Apricot Silk' roses in glass. Because the neck of the glass is small most of these roses were arranged and tied in the hand. The two lower blooms were arranged separately. They wedge the bunch into position and hide the tie.

Secure a smaller piece of wire-netting in the mouth of the glass only. If you have doubts about its stability, secure it in a few places, and on the outside of the glass where it will not become damp, with a few strips of adhesive tape. The flower stems can then pass down through the netting which will hold them as you wish, into the water, while the means of holding the stems is hidden. You can always arrange a few leaves or flowers below rim level so as to hide the least trace of the netting.

When using glass containers, put in a nugget or two of charcoal to keep the water clear. If, however, the water becomes cloudy as it does sometimes during very hot weather, do not disturb your arrangement but take it to the sink, part the stems a little at the back of the arrangement and let a cold tap run with force into the vessel. This will change the water and aerate it at the same time.

When you push the netting into any container, push the folded end in first and hold the netting so that the ends of the cut edge are uppermost. These can be used to advantage. You can crook them over a rim to hold the

Right
This bright mixture of annuals mixed with a shoot from a pot coleus, is arranged in a bowl standing on a flat green pedestal dish. Low-lying flowers hide the water vessel.

Left
Pink peonies, delphiniums, spirea, scotch mist, sweet peas and pinks. The contrasting shapes of the full blooms and the spikey delphiniums give this arrangement fullness and definition.

Below
A copper jelly mould keeps water cool and sweet and brings a lively and natural air to the simple garden flowers.

netting firm – do this in three or four places if necessary. You can also use these little snag ends to embrace any very tall stems that need to be more restrained than others or which are heavy or inclined to turn about as some do, the forced guelder rose is an example.

If you want to make some stems hang down really low below rim level you can do this by hooking an end or two round them quite near rim level where the wire will not show. You can then exert gentle but firm pressure on the wire until the stems fall into the position you want. At other times these wire ends can be pushed through a stem, just as though they were pins. This will hold a stem just where you want it and yet do it no harm.

To return for a moment to glass containers. You can dispense with wire-netting altogether for these if you wish to arrange just one lovely branch or perhaps a group of flowers flowing at some special angle in the oriental manner.

Obviously whatever method you use, the important thing is that the holder should not show through the glass. It is possible, when you are using a narrow necked glass – or an opaque vase – to wedge one stem, or a very few stems, in place by pushing short, thick pieces of bare stem between the branch and the side of the container.

You can also use a lump of modelling clay the same way but if you do, remember that clay will stick only to perfectly dry surfaces so get it in place and the stem arranged before adding the water.

Simple and effective are the ancient Japanese 'kubari', either the forked or cross stick type. Kubari should always be cut from living twigs – cupressus is excellent for this purpose. First cut the twig so that it fits tightly in the mouth of the container. This may not necessarily be across the widest portion because the stem may look best flowing from some point near the rim, so test first. Split the wood and wedge it open with another small piece of the same twig so that it resembles a Y.

Cross twigs should first be measured in the same way and then simply fastened together at the centre with raffia or fine twine.

A very modern form of kubari is simply to cut a block of Oasis, about which I have more to say later, and wedge this in the mouth of the container.

Another effective way to hold one single stem, a branch of blossom for instance, is to bend but not break the base of the stem so that it makes a 'foot' at right angles to the main stem. This should fit snugly from one side of the base of the container to the other. This being so the branch will stay upright and firmly in place.

An invaluable aid is the pinholder which holds stems impaled upon its points. Woody stems can be cut on a slant, or even split and then can be arranged at almost any angle. Pinholders come in all shapes and sizes. You can buy one, or a series of them, small enough and dainty enough for a wineglass. Actually, these little holders can be pressed against the side of a glass to hold one stem. Other pinholders are so large that they are heavy to lift but they are invaluable for holding a really heavy branch in place inside the vase.

Although they can be used inside a tall vessel, pinholders are most useful for arrangements made in shallow containers. It is important that the pinholder does not move or slip about if the arrangement is moved. To prevent this happening simply make three or four peasized pills of modelling clay and press them under the *dry* holder. Do this lightly but firmly so that they adhere but are still rounded. Then turn the holder right way up and press it down on the container in the spot in which it is to stand. As the pills are flattened they provide a bond between the two which can later be easily removed.

If you would like to use a dish or a plate or some other object which is really too shallow to hold water, use a tin or small deeper supplementary container to hold the water and the pinholder. Place the clay pills under the water vessel as well as under the pinholder in this case.

Foamed plastic stem holders, such as Oasis, are great aids to the flower arranger. Made of foamed urea, their texture is soft, sponge-like and unresistant. They are available the world over.

Probably the most important thing about them is that you can so easily insert a stem into the surface where it will immediately hold firm. If the stem is very short, you need insert no more than 1 inch or even less. As you will appreciate, this is a great advantage because many lovely subjects, leaves in particular, are often very short stemmed. Should you wish, and you might if you were making Christmas decorations, you can even insert stems upside down and they will still stay in place.

Because the plastics absorb and hold water they can be used ex-container, that is to say, on a plate rather than inside a vessel. However, when it is used this way one should realise that the moisture will evaporate constantly and that the plastic will need re-soaking each day.

When used inside a container it is most convenient to put a square peg in a round hole, in other words, a rectangular block in a cylindrical vessel. This then leaves four spaces near the rim, and water can be poured into whichever one is most conveniently placed.

Obviously, it is a great advantage to have a variety of stem holders but where the arranger is working to a limited budget and in cases of emergency it is possible to devise many simple means of holding stems. Long ago, wet clay, straws bunched and pressed into a vase, and box snippets arranged to come just to rim level, were some of the means employed. The important thing is to ensure that the stem holder is so firmly wedged or anchored that it cannot move while the flowers are being arranged. As a rule, it is the first few stems that need most careful placement. Once these stand firm and as required, other stems which cross them below rim level inside the vase become locked and these then make a stem holder for those which follow.

For those who have no pinholders a large potato offers a good substitute on occasions. Its base should be sliced so that it holds firm. Woody stems can be cut on a slant and thrust into this. Larger holes can be made with a peeler or an apple corer to take small and frail-stemmed flowers which should be bunched beforehand. The potato is hidden with a cluster of stones which also anchor it.

Those new to flower arranging may find it interesting to note that hiding the stem holder in a low arrangement often anchors the flowers in such a way that they become welded to the container. And the way one decides to camouflage a stem holder can add to the interest of the arangement as a whole. Often it is sufficient simply to arrange the largest leaves or flowers so low that although they are not actually in the water they are so near to the surface that they screen the holder. If the arrangement is in a vertical style to do this may not be right and then one resorts to the use of shells, stones, small gnarled pieces of driftwood, cork, bark, fungi—these can be dried and used again and again, actually, any natural material which has some beauty or interest to commend it. Pet shops stock certain items which make good accessories, coral, rocks, sea-fans.

Where it is essential that objects are kept out of water it is usually a simple matter to lay a piece of bark, plastic, cork or even a flat shell, across the container from one side to the other near the pinholder, and to arrange them on this. Wire-netting can be used as a nest for the same purpose and in this case one can use leaves to hide it and place the other things on these.

Wire-netting can be cut and rolled to make a cone. Cut out a paper pattern first. The base can be pushed into the container and the flowers inserted all over the surface of the wire shape, through the netting, their stems down into the water. Alternatively, a cone can be stuffed with moss or damp foamed plastic. However, it is much simpler, especially if you are making several Christmas decorations, to buy the foamed plastic shapes ready-made for this purpose. These come in several sizes. They are also available in spherical form. These can be used to make floral bosses which can either be mounted on a stem like a little tree-trunk or suspended from a cord or ribbon.

96

Styles

Left
Many kinds of annuals fill this Victorian vase designed for two levels of flowers. The tall bugle-shaped container fits inside the bowl. One can improvise similar containers from everyday objects quite easily.

Right
Alliums and driftwood. Formal flowers fit naturally into formal patterns but there are many simple ways we can introduce a little informality without diminishing their effectiveness. Driftwood adds curves and hides the stem holder.

Below
Ranunculus in a Queen conch shell. There is really no limit to the type of containers you can use. So long as whatever you would like to use can hold water or some moisture-retentive material it will do. Shells and flowers go beautifully together.

One of the best pieces of advice I can give relating to flower arrangement is this: don't be tied in any way. Don't think that you have to have special vases, that you have to follow special rules, that you have to use only certain kinds of flowers, materials or colours. The way you arrange flowers should depend entirely on how you want to see them. However, I think that it needs stressing that flower arrangement proper means value for money and reward for time spent, which the mere placement of flowers can never be. Think in terms of buying a few beautiful flowers and spinning them out with foliage and other accessories. Collect a wide range of containers because these will help you ring the changes constantly and you can elect to use the same cheap flowers for weeks on end without ever becoming tired of them. Collect containers with the same liberal point of view as I suggested you should adopt when looking for those suitable for plant ar-

rangements. Apart from true flower vases—and so far as these are concerned do realise that some of these are difficult to use, especially the old fashioned types which need so many flowers to fill them attractively—you can use anything that holds water or which can be made to appear to do so.

If you make a collection of accessories for flower arrangements you will always have a source of decoration and of inspiration. These with your house plants will ensure that you can always rustle up a flower arrangement or a party decoration for some special occasion. Do remember that anything that grows can be used. Driftwood is particularly lovely for this purpose and it is worth while searching the beach to find one piece or more that is beautifully shaped, no

matter how small. If you find only small pieces they can be joined together quite effectively to make a piece which is shaped more to your liking. Such pieces can be given false stems or they can simply be laid or wedged in place.

Cone and certain seed heads, such as poppy, lotus, morning glories, proteas, camphor tree pods, all on sale at certain times of the year, will look like wooden flowers. You can arrange these with fresh materials as well as dried ones.

Most things lifted from the fruit bowl or the vegetable basket will look well arranged with flowers and leaves. Those crisp, vivid yellow-coral, curly leaves from the forced rhubarb, large parsley leaves, especially if they are yellowing a little, frost-blue outer leaves of cabbage,

even a whole little cabbage can play a part.

Many leaves will eke out a few flowers and give substance as well as beauty to an arrangement. Fern fronds and fallen leaves, picked up in the park perhaps, can be used fresh and then pressed and kept for some other occasion. If you have a vigorous leafy house plant, borrow a leaf or two from it. If possible, select those which you know you can treat as leaf cuttings after they have served their term in the decorations – the beautifully coloured leaves of *Begonia rex* are ideal for this purpose. Use trails of tradescantia, ivies, plectranthus and rhoicissus with all uniform flowers which could do with a little informality and root the cuttings afterwards.

A fruit bowl can become a flower arrangement with such little effort. Put a piece of well soaked Oasis in a waterproof plastic bag and hide it among the fruit. This will hold the flower and leaf stems. If necessary use two or more of these containers so that you can distribute the flowers well. Generally speaking, shiny blooms look better and cleaner with fruit than do those with soft petals. You can also use children's party balloons filled with water or tablet tubes to hold the flower stems as we do in pot-et-fleur arrangements.

The lovely texture of gladioli can take any of the brightest fruits, for none of these are likely to overpower the flowers themselves. This is a good way to use these flowers when they have past their best and the spike is no longer the complete beautiful thing it was. Snap off the tip on which there are still good florets and renew these by arranging them in a completely different manner. This is one example of what I mean about studied flower arrangement being value for money.

In its widest sense, flower arrangement falls roughly into two groups, formal – into which group fall the traditional arrangements, and informal. There are subdivisions of these groups. Generally speaking, the type of flowers often, but not always, guide us as to what style to use. As you will appreciate, uniform flowers, especially where only one kind is to be used in an arrangement, tend to fall into formal patterns. Indeed, so far as shop flowers are concerned, their perfect uniformity is often best exploited.

In our homes, we find that certain styles suit one place better than another. For example, on a table that stands in the centre of a room or round which people pass the flowers should be arranged so that they look good from any angle.

Decorations of this kind are called, for want of a better name, all-round arrangements. For a buffet or for a decoration that has to be set against a wall it is necessary only to face the flowers so that they look out into the room. Actually this is a very economic style because you will not need so many flowers. These are known as faced arrangements.

On these two themes we can play many variations. Flowers for special little places about the home may not need to conform to any particular style any more than any other ornament in the house. These can be made truly pictorial or scenic. Alternatively, they can be sparse and oriental in style, expecially if some furnishing or other decoration nearby is in the same mood.

So far as traditional styles are concerned, think in terms of shapes, the shapes which you would get if you were to draw a line round the flowers' tips after they were arranged. This may sound complicated to a beginner but it is true to say that after doing only very few flower arrangements one can see how these shapes emerge, and by the same token, one can quickly appreciate which are likely to be the most suitable for one's own needs.

Let us take first a bowl of flowers arranged for a table

Previous page
Single chrysanthemums,
daffodils, holly, cotoneaster,
mistletoe and leucothoe.
Strong colour contrasts are
warm and welcoming in
winter and at Christmas also.
The forced daffodils should be
bought or picked in bud for a
longer vase life.

Top left
Mixed dahlias with parsley,
fennel heads and santolina
buttons. Short-stemmed
flowers look well massed in a
simple manner. Even so, each
one should be arranged
separately. Wire-netting holds
these blooms in such a way that
each one can be fully admired.

Above
Marigolds in a bowl raised on
a pedestal. Like some other
flowers, tulips and Iceland
poppies for example,
marigolds tend to go their
own way in an arrangement.
Vary stem lengths to give each
bloom space to display itself.

Left
Tulips, freesias, hyacinths and
mimosa in a work basket.
Wickerwork and flowers go
well together. Either line the
basket with foil or plastic or
install a water-tight container,
a tin for instance. Prop the
lid open before arranging the
flowers.

Above
A bowl of growing plants and
cut flowers arranged together
originally made as a gift.
Saintpaulia and crocuses are
combined with cut stems of
catkins, heather and snowdrops
all placed in a kitchen bowl.
Other plants could be added
quickly and without trouble
when the cut flowers have died
to make a lasting plant
arrangement.

Below left
Wayside grasses, *Hedera
canariensis*, and gloxinia. If
small flower arrangements
and pot plants are concentrated
in one area their decorative
value is often greater than if
they are dispersed. Grasses
are long lasting and can be
left to dry in place.

Right
The growing plants framing the
carnations are sansevieria,
Hedera helix 'Glacier' and to
the left is the pretty marbled
scindapsus and opposite the
yellow blotched sedum. Cut
sprigs of the silvery senecio to
hide pots and flower container.

Left
Narcissi in variety, tulips,
irises, hyacinths and guelder
roses (*Viburnum opulus*) red-
leaved maple and broom tips
in candlecups. When making a
pair of arrangements do them
together (arranging one stem
in each at a time) so as to make
them twins. Candlecup designs
like these can be used with
other flowers at any season of
the year. The all-round shape
of table-centre arrangements is
particularly important.

Below. See following page.

centre. Here you have the choice of several shapes. Which one you select will depend upon the size of the table and the occasion. If no one is to sit at the table the arrangement could be high, wide and handsome. But, if you were arranging the flowers for a dinner table it would be best and more polite, to keep them low. A small table needs only a small decoration at its centre while a very long table could have flowers along most of its length – or perhaps a line of three or five bowls.

The pattern most often used is a half-sphere or globe which is resting in its container which may itself be another half-sphere but this is not essential. This pattern can also be made in a rectangular trough.

As a variation, the side flowers may be elongated so that their arrangement is in the shape of an egg sliced through the centre. In a different manner, the tallest stem may be much longer than the side stems and the intermediate stems adjusted accordingly and then you have a cone.

No matter which of these three basic patterns you select, there is one rule to remember for all-rounders if you want to learn to do them quickly and effectively. The centre stem should always be plumb in the middle of the container and it should be the only stem that is upright. This is where you will find the little wire-netting cut end hooks so useful. They help to make a bent stem upright. Hook one or two round the stem where it stands up from the netting and gently press on

the wire until the flower head or the tip of the stem is dead centre. After this, every other stem which is arranged should lean away from this central stem even if the angle is only very slight.

The side stems, which should be arranged next, should be at a really wide angle to the centre stem. While the centre stem defines the height of the finished arrangement, the side stems will define its width, and all the other stems should be kept within these dimensions.

For formal faced arrangements, imagine that we slice an all-rounder down the centre so that it becomes a semi-circle, a half oval or a triangle in outline. The centre stem is still the only one that is perpendicular but now it is moved to take up a central position but, this time, as far back against the rim of the container as possible. This is so as to leave plenty of room for all the flowers that are to be placed before it.

Flower arrangements need to have depth and this is an easy way to achieve this effect. Given so much space in front of this centre stem you will be able to arrange the blooms at different levels and to recess some, thus adding to the general interest and avoiding a flat over-formal surface.

Once again all the stems which follow this centre stem placed well back against the rim should lean away from it either to the left or the right, as the case may be. Stems should never be seen to cross each other above rim level. Instead, try to make every stem appear as though it had sprung from a source at the base of this centre stem.

If you can, let the decoration taper at the edges. If you have twelve or ten flowers almost identical and little else to arrange with them, you will find this impossible – one reason why I suggest that it is helpful to collect some accessories. Where flowers seem too much alike, introduce contrast of shape, slender stems such as grass, gladioli leaves, pencil rushes, small-leaved ivy trails, or the spike like flowers of a delphinium. However, even if you have only a bunch of flowers all exactly alike you can still create a flowing or growing effect.

The all-round arrangements just described were for bowls and fairly low containers but there are occasions when this type of arrangement has to be made in a tall container. In such cases one simply follows the same procedure.

To avoid a squat appearance or one in which the container appears to dominate the arrangement, try to make the central stem at least one and a half times the height of the container when measured from the point where it rises from the rim. If by doing this – and because you have no choice of container – you find that the arrangement would be too tall for a table centre, adjust the proportions by making the tallest stem reach the required height and arrange the side stems and all the lowest materials so that they flow over the rim and down the sides and so conceal the true height of the container.

Many arrangements in low shallow vessels have the flavour of the orient about them even if they do not precisely conform to the rules of the ancient and traditional Japanese flower arrangements. These were very strict but even in today's styles they can be helpful. You may not be sufficiently attracted to true Japanese styles to want to copy them but you may find that by studying the principles which underline them you could benefit greatly for they are based on observation and sound common sense.

The basic shape is an irregular triangle and quite often there are only three flowers or stems in an arrangement. These are known as *shushi*. If additonal stems are used these are known as *jushi* and when they are arranged they are always placed within the pattern,

Previous pages left
'Super Star' roses match scarlet sweet peas. Styles of flower arrangements have to be based on the role of the arrangement itself. Those which are to stand on a dining table should be low so as not to be in the way. However, you will still need some long stems to obtain the length of this arrangement – remember to check that all stems are in water all the time.

Previous pages right
Delphiniums, roses, anthemis and gypsophila in copper. When round flowers are massed, use spicate shapes to taper the edges of the arrangement. As well as delphiniums, grasses, rushes, leaves and sprays of foliage, blossom and berries can be used.

Above left
Lilies and driftwood. The method one uses to camoufla a stemholder can add to the interest of the arrangement as a whole. Three small piece of driftwood, carefully placec here look like one wonderfull contorted piece.

Left
Gladioli and desert spoons. Really the bases of faded agave stems, desert spoons are just one example of the many natural, long-lasting plant materials that one can buy or collect to use in flowe arrangements.

Right
The fleur-de-lys outline of irises is so lovely that one should give each flower roon to display itself. Their uniformity is softened by the curving driftwood which also helps to hold the shell in place.

outline or dimensions set by the *shushi*.

These three main stems are said to represent heaven, earth and man, *shin*, *soe* and *hikae*. The important stem is *shin* and this one should always be the tallest. It should also be curved and its tip should always be over its base. No matter how curving or undulating this stem might be it is controlled by this rule. The next in importance is *soe* and this second stem is placed to the side of the main stem, and indeed, as it rises from the surface of the water or from the rim of a tall container, it runs so close to *shin* that the two look like one stem. After a little space *soe* should move away to follow

its own way but it must never reach more than two-thirds the height of *shin*. *Hikae* is the lowly stem, as befits its name. It should always occupy a low position in an arrangement. It should flow forward but never downward.

When *jushi* are used, these are always added last, and as a rule just three or five are considered sufficient.

From this basic traditional style many others have evolved and even break-away groups have evolved their own styles also and so it is not possible to speak of one modern Japanese style. Apart from the rigid rules, which not everyone appreciates, the value of these

Left
This arrangement is in the Japanese ikebana style. The tall curving stem and mauve blooms of the Chinese wistaria (right) balance the slightly darker tones of the dwarf bearded iris (left). The low-growing white flowers of the cyclamen (below) provide a contrast.

Top right
Sweet peas and petunias, both of which are quite long lasting if they are gathered young enough. The first should have only the lower flower on a stem open wide. Petunia buds should be well coloured.

Far right
Sweet peas in a Wedgwood comport. Cut or buy sweet peas with at least one bud still to open. Arrange them in shallow water or in foamed plastic. Petals must be kept dry or the flowers will rot, so shake off rain or dew before bringing them indoors.

Right
Roman hyacinths, Christmas roses (*Helleborus niger*) and double tulips. With only 1 inch or so of their stem ends in water, these hyacinths are stretched to their limit. This way just a handful of flowers will make a good-sized decoration. Water should be topped up daily.

styles lies in the fact that they teach one to use very few flowers. This is a contrast to western traditional flower arrangement in which masses of flowers were and are used, but it is important to stress that you do not have to follow the rules of Japanese flower arrangements to make attractive decorations in which only few blooms are used.

When we use few flowers we concentrate on the beauty of line. For those who have to buy all their flowers line arrangements are both fun and quick to assemble. For instance, for a quick and attractive arrangement, take five irises, daffodils or any uniform flower. Arrange the flowers in your hand so that each bloom stands a little above the other. Cut the stem ends level. Stand them on a pinholder in a low dish. Move each one slightly away from its fellow to give it room to grow. At the foot of the stems and to hide the holder, arrange leaves, shells, fruit, seed pods, coral, whatever you have. To make a simple variation on this theme arrange the stems on the holder so that the flowers form a curve, a crescent or an S. This curving line need not be upright. There may be occasions when you think that it would look better flowing to left or right.

Arrangements in which a branch, bare, leafy, berried, blossomed or lichen-covered, or even driftwood, is featured with a few flowers can look very lovely in spite of the fact that they are also very economical. Choose a branch for its own sake, the more twisted and curved the better. Failing this, prune a fairly straightforward branch so that it assumes more the character you want.

For such arrangements, set the pinholder in the dish either in the centre or to one side—often the latter is more effective. Set the branch on the pinholder and then begin to work on it. Pull at the stem gently until the tip is over the centre of the base of the container and only when you get this to your satisfaction begin to introduce other materials. As we have already seen, the manner in which you hide the pinholder can contribute to the effectiveness and beauty of the whole arrangement.

If you buy foliage to eke out your flowers you will find that most branches are too heavy, too dense or the wrong shape. These need breaking down and dividing and even then you are likely to find that some foliage needs removing. Often the leaves you remove can be used elsewhere.

Opposite page
Iceland poppies (*Papaver nudicaule*) and briza grasses. Some flowers, including all poppies, are best cut in bud, just before they are ready to open. They will then last many days in water. Poppies should always have their stem ends singed before they are arranged to prevent loss of latex.

Left
Poppy anemones, physalis (Chinese lanterns), adiantum fern, holly, clematis seed, blue spruce and autumn coloured foliage. There are only three fresh flowers in this arrangement. The added value of an arrangement such as this is that you can keep it going for weeks if you change the water regularly and remove and replace the flowers as they fade.

113

Often one bunch of flowers can be broken up to make several arrangements which contain three, four or five flowers. The effect of the arrangement will depend on the placement of the blooms and the accessories. These do not necessarily have to be arranged in low containers. For instance, three tall chrysanthemums can be arranged, one above another in a tall vase with a flurry of some other materials at rim level, perhaps some berried bunches, leaf clusters, or even a bunch of some other flowers, say a posy of scarlet anemones, depending upon the colours used.

Three flowers of medium length can be given height by using branches, pencil rushes, gladioli leaves placed behind them. If these are all arranged in a tall vase the desired effect will be even greater.

One way to save both time and flowers is to make a permanent framework of leaves before which you can arrange a few flowers helped out with fruits, foliage or whatever you can find. As the fresh blooms fade, these can be easily replaced, even with a different kind of flower altogether. Some foliage is so long-lasting that such an arrangement can stay in position for weeks. In spring you can adopt the same principle but with different materials, using burgeoning blossom and spring flowers with perhaps, a flowering house plant or two.

There are some flowers that flag or wilt badly, examples are pyrethrums, hot-house roses, forced tulips, yet once we can get them to take water they perk up and last well. Almost always the cause of flagging is an airlock which forms in the stem and this affects some flowers more than others. Usually the woodiest or the most fibrous stems, such as stocks, are the most temperamental.

Never begin arranging flowers as soon as you get them home except all narcissi. These have tough, hollow stems and even if the flowers are a little dry and flagged they quickly drink and perk up.

When flowers have been out of water for some time, often really hot water treatment is best. Otherwise,

stand them in luke-warm water – baby-bath heat, for at least an hour, longer if possible. Those which are really badly flagging and any which have been stood in luke-warm water but which have obviously not taken any, should be stood in 2–3 inches of boiling water. Let them remain there until the water has cooled and then arrange them in unboiled but luke-warm water. There are exceptions, never stand bulb or corm flowers such as narcissi, tulips, lilies or gladioli in hot water. The stems will just collapse. Always stand paeonies, delphiniums, chrysanthemums, scabious, pyrethrums and most annuals in hot water to begin with.

Frail, delicate-looking flowers such as annual gypsophila and saponaria and fern fronds and small-leaved soft subjects such as maple are best drawn through the water, shaken gently to remove surplus moisture and then arranged. Very young and immature foliage often needs immersing for a few minutes, but if you buy this it should already be hardened or conditioned.

Stems that bleed, that is, exude a white sticky sap or latex, can be sealed best and most quickly by pushing the cut stem into sand, but of course this is not always handy. It is possible also to stem bleeding by pushing a little dry Oasis on to the wound. You must treat the stem again if you cut it shorter when arranging. Plants of this nature include the poinsettia.

It should not be necessary to change the water each day for flower arrangements. What is important is that there should be no vegetation under the water except the stem. Leaves, except those of tough evergreens, quickly decompose and turn the water smelly. Even the evergreens will rot in time if they are left under water long enough. Always strip the leaves from any portion of stem which is to go under water. A word of warning, do not overdo this or you may find that there is a very bare zone above the rim of the vase. Top up with fresh water each day.

Take care though that no leaf touches the water while its tip is over or on the rim of the container because this might create a siphon and you will then find a pool of water on some precious piece of furniture and an empty vase.

Some flowers last best in shallow water. If you have had gladioli that snap their stems after arrangement they are probably getting too much water. Just 2 or 3 inches is sufficient for them and most other bulb or corm flowers. Forced tulips however, need a deep drink before arrangement. Sweet peas last best in bowls in shallow water than in deep vases although if these are all you have they can hold a little rather than a lot of water.

A lump of sugar or a teaspoonful to a pint of water will help to feed flowers and keep them looking lovely for a little longer than usual. You can also use a saltspoonful of honey to a pint of water or even a glucose tablet. Most of the proprietary life-lengtheners have sugar in them and are well worth using if you are not budgeting very carefully. An aspirin tablet or a copper coin does not help the flowers to live longer because they do not check bacterial activity. Flowers live no longer in metal containers for the same reason. For evergreens and branches you hope to force into early blossom, use a few drops of liquid plant food or a half of a plant food tablet in the water to keep them going. Do not stand glass vessels in a window or in sunlight or the water will soon be so active that the flowers it holds will die.

Although it helps some flowers and plants to be lightly sprayed with clean water from an atomiser, others will simply discolour if water falls on their petals. Fortunately, these are not numerous, most prone are all kinds of violas and sweet peas.

Container Gardening

The area immediately adjacent to the home should never be neglected. Now that space is at a premium it is so important that the fullest possible use be made of whatever is available. Gardening in containers is the obvious solution for the many who find themselves without the traditional garden. As more and more people move to live in blocks of apartments and small terraced houses with miniscule plots it is important to take stock of what is available and then use it to the best advantage.

The space in question can vary in size and attract a number of names; paved area, patio, terrace, roof-garden or courtyard. It need not be a definite floor area but a space or ledge on which window-boxes, pots or urns can be placed or from which hanging baskets can be suspended. Even the smallest area that is capable of being walked upon should be considered as an extension to the home, one which can be sat in; a place where *al fresco* meals can be taken; or where friends can be entertained during the better weather. When well planted and carefully sited, containers can liven up dull areas. They can give a great deal of pleasure to their owners by providing an interest and a contact with growing things and, in addition, they give pleasure to the public at large who chance to see the window-boxes, hanging baskets and other containers as they pass by. As with plants or furniture in a room, containers can often be moved about to suit the occasion or whim of the grower. If plants do not flourish in the first position chosen for them, the container can be moved into more sun or more shade; when friends arrive and more outdoor circulating space is needed they can be transferred to another position, returning them to their regular home later.

SITING

The positioning of containers is very important to the plants growing in them. It is a mistake to attempt to grow sun-loving plants in heavy shade, or vice-versa. Happily the majority of plants are very tolerant and will thrive in all but extreme conditions. Most plants like some sun but types can be found which will tolerate even the worst positions. Sun-loving plants, such as the pelargoniums, will bloom profusely through-out the summer and autumn months in a sunny position but get all leggy and be sparing with their flowers in a poorly-lit courtyard. Conversely, the shade plants will get burnt if they are used in a position totally alien to their natural environment.

Small areas sandwiched between high city walls can appear damp and sunless, but such a daunting sounding prospect need not deter the would be container gar-dener. For, with only a little effort, such places can be turned into a restful green oasis for such plants as ferns, ivies, shade-loving plants and shrubs, and prove an ideal refuge for the city dweller home from the heat, noise and clatter of business in the city. Areas such as these are rarely capable of supporting a lawn and are usually best paved over. Plants in containers strategic-ally placed can prove very attractive when seen against a background of paving. There should be a willingness to accept the limitations of the site and to resist the temptations to be over elaborate. A simple plan is usually the most effective.

The word 'patio' can conjure up a hot sun-bathing area adjacent to the house. It could be furnished with restful cool-looking plants such as the lovely white and greeny-white nicotianas (flowering tobacco), fuchsias, iris or dwarf bamboos. Or the gardener may prefer to evoke tropical climes by using exotics such as agaves, cordylines, the practically hardy palms *Trachycarpus fortunei*, the Chinese Fan Palm, or the date palm *Phoenix canariensis*, pelargoniums and the scented heliotrope. Many succulent plants grown in the home during the winter months such as aeoniums, echeverias, crassulas and sedums certainly enjoy a sojourn in the open-air, they colour up, toughen up and are often induced to flower when given a summer vacation out in the sunshine. Pans of these succulents look best near to the house and are very easy to care for.

Balconies and roof gardens are also places which allow the grower an escape from the confines of the home. They can provide a sitting space in sun or shade —ideally both—and balconies can add an attractive view to the windows they serve. A word of warning, however: ensure that the structure is not overloaded, the combined weight of the containers, the compost and plants within them, the owner and friends quickly adds up and must be considered. Small balconies must not be cluttered up with too many pots. Often it is best to keep most of the floor space free and to use hanging baskets and boxes fixed to the railings or surround to the balcony. Sometimes just one really dramatic single plant or a mixed planting in one container placed outside of a balcony window so that it can be viewed from within is best.

Roof gardens prove something of a challenge as they are often areas which receive a lot of sun and wind. Large containers filled with mixed plantings are usually the solution as these retain the water better than a collection of small pots. Some staking of the taller growing plants and shrubs will be necessary to avoid wind damage and sometimes screens are needed to break its first force.

Window-boxes can be a joy twelve months of the year. They provide an attractive frame for the windows,

Left
Solanum capsicastrum, a delicate plant which looks good in a suitable container.

121

whether seen from inside or outside, and bring the plants in them into close contact. Many small plants are extremely beautiful but much of their beauty goes unnoticed in the large garden because the dominant plants are the larger and bolder specimens. Leaf marking and flower detail is only fully appreciated when the plants are in close-up. Scent too is fully enjoyed when it comes in through the open window. Window-box plants should be attractive at all times and if they are grown for the sake of their flowers should flower easily, profusely and over a long period. They need not however last forever and an attractive idea is to have seasonal boxes; one perhaps for the spring and summer months and another batch of plants for the autumn and winter. Gay flowering plants can be used in the first, possibly against a permanent background of low-growing evergreen shrubs and miniature trees. For the later planting greater emphasis might be placed on the evergreens, brightening them up with berried plants, chrysanthemums and early flowering bulbs. For the imaginative there are bonsai trees and the naturally dwarf trees which can represent their bigger counterparts and give the grower the illusion of a collection of forest trees.

CONTAINERS

Plants can be grown in anything that is capable of holding soil. Garden centres use old tin cans as a temporary expedient and these are standard equipment in the Far East and in South America. The commonest containers are clay pots with drainage holes in the base. They have been discussed earlier in this book. The square, oblong and circular terra-cotta seed pans are of similar material and are very valuable for plants that do not need a deep root run but like a quick-draining compost. They are very suitable for sempervivums (house-leeks), the mossy saxifrages and the dianthus. They have a nice chunky look and fit well into a collection of pots of different dimensions, they are also attractive topping a low oblong wall, such as is sometimes found at the top of a short flight of steps. Glazed pots have a slight advantage over their porous cousins by not losing so much moisture by evaporation. Glazed pots need much less watering than unglazed ones. They are often more decorative but beware of strong colours which may add nothing but a discordant note to the composition. Plastic pots, provided that they are not offensive in their colouring, look good and are in common use and also retain water. The terra-cotta, black or dark-green coloured ones are quite acceptable. Tubs can also be of plastic and these have the advantage

A wide selection of containers will help to show each plant to its best advantage. A hanging basket suits the trailing varieties, such as begonias and trailing lobelias. A tall curving pot makes a good contrast to the spiky leaves of a dracaena and the delicate tendrils of variegated ivy. Shallower containers such as flowerpots, seedpans, urns, or stone sinks, set off plants with more compact foliage. Back row, left to right: *aubrieta*, thyme, mesembryanthemums, dwarf juniper. In front, left to right: *Solanum capsicastrum, impatiens, dianthus.*

that the container adds only marginally to the total weight and makes for slightly greater mobility. Wooden tubs should be fairly resistant to decay and are useful in sunny situations as they do not take on solar heat. Hardwood tubs need little preservation but softwood ones should be treated with a wood preservative. Blocks or cleats should be kept under the bases of wooden tubs to prevent decay of the bottoms and allow a free passage of air beneath them. A real refinement is to have tough outdoor casters fitted to allow ease of movement. For a really large specimen or for a good-sized group planting there are lovely large khaki-green glazed pots to be found in Chinese shops. They often have a decorative and effective key pattern around the top edge and have been used for transporting the ancient pickled eggs beloved of the Chinese community. Drainage holes for these are essential if plants are to be grown directly in them and as the pottery material is very tough it could prove a job for a professional.

Most containers need adequate drainage holes to allow excess water to run away. These can be provided with a hand drill and a masonry bit if necessary. Earthenware crocks such as were used for storing bread or flour, or for preserving eggs are often available cheaply and, with drainage holes provided, make very attractive containers. Cracked casserole dishes and stew pans which have been thrown out from the kitchen can be brought into use if they are of an attractive shape and appropriate size.

Many other articles can be used as 'planters' or 'cache pots'—which are used merely to hide the pot in which the plant is growing. The classical lead urn is usually seen with a clay pot slipped into it. Beautiful fibre-glass copies of traditional lead urns are available and these have the advantage that they are very light and easy to move. Wooden tubs and wicker baskets which have been used for transporting fruit, vegetables or fish can in certain situations look exactly right and while these will not last forever they will be good for a few years if their function is only to hide the pot.

Window-boxes can be of timber, asbestos, clay, plastic, concrete or fibre-glass. All have their own advantages. Boxes should be at least 15cm (6in) deep and preferably 25cm (10in), allowing a reasonable quantity of compost to be put into them so that plants with an average root system can be used. Often it is advisable to line wooden boxes with heavy duty polyethylene to help retain moisture and to delay rotting of the timber. Boxes used on or below window-sills must be completely safe. Those fitting into window recesses will have the weight taken mainly by the ledge on which they sit and it is usually sufficient in those cases to see that they are additionally fixed to the framework of the window—possibly by hooks. Wooden wedges will level up boxes on sloping sills. Those which sit on brackets below the window must have adequate and possibly substantial brackets to support them. Remember the possibility of drip from the boxes after they have been watered and the excess water is running away. Care should be taken that this will not fall on something it shouldn't below it or to the annoyance of people living below.

Hanging baskets provide a welcoming feature over and near to entrance doorways and can also be used in other places with equal effect. The simplest form is one made of galvanised, painted or plastic coated wire, shaped like a half globe. Their season is usually limited to the summer and autumn months. Traditionally, this kind of basket was lined with sphagnum moss and then filled with good compost leaving 2.5cm (1in) or so at the top to facilitate watering. Recently there has been a move away from the use of sphagnum moss and black or dark-green coloured plastic sheeting has been substituted. The sheeting is pierced with small holes to allow an escape of water and while this does not look as attractive as the moss it does allow more soil to be used and helps to retain moisture more efficiently. Small plants can be tucked into the sides of the basket as planting progresses with either liner and these tend to cover the material quite quickly. Half baskets exist which are a quarter of a globe and are filled in exactly the same way but are mounted against a flat surface such as the wall on either side of a door or window. All of these open baskets need regular watering once the plants in them have established themselves. They should be placed periodically in a bucket or deep bowl of water to give them a real soaking.

An excellent new development is a rigid light-weight plastic basket pierced around the sides with tiny holes, with built-in chains to support it and a saucer drip-tray attachment which overcomes the annoying habit hanging baskets have of dripping for some long time after they have been watered. The saucer also provides a tiny reservoir of water which if not taken up by the compost will at least increase the humidity. These are very neat appliances and a real improvement. Regular feeding will keep baskets of colourful plants, such as fuchsias, lobelia, pelargoniums and begonias, going from May to frosts.

A few ceramic hanging pots are to be seen. In sun these tend to get quite warm and dry out rather quickly.

Shallow stoneware sinks are also popular containers for plants. Although a little heavy to handle they are tough, have thick sides which tend to insulate the soil mix inside them from the extremes of sun and frost, and allow enough surface area for some form of landscape to be built up. Sinks are very effective on a terrace outside of French windows or by a balcony window when they can be seen from within the home. They are usually best when lifted from the ground on piers or a pedestal, allowing for greater ease of inspection, tending and effect. Good drainage should be provided by spreading a quantity of small shingle on the base—keeping the drainage plughole free with a piece of upturned clay flower-pot. Good quality soil should then be added, plants and possibly some decorative stones set in place and the surface of the soil sprinkled with stone chips or gravel to provide a scree effect and perfect top drainage. Suitable plants for inclusion in such a garden might include some of the really dwarf conifer trees and evergreen shrubs and numerous low-growing alpines. There is no shortage of suitable material for use in the sink and planning of the miniature landscape can be very entertaining. Occasionally whole sinks are devoted to just one type of plant; miniature roses, or just dwarf trees or sempervivums. Small rose gardens can be achieved, or the cob-web houseleek (Sempervivum arachnoideum) is equally effective when grown in this way in quantity.

Some highly decorative containers are now available —the Italian terra-cotta decorated pots and the oblong troughs are excellent although the latter do not really have sufficient depth for some plants. The tall oil jars are decorative in their own right but are not very practical planted as their necks are too narrow and they seem disproportionately tall.

Those who wish to have (or are compelled because of awkwardly shaped surfaces) tailor-made containers must either go to a potter and put in an order or settle for the more adaptable wooden container. Many lumber yards are perfectly happy to cut wood to size for customers and it is then up to the home handyman to assemble the pieces with screws or nails. Exact measurements will of course be needed.

HOW TO TREAT CONTAINER PLANTS

Good soil is the first essential when growing plants within the narrow confines of a container. Without the free root-run that plants in the open ground enjoy, container plants rely entirely on the quality and suitability of the medium in which they are planted. A soil mixture rich in nutrients is needed for most plants and, with rare exception, one which is water retentive is advantageous. The former involve plenty of organic or artificial fertilizer and for the latter such ingredients as peat or leafmould which are capable of retaining considerable water.

Soil preference is not normally any problem in containers as they can be filled with the particular type of compost suitable to the plants that are to be grown in them; lime-free for plants which like lime and *vice versa*. Problems are only likely to occur when plants of totally different needs are grown together in the same container. A degree of compatibility is essential in mixed plantings otherwise one sort will suffer. Being compatible must also apply to sun and shade needs and the pace of growth of the several plants used together—otherwise the strong growers will swamp the more delicate.

Plants which are grown for their flowers will need to be fed with a fertilizer low in nitrogen. Nitrogenous fertilizers are excellent for helping to produce lush foliage plants such as coleus but would make the leaves of pelargoniums huge at the expense of flowers. Ringing the changes with two or three fertilizers is always a good thing and certainly to be recommended with mixed plantings. Most large specimens which are planted in more or less permanent positions will benefit from a mulch of well-decayed leafmould or compost in the spring. If top dressing with peat, ensure that the peat is moist before applying, otherwise it will shrug off water and prevent seepage to the soil proper below. Foliar feeding (the taking in of nutrients through the leaves) helps considerably and should be undertaken during the growing season. This is best done from a watering can with a rose attachment. Overhead spraying with clear water is also advantageous (fuchsias love it) particularly after a hot sunny day.

The soil mix in all containers will eventually need replacing but this stage can be delayed for quite a while by regular feeding and by stop-gap methods. Regular feeding of course helps to keep the soil in good heart but if the top 5cm (2in) of soil is scraped away and replaced by good rich mixture it may suffice for a season or two. The need for renewal will, however, occur and will be apparent by an obvious loss of vigour in the plants and perhaps some yellowing of the leaves. Spring is the best time to carry out this task, enough fresh soil should be at hand, and it provides an opportunity to repair or to strengthen any wooden containers—they may also be painted. When window-boxes are totally emptied at the end of the year the soil should at least in part be replenished before any new planting is attempted. Where boxes have permanent occupants, such as a background nucleus of shrubs, the soil should have some slow-acting fertilizer (bonemeal) and fresh soil worked in when temporary flowers are removed.

Do not overfill containers with compost or there will not be enough space between the top of it and the rim of the container for a reasonable amount of water to be flooded in, 5cm (2in) should be left whenever possible. Plants which have been acquired in temporary pots—plastic or whalehide—can be planted at any time of the year provided that care is exercised in removing them from their temporary homes. Shrubs

and trees lifted from the open ground must be treated more carefully until such time as they are well settled again after their disturbance. Generally speaking, April and May are the best months for establishing evergreen shrubs. Firm planting is of vital importance and any staking that is needed should be undertaken at that time. See that the roots of the plant are well below the surface of the soil and not heaped up above it, which results in any water applied running off the place where it is really needed. Some thin supports can be useful for plants such as nigella (love-in-a-mist) which will grow through any twiggy pieces and gain support, and some of the taller growing plants should be staked with strong canes and tied in. As tall and climbing plants grow they should be guided to, or be tied to, their supports. A watch should be kept for insect pests which should be dealt with promptly by either a systemic or contact insecticide.

Container plants want watering, like any other plants, when they need it, that is, just as they start to dry out a little. Out of doors, however, containers are not totally dependent upon the grower for water as some arrives (often unexpectedly) in the form of rain. The air outside may also be more humid and the degree of humidity changes, sometimes daily. This may mean that the soil after a few days of cloud and high humidity is still moist whereas under sunny conditions and with drier air it would have needed watering much earlier. Climatic vagaries such as these and the effect they have on plants in containers are for the gardener to deal with by checking and testing for moisture at the right time but a number of remarks might alert the grower to points he may not have considered.

It should be remembered that hanging baskets which are under the roof of a porch will receive virtually no rain. The same is true to a lesser extent of window-boxes which sit in the recess of a window, particularly if the house has generous overhanging eaves. The area immediately next to a wall is also often protected by window-sills, storm guttering and the wall itself and prevents rain from reaching plants in containers right against the wall. When first planted up, window-boxes and other containers which have been given a reasonable depth of soil will have a lot of unoccupied soil which will be comparatively slow to dry out. Fairly dry soils will encourage roots to go searching down into it for water with resultant top growth. A cold,

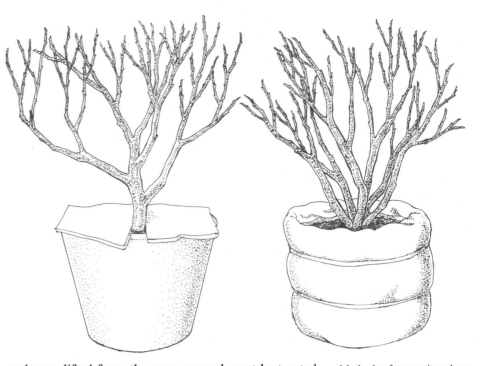

Methods of protecting plants from severe cold. Left: the soil surface can be covered with slate. Right: the pot can be wrapped in insulating material.

wet, (unoccupied one) will prove no such attraction for the roots. As the season progresses and the plants produce lots of top growth and the containers become filled with roots so they will need regular and generous watering.

The faded flowers of all plants should be removed as soon as they are past their prime. Plants with sterile flowers, such as hydrangeas, do not set seed and do not therefore need this attention—also their flowers remain attractive for several weeks after they have faded. This 'dead-heading', as it is called, prevents the formation of seed pods and extends the flowering season considerably. With some subjects this can be done with the finger and thumb, just pinching the soft flower stalk away. Others of a woodier nature will need pruning shears and this affords an opportunity for a little light summer pruning. Soft flower stalks should be removed completely and the tougher types cut back to a growth bud in a leaf axil from which the next flowering shoot will emerge.

Half-hardy and tender plants must have been thoroughly hardened off before they are planted in the open. This may already have been done when the plants were purchased but it is as well to ask. If at all possible, a mild period should be chosen for planting, the more tender plants will not then feel such a shock. Hardening off involves gradually acclimatising plants to the open air. As nights are almost invariably cooler the grower begins by standing plants out during the daytime but putting them back under cover at night, gradually extending the period out until it becomes 24 hours. This exercise is not attempted if the weather is very bad—the grower waits.

At the other end of the year there is the question of how well some of the more permanent items will come through the winter. Happily, the shelter that city walls provide protects them somewhat and any which are mobile and in a particularly exposed position might perhaps be moved temporarily to a more favoured spot. Many plants are quite capable of withstanding severe cold provided that the soil is not unduly wet at the time. If necessary, divert excessive rain water away from the soil in the container by covering the surface with a piece of slate or polyethylene. Thin-sided containers should be avoided whenever possible in cold districts as they do not give much protection to the roots of plants which are most likely to be hugging the sides of the container. Should very expensive containers be used, they should be moved to a protected place or wrapped in some way.

As the winter months approach, some tidying up of the containers will be necessary. Annual flowering and foliage plants and the half-hardy and tender subjects, which will perish or suffer badly from cold, will need removing. The annuals, and those which cannot be overwintered by the grower, should be taken out when they are past their best and an opportunity taken to replace or improve the remaining soil. Tender plants which are to be saved should usually be cut back a little, moved into small containers for housing under cover or, in the case of bulbs, tubers or corms, be dried off for winter storage. The tuberous-rooted should be stored in peat. Perennial plants that remain may need some of their top growth removed to prevent them from being blown about in winter gales. Some are better left with top growth attached when this provides a little protection for the more delicate growing crowns— this is true of hydrangeas, the faded flower heads protecting the succulent growth buds just below them.

Plants which are clump-forming and which have become crowded should be thinned out. The autumn months are the right time for this task. The newer growth should be retained and the older parts disposed of; this usually means cutting away the outer edges and leaving the inner growth. Pruning, when it is required, has been included in the descriptive list of plants that follows. In very confined spaces it may be necessary to be more drastic, or to prune or at least thin out plants, shrubs and climbers more often. Beware, however, of perpetually snipping away at plants or they may not flower properly. Weeds are not often much of a problem in containers as most soil mixes used have been sterilized, which kills off all weed seeds and pernicious roots which appear with alarming regularity in the open ground. Any that do appear, however, should be removed as soon as they are identifiable, as there is no point in their remaining and taking up nourishment and proving disruptive to remove at a later stage. Sometimes self-sown seedlings from the cultivated plants appear in very unlikely positions but invariably they are able to survive in such positions and, if they look right, they often prove very valuable and much more natural looking than those planted by hand.

Throughout the year try to ensure that the soil does not pack down and become very hard through regular watering—try to prick it through with a hand-fork occasionally to let in air and prevent water which is applied from swilling straight off.

This shows the effect of wet and dry compost on the roots and top growth of an asplenium plant. On the left, wet compost; on the right, dry compost.

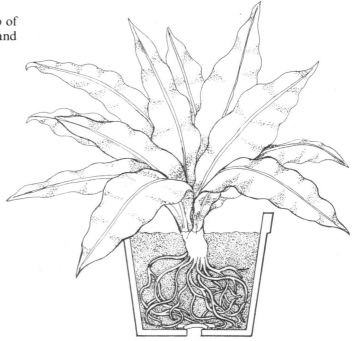

125

Indispensable plants

Some plant families are so adaptable that they are constantly in use in all forms of gardening and it is to those families that the grower is most likely to turn for his plant material.

It would be difficult to imagine life without begonias. The small bedding begonia, *B. semperflorens*, is indispensable for all sorts of containers and will do well in practically any situation. The modern hybrid semperflorens have fibrous roots, glossy leaves (hence one common name wax begonias) which can be bright-green, chocolate brown or purplish in colour and continuous flowering capabilities (the name means constant flowering). Flower colour ranges from pure white through salmon and other pink shades to carmine-scarlet. All begonia seed is minute and care is needed in the early stages when raising plants from seed. Young pricked-out plants are, however, available in the early summer and cuttings root easily. Window-boxes devoted to these low-growing plants make spectacular features and odd plants can be fitted into any form of mixed arrangement. There are a few double-flowered sorts, like New Yorker with strong pink flowers and chocolate coloured leaves, but these do not stand up so well to adverse weather.

The pendulus or basket begonias are tuberous rooted and invaluable for use in hanging baskets. Seen from below, as they usually are, the full beauty of their flowers is apparent; these can be single (very pointed and recurved) or double camellia or carnation flowered. Orange shades have been added to the colour range.

Tuberous begonias produce splendid double flowers in the usual colours and attractive foliage throughout the summer months. The dormant tubers are started into growth in some warmth early in the year (this is usually done in shallow trays of peat) and are planted out when all danger of frost is past. They enjoy a position of some sun and some shade and will go on producing their flowers in such a position until they are touched by frost. Some form of support should be given as the heavy double flowers need it and thin canes are satisfactory for this. Avoid piercing the tuber when inserting, and tie to the cane with raffia. Additional ties should be made as necessary.

Multiflora begonias are also tuberous and as the name implies they produce numerous flowers but of a smaller size. Most of the flowers are semi-double but very effective. The large double-flowered sorts will need a position sheltered from winds as they are liable to snap off in a gusty situation but the multifloras are tough and will stand up well to reasonable treatment. All of the tuberous rooted kinds need a good rich soil and regular feeding to support the wealth of flowers produced. As the season finishes they should be carefully lifted and their tubers dried off and stored in peat until the following spring.

Petunias, too, can be used in all sorts of situations—they are happy in full sun or some sun and shade. Great strides have been made in recent years to produce types which will stand up well in bad weather. The huge rather floppy singles are very beautiful—there is a single White Swan—and some lovely clear self colours. Multi coloured sorts have a certain brilliance and the full doubles can look more like carnations. Some of the purples and those with purplish veining are often sweetly scented. They have a long flowering life and need to be kept well watered and regularly fed. Small twiggy sticks will support plants in tubs and boxes but those used in hanging baskets should be allowed to tumble about.

The Impatiens gained their name from the impatient way that they dispose of their seeds—they shoot them out—it could equally have described the speed with which they start flowering for they begin to bloom at a very early age and continue to do so while the weather is with them. The attractive F1 hybrids have a much better habit than all the old species and have brought with them a whole new range of colours. The biggest improvement has been to make them short, bushy and spreading instead of tall and flowering only at the terminals of the shoots. Flowers are available in white, some lovely pastel shades and the strong fluorescent colours. Some flowers are striped and a few are double although the latter do not stand up well to bad weather. Sun and shade suits them best and they must be kept well watered. The newly-introduced sorts with multi colored leaves are particularly attractive, even without their large flowers. Cuttings of a particularly admired form will root with ease—even in water—and quickly develop into a nice flowering plant. Quite warm indoor conditions are needed to overwinter plants and this may not be worthwhile as it is so easy to get replacements for them in the late spring of the next year.

In a position of full sun pelargoniums provide a startling and long lasting display. They will do tolerably well in a spot giving them only some sun, but will become much too leafy and flower poorly in shade.

Some of the best varieties have been around for years but new sorts are constantly being introduced and the choice of types of plants and the range of flower colouring is very wide, Pelargoniums fall roughly into groups

The Martha Washingtons (*P. domesticum*), which flower in the spring and early summer are perhaps the most beautiful, but unfortunately they flower early and are easily spoilt by adverse weather and are the least useful for outdoor work. They have large trusses of flowers in shades from deepest burgundy to pure white —almost invariably with a throat or blotch of a different colour or shade. They are showy but temporary.

By far the largest group consists of the zonals (*P. × hortorum*) which have a dark green zonal patch on their leaves and an ability to survive under adverse conditions—including some slight frost provided that they are dry at the root at the time. Zonals flower continually. They usually flower more profusely in containers than they do with a free root-run—particularly so if the season is a wet one. Although poor soil is often recommended for pelargoniums this is certainly not appropriate to container-grown pelargoniums. Once the roots of the plants have penetrated the whole of the soil allotted to them they definitely benefit from regular feeding—masses of good sized flowers cannot be expected from a poor soil. The zonals cover the full pelargonium colour range.

Those with ivy-shaped leaves and a trailing habit (*P. peltatum* and its hybrids) are very useful in hanging baskets and for breaking up the hard lines of window-boxes etc. L'Elegante is internationally known with its white flowers veined with deep purple and cream-edged leaves which acquire a purple tinge in sunny and rather dry conditions. La France, a semi-double lilac with maroon markings, and the rose-pink Galilee are also well known throughout the world and these three are some of the best.

The zonal group also includes many types with variegated leaves, and the most spectacular of these is Henry Cox (sometimes listed as Mrs Henry Cox) with red, gold and green markings fused with shades of these colours. Other forms have gold, bronze and chestnut brown markings.

The dwarf scented-leaved pelargoniums are excellent for window-boxes. *P. fragrans* and its variegated form *P. f. variegata* have a nutmeg scent and *P. crispum variegatum* a spiral growing habit, crinkled variegated leaves and a lemon scent. When more space is available there

are a number of larger growing types with scents of peppermint, rose and orange. All of these plants exude a pungent smell when touched and a faint aroma at other times. Flowers are insignificant but the scent compensates. The miniature and semi-miniature are also valuable in small window-boxes where they are unlikely to grow taller than 20cm (8in) and 30cm (12in) respectively. A good number of these dwarfs have very dark leaves—Black Vesuvius with red flowers and its salmon form are examples. Some have delicate five petalled 'butterfly' flowers. The miniatures often have individual florets as large as their bigger relatives; it is only that there are fewer florets on one head of bloom. Some are miniature in all of their parts.

None of the pelargoniums is hardy—the Martha Washingtons are the most susceptible to damage. Although a number of all kinds will survive a normal northern winter in a sheltered place they are usually slow to come into bloom again the following year after their ordeal and it is debatable whether it is worth while trying to continue with them a second year. If they can be lifted and overwintered in a light and frost-free structure they will come into bloom early the following year and can be planted out when all danger of frost is past. *Alchemilla mollis*, (Lady's Mantle) is totally different from the gaudy pelargoniums but should be in every garden of every type. It has beautiful downy foliage which is shaped in such a way that the individual leaves catch rain-drops and produces frothy, finely built, lime-green flowers during the summer months. Alchemilla thrives in sun or shade and seeds freely. Small plants can always be tucked into small spaces and the resulting plants are absolutely no trouble.

Fuchsias for a time went out of fashion but sensibly they are now back in favour. All over the world fresh interest has arisen in these very dependable plants which are so prolific with their flowers and so easy to care for. They should be in every garden; they do well in practically any situation (preferring a position between full sun and shade). Their flower colour is very varied, they offer a wide range of flower shape and size and with few exceptions do well in containers out of doors.

The trailing varieties have a habit particularly well

A plain paved courtyard can be brightened up immensely by several troughs and pots filled with a wide variety of colourful plants and flowers. From left to right: hydrangea, *Calendula officinalis*, lavender, lobelia (in urn), *aubrieta*, begonias, *linum*, *chlorophytum* (spider plant), clematis (growing up trellis), *impatiens, alyssum*, oxeye daisies, ivy-leaved pelargonium, petunia. The hanging basket contains fuchsia.

suited to the hanging basket; the trailers also look good as standards and half-standards when the underside of the flowers on the pendulous growth is seen to best advantage. They are also used in window boxes and at the edges of tubs. For standards, a 'whip' (a young tip cutting) is taken, rooted, and then trained to allow development only of the tip growth—all side shoots which develop are removed from the leaf axils as soon as they can be handled. In this way a straight single stem is built up. When the stem has reached the desired height—this is usually at one metre (3ft) for standards and half a metre (18in) for half-standards—the tip is pinched out and the resulting laterals at the top are allowed to grow to form the main branches of a 'head'. The laterals are stopped at least once to build up a good framework and at the end of the first season a dense head of growth should have developed bearing many flowers. The main stem should be secured to a cane to prevent wind damage. Fuchsias are very amenable to training and can be formed into many shapes; bush, standard, espalier, fan and trailing.

There are hundreds of varieties from which to choose; dwarf forms like Alice Hoffman and Tom Thumb for use in small window boxes and small containers; trailers and those which are fairly hardy. Some have flowers of a single colour, some are in two or more shades or colours. A number have slim, tube-shaped, single flowers while others flaunt big, fat, double flowers, with semi-doubles to add to the number. The skirt-like piece of the flower is called the corolla and the up-curling pieces, next to the tube, the sepals. Some of the single and tube-shaped sorts are particularly floriferous, so are some of the doubles, but a number of the larger flowered doubles tend to take a rest between bouts of producing their huge flowers. White forms, either single or double, are particularly attractive in some shady positions, when their slightly luminous quality shows to best advantage. The typical fuchsia colour when linked with deep purple is very lively and some of the most popular are in this colour combination. Some of the very large flowered forms are really only happy when protected by the greenhouse but the vast majority are happy when given that slight protection of the close proximity of house walls. In general fuchsias are not winter hardy (although some are fairly so). If the plants are set a little deeper than would normally be the case in the first instance, the covering of compost over the rootstock will ensure its survival in winter areas like the Northwest and although the whole top growth may be killed the root will send up new growth in the spring from below the surface. Lifting the plants and storing them free from frost is a safeguard. Fuchsias love a cool moist root-run, a moist atmosphere, some shade whenever possible and, when flowering profusely, regular feeding. They should not be allowed to dry out completely and appreciate an overhead spraying or a dousing from a watering-can with a rose on a regular basis. Rich soil at the start followed by a regular feeding programme will ensure that the season from May to October will be that of the fuchsia.

Pansies and violas flower over a long period and are of a suitable scale for use in window-boxes and other small containers. The individual blooms of some of the giant-flowered pansies can be as much as 10cm (4in) across but the most useful plants are usually those which produce a larger number of smaller flowers over a long period. Young seedlings of both plants flower at an early age and tip cuttings root easily during the better months of the year. Some of the violas have bright, clear, self-coloured blooms while the subtle colours and face-like markings of some of the pansies are also very interesting. At the end of a season a number of

plants can usually be cut down hard when they will send up short young growth from the root stock. Some pansies flower from late autumn through to May where seasons are mild enough and are commonly known as winter flowering.

Chrysanthemums are traditionally autumn flowering but the comparatively new technique of blacking out plants for a given number of hours and thus decreasing the length of daylight they receive, induces them to flower at a time calculated by the specialist grower. Chrysanthemums can now be bought in bud and in flower every single day of the year. Coupled with the blacking out technique the specialists also apply a dwarfing agent and the result is long-growing plants which flower to order, pack for market and travel easily and prove attractive to the customer. All of the artificially dwarfed plants will revert to their natural and full size in subsequent years and are of little direct value to the container gardener after their initial flowering. Chrysanthemums bought in small pots or half-pots and used during the cooler months of the year will last a very long time in good condition in window-boxes and other containers that can be watered adequately.

Some of the naturally lower growing chrysanthemums such as the pom-pon types with double white, yellow, bronze or wine coloured flowers can also be purchased when in bud in September and will usually last two or three months in good condition.

Fuchsia 'Golden Marinka' trained as a standard to display effectively its hanging flowers.

Plants for sun and shade

Clematis, such as this Ville de Lyon variety, can look very attractive climbing up a trellis.

The majority of plants are happy if they receive some sun each day. Some demand longer hours of sunshine to bloom profusely and others prefer shade. Shade should perhaps be defined. An area which is surrounded by high walls yet is open to the sky above can be shaded because the walls prevent the sun from reaching it. A similar spot can be shaded because a large tree obscures the sunlight and worst of all there is the area immediately below the branches of a tree. The last situation creates real problems as the plants used there will not only have to accept the poor light but must also content with the drip from the branches after every shower. The position open to the sky and receiving some sun is the type most often found in towns and the choice of plants that will thrive in that sort of shade is very wide.

SUN PLANTS

Pelargoniums and petunias thrive in the sun, the low growing mesembryanthemums and *Portulaca grandiflora* open their brilliantly coloured flowers there and the plants with grey or silver foliage acquire their proper hue. Most annual flowering plants enjoy sun. Tagetes—African and French marigolds—enjoy full sun. The African marigolds have large fully double flowers in orange or lemon-yellow while the French which are smaller growing, can have either single or double flowers and move into rust and bronze shades as well. Their flowering season in sun extends from mid-summer to frost. Lobelia, in all shades of blue, and the white and mauve alyssum (although not necessarily together) enjoy the sun—the lobelia should be kept well watered. Lobelia grown in quantity, as opposed to alternating it with other plants, makes a wonderful display. The tall growing, red-leaved, red flowered *L. cardinalis* is ideal. Nasturtiums (*Tropaeolum*) grow easily and quickly from seed and are highly valued for their orange, red, flame and yellow flowers. The very delicate *T. peregrinum* (canary creeper) with small, canary-yellow, tufted and frilled blooms likes to clamber into and through taller plants and fastens itself to whatever is to hand by twisting a leaf stalk half way round its host. This climber will also do well in some shade. Most of the climbing annuals like sun.

The half-hardy Morning Glory (*Ipomoea rubro-caerulea*) comes from tropical America and enjoys all the sun it can get. The lovely blue variety 'Heavenly Blue' has possibly the clearest colour of any flower. The botanists have recently decided that it should be *Pharbitis tricolor*. Seeds germinate easily when there is enough warmth—the seed should be soaked in warm water for 24 hours before sowing to soften up the hard outer casing. The young plants hate root disturbance and should either be grown singly in small pots and be very carefully transplanted to their permanent positions when large enough or should be sown *in situ* where they are to flower.

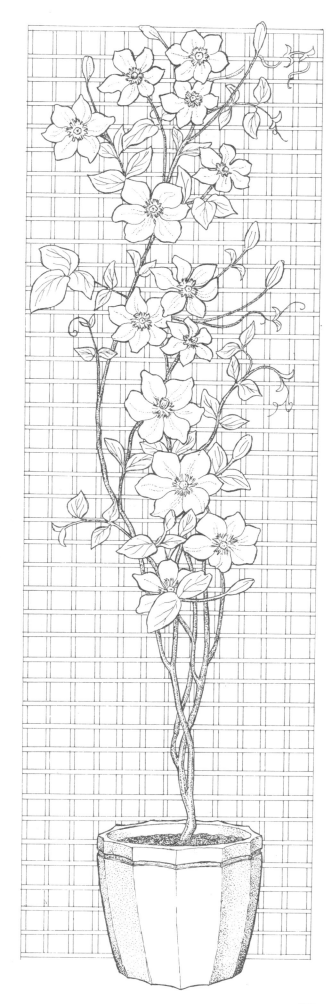

A varied arrangement of sun-loving plants on a windowsill. From left to right: *alyssum*, zonal pelargonium, *tagetes*, lobelia, ivy-leaved geraniums and petunia.

Cobaea scandens (cup-and-saucer vine) is a tougher and stronger growing perennial which is usually treated as an annual. It grows rapidly and needs a strong support—clinging by means of tendrils. The flowers are bell-shaped and start a pale green colour but darken with age to a violet-blue. There is also a white form—*alba. Thunbergia alata,* the black-eyed-Susan, is an easy climber with 5cm (2in), yellow or orange coloured flowers with a deep brown eye. Thunbergias twine around supports. All of the three climbers mentioned above can usually be bought as young potted plants in the early summer months and will quickly take to their supports when planted. Sweet peas (*Lathyrus odoratus*) are useful both in their climbing form and the newer non-climbing form. They need sun and a really good fertile soil to grow to 1.8m (6ft) to 2.4m (8ft) and to produce multi-flowered stems. The dwarf Knee-Hi varieties are very suitable for sunny window-boxes keeping at around 30cm (12in) high.

More permanent plants are the lovely climbing clematis. These like their heads in sun but their feet in shade. The shade can be provided artificially by placing a large stone, slate or attractive piece of driftwood over the roots or by planting low-growing creepers over the root. Hundreds of beautiful varieties exist and it is often best for the grower to go to see a selection of plants in flower during the summer months and to choose whatever most appeals. Clematis fall into three broad groups. The spring flowering sorts—including *C. alpina* and *C. montana*—need very little pruning, but what they do need should be undertaken immediately after the flush of flowers fade. These can get very large and cause some embarrassment in small spaces. The second group flowers at the ends of young shoots that have been made in the current season. With these, pruning is undertaken very early in the year when all old growth is cut away except a pair of growth buds near the base. This creates a thick stump over the years but dispenses with a nasty tangle. With established plants a good quantity of this old wood can be removed for tidiness in November. As flowers are only produced on new growth there is no point in leaving a lot of old wood about. Varieties falling into this group include Jackmanii, Perle d'Azur, Comtesse de Bouchaud and Star of India, and flower

from late June. The third group have flowers on short young laterals made on the previous years wood. They bloom in late spring and early summer and have some of the biggest flowers—they also often have a smaller batch of flowers later in the year. These should have any dead wood removed and the old growth shortened to plump buds in December. Sorts falling into this group include Nelly Moser, Lasurstern, and the double-flowered, Countess of Lovelace, Duchess of Edinburgh and Beauty of Worcester. Very large containers are needed for any of the three types of clematis—the middle group (those flowering on new wood) are really the most profitable. Good soil, some lime in it, lots of water and regular feeding once the growth has advanced will produce some good plants.

Small specimens of the Australian eucalyptus can be grown in good sized containers, until such time as they outgrow their usefulness. The blue-gum *E. globulus* and the hardier *E. gunnii* can be grown easily from seed sown in heat early in the year, or, alternatively, small 30cm (12in) high plants can be bought. Gums have a beautiful, glaucous grey appearance and the almost circular leaves add a new leaf shape and colour to the scene. If size does become a problem they can be cut back once or twice, and when a desired height has been reached the growing tips can be nipped out at fairly regular intervals. Sheltered positions suit them best and they will take quite a lot of water. A position in sun brings out the best leaf colouring but they will prove to be very attractive in some shade.

Silver foliaged plants are normally native of dry sunny slopes in hot and arid areas. Their attractive covering of hair (woolly, silky or felt-like) is in fact a defence against the sun and wind drying out the green leaf below it. Few will tolerate atmospheric pollution in towns during the winter although a lot can be grown on very much a temporary basis during the summer months. All love sun. *Senecio cineraria* White Diamond and *S.c.* Ramparts are two named cultivars of the Mediterranean species and are very useful in sunny window-boxes and similar places when they show up well against the green foliage and brilliant flowers of bedding plants. They should not be planted out until fear of frost is past but in the right position in mild climates are capable of overwintering in a dry spot. They will, however, grow very tall and leggy. In large containers they could be retained provided that they are cut back hard in late Spring but young plants are usually best. Flowers are uninspiring and possibly best removed. *Helichrysum petiolatum* from Australia, has small, heart-shaped leaves of a pale-green colour covered with a very short white pile and a spreading habit. The arching stems are very attractive and the plant can be used in hanging baskets and other small containers as there is little root. Some of the dwarf growing Artemisia, small spreading shrublets from mountainous regions, are excellent for shading the roots of such plants as the tiny dianthus in a hot position. Their foliage is very feathery and silvery-white.

A number of the half-hardy gazanias have grey or white leaves in addition to their bold daisy-shaped flowers. They are very useful in baskets and boxes during the warmer months. The flowers only open in sunshine and close early each evening.

Some succulent plants are useful in sunny positions for providing an edging and the most popular for this purpose is the echeveria. The blue-leaved *Echeveria secunda* and *E. glauca* are usually used for carpet-bedding and are ideal as low-growing rosette shaped plants in bowls and shallow pans. These flat shapes are also of value in window-boxes. Echeverias produce clusters of pink, red or orange flowers at the top of 15cm (6in) stems from May onwards. They love sun and to be fairly dry at the root. Plants will produce lots of offshoots and there should never be any problem in finding small plants to overwinter indoors—in the brightest possible light.

Commonly known as the Livingstone Daisy, the annual *Mesembryanthemum criniflorum*, and the fantastically coloured *Portulaca grandiflora* can be bought as small seedlings early in the summer and will, in a sunny spot, provide a mass of star-shaped blooms when the sun shines—they refuse to open up on a dull day. All will do well in a dryish compost and quite shallow containers.

Some small annuals that thrive on sun can be sown directly into the containers in which they are to flower. The two annual flax, *Linum usitatissium*, the beautiful, clear-blue flowered plant, and *L. grandiflorum rubrum*, with brilliant scarlet flowers, are examples. Both bloom in only a few weeks from sowing and continue right through the summer months. If seed is scattered thinly over the surface of the soil and then lightly raked in, enough seedlings should appear without the need for much thinning out. The spot where the seeds are sown can be marked with a thin cane, or, a much better idea, a sprinkling of sand can be applied, this not only marks the spot but also provides a suitable germination medium for the seed. The clarkia is half-hardy and, because young plants resent disturbance, are much better if sown in place. A wide colour range is available and the double-flowered hybrids derived from *C. elegans* are much the best. Larkspurs, the annual delphiniums, with finely divided foliage and single or double flowers in delicate and subtle shades of blue and pink, can be sown directly into containers or young plants may be transplanted when small. An autumn sowing is possible in many situations when the young plants will stand up well to the winter and flower that much earlier in the spring. The same is true for antirrhinums. F_1 hybrids of antirrhinum are excellent. They do not exceed 30cm (12in) in height, are cheap to buy as small plantlets, easy to grow and flower for weeks on end. Most antirrhinums are sold in mixed colours and these usually blend well together, but seed and plantlets are sold in single colours for those who have a particular colour in mind. Ageratum is an effective edging plant and thrives in either sun or some shade. Flowers are in subtle shades of blue, thickly clustered together in terminal groups.

Hebes, formally known as veronicas, are small evergreen shrubs just on the borderline of hardiness. Usually the proximity of house walls provides sufficient protection to keep these plants from harm during mild winters. The smaller growing types are particularly suitable for use in window-boxes. All hebes enjoy some sun. Some of the best are *H. pinguifolia* Pagei with small blue-grey leaves and white flowers in May, *H. glaucophylla* Variegata with creamy-white margined leaves, *H. deliciosa* (pale-pink flowers) and the hybrids Alicia Amherst (deep blue-purple) and Simon Delaux (dark crimson). Hardly any pruning is required with these low-growing plants.

Laurus nobilis, the sweet bay, valued for its culinary flavouring, is a perfect specimen for training into a formal shape for use on either side of an entrance. Clipped into the shape of a tall pyramid or as a mop-headed standard, the bay will tolerate cramped root conditions, some atmospheric pollution and regular clipping. Grown as they usually are in small containers, they need a regular soaking in water and some feeding. Some small plants are now about which are intended for use on the kitchen window ledge, allowing the cook to just slip outside for a sprig. Try to avoid draughty corners as they are not totally hardy.

Stachys are very easy, ground covering plants with silver grey foliage covered in very soft, silky hair. The common name of *Stachys lantana* is 'Lamb's Ears'. They hug the ground and in June, July and August produce magenta coloured flowers on 30cm (12in) stems. *S. macrantha* Robusta is almost twice as tall with bright pink spikes. They love the sun but will grow and flower in some shade. The dense foliage of the geums also provides some ground cover; the rather coarse leaves being arranged in a loose rosette, and from May until August brilliantly coloured flowers are produced on wiry stems. The flowers of the variety Mrs Bradshaw are fully double and a vivid scarlet, those of Lady Stratheden semi-double and a golden yellow, and the species *G. borisii* a rich orange scarlet. All are extremely easy to grow under the right conditions.

A shallow trough containing low-growing creeping plants. From left to right: *geum, stachys* and *dianthus*.

SHADE PLANTS

In areas where there is only deep shade it is pointless trying to grow the brilliant flowering plants which love the sun. Instead use must be made of the wide range of plants which will produce their mainly green foliage (variegated plants are less common in this group) and usually subtle coloured flowers.

Ferns are an obvious choice. Hundreds of hardy ferns exist ranging from the hart's tongue (*Phyllitis scolopendrium*) with long, leathery, strap-shaped fronds to the featheriness of the shield fern. The fronds of the hart's tongue are very tough and overwinter fairly well, lasting until the new crop begin to unfurl in March and April. Old fronds should be removed at that time avoiding damage to the new ones coming up. This plant is quite capable of growing on walls and in other dry positions but for really large fronds a moist shady position is best. Crested and undulated edged forms are occasionally seen. Once established, the hart's tongue will reproduce itself from spores in any cranny in which it can get a foothold. The common male fern (*Dryopteris filix-mas*) will thrive in almost any position. It grows from a central crown and produces rather upright feathery fronds of a lightish green. Well grown, it is a big plant but very effective. *Polypodium vulgare*, the common polypody, has a creeping rootstock and will spread nicely in a damp shady area. Its fronds are lance-shaped, much divided (like comb-teeth on either side of a central stem) smooth and leathery. There is an attractive crested form of this fern.

A number of ferns do not have a substantial root system and shallow soil, provided that it can be kept moist, is quite sufficient. When planting it is often best to bury the roots only shallowly and whenever possible to place a large stone over the root. This not only anchors the fern in the first instance until it establishes itself but helps to keep the root-run cool and moist in dryer periods. Feeding is not often necessary but a moist leafy soil suits most ferns and regular overhead watering will ensure large healthy fronds.

Ferns are flowerless, they reproduce themselves from spores which develop in thick clusters on the underside of the fronds. Ferns pre-date flowering plants in the evolutionary system.

There has been much confusion in the past over the proper naming of hostas and it is feared that this will continue for some time to come. Most of the hostas prefer shade although some do very well in sun. They are grown chiefly for the sake of their foliage which can be striking. The boldest is *H. sieboldiana elegans* with large, heart-shaped, glaucous (bluish) leaves with a rippled surface. Smaller but also blue is *H. tokudama* (previously called *glauca* or *fortunei*). Neither have particularly attractive flowers and can be ignored in this respect. *H. sieboldii* (note the similarity of the name to the one mentioned above) used to be called *albomarginata* and has a narrow white edge to its leaf. *H. crispula* is the most handsome of the variegated leaved hostas and is one which really does need moist shade to enable it to keep its white edged, pointed leaves in good condition. Smaller leaved but also variegated is *H. undulata*. It has in fact much more cream colouring then green—the green being at the edge—and a happy medium is needed between sun and shade as it will get scorched in too much sun and darken to too green if not given enough. Several variants of this plant exist with more or less leaf margins. *H. fortunei* 'Albopicta' (a misnomer as there is no white whatever) has early in the year lovely, soft-yellow, broad but pointed leaves with a pale green margin. Later in the year the leaves

turn plain green. Hostas are particularly suitable for courtyard gardens and for growing in tubs and other large containers as they like an adequate and cool root-run. Be especially careful that they are not attacked by slugs which love them and do great damage to the leaves while they are still rolled up by eating through several layers.

Often associated with hostas is Solomon's seal (*Polygonatum biflorum*). They have thick creeping rootstocks and send up 50cm (20in) long, arching leaves from which dangle small, bell-shaped, creamy-green flowers. They should not be allowed to become too invasive and should be cut down to ground level in the autumn.

The hellebores are also shade tolerant and their evergreen foliage has a certain sculptural quality. *H. lividus corsicus* is rather shrubby with dark-green leaves with mock prickles to the edges and lime-green flowers early in the year. *H. foetidus* has palmate leaves with nine leaflets, greenish flowers which become stained deep red as they age. *H. niger*, the not too easy Christmas rose, with its pure-white flowers and black root is low growing. When purchased, extra care should be taken to see that they do not dry out at the root as they are difficult to establish if out of the ground too long. Buy only from a local and reputable nursery and, whenever possible, just as they have finished flowering. The Lenten rose *H. orientalis* also flowers early in the year and the blooms can vary considerably in colour from cream through pink to mauve. They all enjoy a deep moist soil and to be left undisturbed. Bergenias have large glossy green leaves, which take on a red or purple colouring as the weather gets colder, and dense clusters of pink to red flowers from February onwards. They make excellent town plants being able to stand up well to really adverse conditions.

The Japanese anemones are surface-rooting perennials which flower on 60cm (24in) stems in the late

Group of shade-tolerant plants. From left to right: *Dryopteris filix-mas*, (common male fern); *Phyllitis scolopendrium*, (crested hart's tongue fern); *Helleborus foetidus*; camellia. In front is a *Hosta fortunei*.

summer and early autumn, when flowering plants can be scarce. They dislike being moved, but once well established flower freely in some shade and in practically any kind of soil. The common white form *Anemone japonica alba* and the lilac-mauve *A. j. elegans* are most often seen, but there are deeper, rose-coloured sorts and some purplish-red which are even smaller. Once re-established these plants present no problems. Foxgloves thrive in shade, (and also do well in full sun—provided that they are moist at the root), and some of the new varieties which flower all round the stem are a definite improvement. Lovely subtle colours have appeared—mostly strongly spotted with a contrasting shade. Foxgloves are biennial plants. The seed is sown in April or May of one year and the flowers are produced in the following year. For containers, small plants are best fitted into suitable positions from September onwards. Primroses and polyanthus are suitable for some shade and these should be purchased and planted when convenient in the late autumn for the spring display. Most of the primulas need moist conditions to do really well. Some of the new blue strains are particularly attractive.

No section dealing with plants that enjoy the shade would be complete without mention of the ivies (hedera). They are capable of being put to so many different uses and their leaf shape and colouring is very diverse. The common English ivy, *Hedera helix*, has dozens of offspring. All of the ones which are used in the home can be grown quite easily out of doors, provided that they are properly hardened off to the cooler conditions found there. This merely involves planting them during the warmer months. The Irish ivy *H. hibernica* has larger leaves of a deep green and is particularly fine when grown up a tall pole or collection of canes. *Hedera canariensis* 'Variegata' (often called Gloire de Marengo) also has large leaves but these are splashed with cream colouring and, out of doors, take on a pink tone at the edges during the winter months. The yellow offspring of *H. helix*—such as Buttercup and Gold Heart—really need some sun to shine to best advantage. Most of the variegated forms tend to lose some of their colour during the dull months but will quickly return to form in the spring. They all look well cascading over the edges of containers as they tend to break up severe lines, and most will give a little height if trained up canes in arrangements which lack taller plants.

Closely allied to the ivies is *Fatsia japonica*. This plant is often used indoors where it is perfectly hardy and very tolerant. It makes a large and impressive shrub—up to 150cm (5ft)—and usually loses its bottom leaves as they age, leaving a bare stem topped by large, glossy, dark-green hand-shaped leaves. This shrub has been crossed with ivy and produced *X. Fatshedera lizei*—also used in the home. Fatshedera is a typical hybrid, having the leaves, stem and habit of both parents. It needs support in the form of a cane, has medium sized leaves, which are tough, and is often more in scale in small areas than the fatsia.

Euphorbias have suddenly become fashionable plants. They range from small trailing plants with succulent-like foliage like *E. myrsinites*, ideal for spilling over the edges of containers, to tall-growing sub-shrubs like *E. wulfenii* with blue-green, evergreen foliage and large heads of greeny-yellow flowers. Euphorbia flowers are in fact tiny and quite insignificant, the showy part is a bract surrounding the flower. *E. robbiae* is of medium stature (inclined to be invasive) but keeping its dark green foliage and displaying typical flowers throughout the winter months. *Wulfenii* needs sun to flower every year but will do so every other year in shade.

Of the taller growing shrubs that will stand some shade, the mahonia is one of the most useful. These plants will provide height, and their elegant leaves, with several pairs of small leaflets and yellow flowers at a difficult time of year, are very welcome. *Mahonia japonica* is the hardiest of the Asiatic species and *M. lomariifolia* and the hybrid Charity are capable of over-wintering in mild situations. Out of doors *M. ognifolium* is the most commonly seen, next is the more tender *M. bealei*. All have fine sculptural leaves and mid-winter yellow flowers. They need shelter from boisterous winds, rich soil, large containers and lots of water. Hydrangeas can be very effective but should never be allowed to dry out completely and require regular feeding and attention. The florists' type, *H. macrophylla hortensia*, is the most often planted—usually when it has been a gift plant and its indoor life is complete—and is the least hardy. *H. arborescens grandiflora*, an American frost-hardy type with sterile creamy-white flowers, and the popular Lace-cap, *H. macrophylla*, with flat flower heads in shades of pink and blue and in white, are notable plants. All coloured hydrangeas respond dramatically to the degree of acidity of the soil and can be turned into deep blue or deep pink shades by adjusting. A collection of hydrangeas in differing soils can produce an interesting display of plants with flowers of different colours. Once the flowers have lost their first freshness there is a very interesting period when their colour changes gradually, but still remains very decorative. These fading flowers should be left for as long as they are of value—probably through to the spring. No pruning, beyond the removal of the spent, dried heads in spring, is usually needed.

Camellias are ideal for growing in large pots and tubs. They are hardy north to about Washington D.C. but can get scorched if flowers which have been slightly frosted are too quickly thawed out by sunshine. A spot facing east should be avoided. They must have an acid soil but will tolerate all kinds of other conditions, half-shade, some pollution (because the glossy leaves are able to cast off sooty deposits), and a certain amount of neglect. They will, however, repay careful attention by blooming profusely.

Ricinus communis, the castor-oil plant, is unusually quick growing. Seed sown early in the year will, during a warm summer, produce an attractive plant 2m (6ft) high by the autumn. The purple leaved form, *gibsonii*, is by far the best type. It has large palmate (lobed) leaves—up to 60cm (24in) across—of a dark purple colour. If a single pot grown specimen can be bought in May, planted in a large container and kept moist, it will prove a startling sight in good light. Staking will be necessary in practically any position to avoid the possibility of the stem snapping off in a high wind. Also grown purely for the value of their decorative foliage, the hybrid coleus are sold early in the summer as small plants and can fit in well into all kinds of situations. Commonly called the 'painted leaf' they bring a vast range of colour to the container garden. Either sun or shade suits them although the leaf colour is likely to be just a little stronger in sun. They must not be allowed to dry out completely—dryness usually makes them collapse—and even though they recover again a number of lower leaves will be dropped. Good rich soil and some regular feeding will produce some fine plants. Very similar, *Iresine herbstii*, particularly the crimson cultivar Brilliantissima, is used in much the same way. *Kochia scoparia tricophylla*, the summer cypress or burning bush, is a rapidly growing, half-hardy annual forming a pyramid shape of finely cut foliage. In the autumn this plant takes on a deep purplish-red colour and can be very impressive when

60 to 70cm (24 to 28in) high. The flowers of all these foliage plants are insignificant and are best removed as they appear.

Cordyline australis is a native of New Zealand where it is known as the cabbage palm. It has a good architectural quality which fits in well with town gardens and containers generally. The tough, pointed but strap-shaped leaves, are produced in a great whirl at the top of a stout woody stem. An attractive bronze form, *C. a purpurea*, is not quite so robust but more interesting. Both sorts do well in either full sun or some shade and will take copious water and regular feeding during the growing season. Older, dried leaves should be removed to keep the plant tidy.

London pride (*Saxifraga umbrosa*), produces its neat rosettes of spoon-shaped leaves and short sprays of beautifully marked flowers in even the darkest shade, and there is also a form of this plant which is golden spotted and prefers a little sun. Also happy practically anywhere, is *Alchemilla mollis* (lady's mantle) with perfectly shaped leaves, puckered and uniformally crinkled and delicate yellowy-green tufts of flowers. *Alchemilla* seeds itself freely and small plantlets appear regularly which can be tucked into all kinds of odd corners. *Dicentra specabilis* (bleeding heart) is a perennial which grows rapidly in the spring. It has delicate feathery foliage and in March and April produces on arching stems, sprays of small, pink, pouched flowers, shaped like a heart. *Dicentra* will flower quite well in some shade. They dislike disturbance, having a brittle root stock, but are very easy and rewarding plants. The double-flowered form of the little button daisy, *Bellis perennis*, are splendid plants for use in window-boxes and other containers. Red, pink and white forms are available—some small, some much bigger. All like to be moist at the root. Some lilies make excellent tub plants. *Lilium regale* is one of them. *Regale* flowers in June in the north with white trumpet-shaped flowers suffused with purple on the outside, and flushed yellow in the throat. These and many other lilies are stem rooting (they produce roots on the stem growing from the bulb to the soil surface) and need fairly deep planting—around 20cm (8in). When planting lily bulbs, set them on a 3cm (1½in) bed of coarse sand which provides good drainage and prevents rotting. They all should have some sunshine. *Lilium candidum*, the Madonna lily, needs totally different treatment; it likes sun and should have only 3cm (1½in) of soil over them. The only suitable time for planting *candidum* is August when the bulbs are dormant. The very fleshy bulbs of all lilies should be planted as soon as possible. *Candidum* is liable to a fungus disease in hot and dry conditions, and any affected plants should be sprayed with a good fungicide.

Trailing plants are invaluable for breaking up the harsh edges of containers. The trailing lobelia, ivies and ivy-leaved pelargoniums will do this, but campanulas excel for this purpose. *Campanula isophylla* is not hardy but is particularly useful. The type is pale lilac-blue but there is a white variety, *alba*, both having smooth, bright green leaves and a pleasant trailing habit. Another form *mayi*, has slightly downy foliage, with a greyish look, and deeper flowers of a mauve shade. In most fairly sheltered positions all three will pull through a winter without difficulty. *C. fragilis*, blue with a light centre, and *C. carpatica* white and several shades of blue, are totally hardy and spread happily. Taller growing campanulas like *C. persicifolia*, with single and double flowers in white and shades of blue, are useful in larger containers. They usually need thinning out periodically to keep them from deteriorating.

Different varieties of dwarf conifer. From left to right: *picea glauca, picea abies, juniperus communis compressa, chamaecyparis lawsoniana elwoodii*. In front: *taxus fastigata aurea* (left), *juniperus pfitzeriana hetzii*.

DWARF CONIFERS

Dwarf and slow-growing conifers are of great value in many kinds of containers. In window-boxes they can provide a background of green for the temporary and colourful flowering plants; in sink gardens they provide a little height and a tree-like accent for a landscape; they often fit the scale of a small paved area and will not quickly outgrow the area allotted to them. There is a very wide colour range in conifers; light and dark green, grey-green, blue-green, golden and silvery, and the best way to choose a few is to visit a specialist nursery.

Very slow-growing, of a medium green and columnar in shape is *Juniper communis compressa. Chamaecyparis lawsoniana ellwoodii* is the same shape, and is commonly seen and usually very cheap, although, compared with the juniper, a little coarse. Tall and very slim, the golden Irish Yew *Taxus fastigata aurea-marginata*, will only grow around 5cm (2in) a year until it is well established, and then only possibly twice that amount, and con- tributes a beautiful, pencil slim, column of fine gold- edged needles. The spruce family provides conical shapes (*Picea glauca* Albertiana conica), low dome shapes (*P. g. pygmaea* and *P. g. mariana* Nana) and a spreading, flat-topped 'nest' (*Picea abies* Nidiformis).

Some of the larger growing conifers are useful in positions such as on either side of an entrance door— particularly upright growing sorts in low Caisse Ver- sailles.

An 'average' soil suits the conifers best and, when planted in such a medium, they will grow true to type, neither too swiftly nor at such a slow pace as to virtually stand still. Slow-acting fertilizer worked into the soil after a few years will keep them going. In their first year after planting, all evergreen trees should be given particular attention to ensure that they settle down well. Firm planting is essential—do not be tempted to pack loose peat around a newly planted conifer, such light-weight material will only inhibit firm planting. Scatter damp peat over the surface of the compost to help retain moisture by all means.

BULBS AND TUBERS

When the grower buys spring bulbs there is within each bulb a perfectly formed embryo flower and all that is needed that first year is to bring the flower bud out of the neck of the bulb and to the flowering stage. To flower the bulbs again another year is another story, and is dependent on how nearly the grower can follow what is needed for the formation of future flowers. The bulbs should be fed and be allowed to retain their

foliage until such time as it dies down naturally. Bulbs which are grown in very shaded positions do not usually do well the following year largely because the bulbs will have not received enough sunshine to ripen them. If large bulbs are grown in an insufficient depth of compost, they too will be unlikely to put up a worth- while show the second year. If possible, spring bulbs should be replaced each year—certainly this should be so for window boxes—allowing them to be taken out when faded and be replaced straight away by some other attractive plants. A friend's country garden could be the destination of the lifted bulbs.

Spring flowering bulbs should be planted as early in the autumn as they, and the space they are to occupy, are available. They will start within a very short time to put down roots although there will be no sign of this above ground. Good potting mixture, and not bulb fibre, should be used. Plant at the recommended depth or as near to it as possible with the containers available. To get them to make a good root system before the severe weather sets in, and before there is sign of top growth, is essential for success. Their only needs are that they should be kept moist (dark, too, if at all pos- sible) and that they should be given some light staking with thin canes and later tied in with raffia. Nothing is more infuriating then to find that large flower heads have been snapped off by a gust of wind. When lifting bulbs, which do have a home to go to, keep them cool and moist and get them to a garden within a day or two.

Some of the smaller bulbs do very well in containers and *Scilla sibirica, Puschkinia libanotica, Chionodoxa sardensis* and *Iris reticulata* are very inexpensive and, apart from the last named, usually appear at least for several years. Reticulata and *I. danfordiae* more often than not do not reappear the next year and should be treated as expendable items, pulling them up after they have flowered.

Summer and autumn flowering bulbs are also easy to grow provided that some sun is available. The hybrid gladioli, and a few of the species like *Gladiolus byzantinus*, are grown from circular shaped corms planted in April or May around 10cm (4in) deep in a sunny position. Some bonemeal worked into the soil at the time of planting will ensure strong growth, large flowers and some bloom the same year. Stak- ing the heavy flower spikes of the large flowered hybrids is obligatory to avoid wind damage. After flowering, and when foliage has died, the corms are lifted and stored dry in frost-free conditions. Some of the small and miniature flowered sorts are particu- larly attractive. The bulbous iris bloom over a long period, starting with the Spanish in late spring, followed by the Dutch, with the English coming last. White, blue, yellow, bronze and purple shades are produced and there are some bicolours.

The *Canna indica* (Indian shot) make splendid con- tainer plants provided a sufficient depth of soil can be supplied. They produce magnificent foliage— particularly the purple-leaved sorts. The strangely shaped tubers should be planted at least 8cm (3in) deep, and be very carefully watered until growth is well under way when they can be flooded with water regu- larly. When flowering is completed, and just as soon as the foliage is hit by frost, the tubers should be lifted and stored in dry peat. The dwarf-growing dahlias, particu- larly those with single or small pom-pon shaped flowers are easy to grow, cheap to purchase and give a long season of flowering.

Agapanthus are not tuberous rooted although they are usually grouped together with plants that are. They have a thick, fleshy root-stock and strap-shaped leaves emerging from short necks. Large umbels of blue, and, less often seen, white, flowers are produced on stems slightly under 1m (3ft) in length. Agapanthus are one of the few plants which appreciate container culture and usually flower best when their roots are confined by one. They need regular feeding and some top dressing with fresh soil each spring, otherwise they prefer to continue in the same container for years when their fleshy roots tend to fill them up. They can scarcely be given too much water during the growing season and can even be stood in water. *A. africanus* has wide evergreen leaves and large clusters of violet-blue flowers in August; *A. campanulatus* has narrower leaves which usually disappear in winter. A new strain known as Headbourne Hybrids is without doubt the best so far. Originating from South Africa, they love the sun.

SCENTED PLANTS

Scent can be an additional bonus in a garden and is particularly valuable near to the house. The scented-leaved pelargoniums offer a subtle perfume and such plants as mignonette, stocks and nicotiana have a heavy and definite scent. Flowering tobacco (nicotiana) is sold in tall and dwarf growing sorts, some which only open their flowers during the evening, but the most useful development has been the introduction of types which open their flowers during both day and night. These give off perfume all the time and come in white, pink, a greenish shade and a dull burgundy colour. Although it is often said that sweet peas no longer smell, this is not strictly true—some scent has been lost to gain bigger and more flowers per flowering stem. Mignonette was never much to look at, (this is also true of night-scented stocks), but grows easily from seed sown where it is to flower, and pervades the air with a strong perfume. Many beautiful, scented roses exist (another family often accused of laxity in this regard), although they need an adequate root-run. The lily-of-the-valley scent of the shrub *Mahonia japonica* early in the year is particularly welcome as are the tumbling strings of pale-yellow flowers. Lilies-of-the-valley have a very long and dull non-flowering period, need shade, but could provide a foliage contrast with other plants and smell beautifully. Catmint (*Nepeta × faassenii*) has a strange but attractive pungency and the scent of lilies is not appealing to everyone. The ten-week stocks (matthiola) can be brought into flower in ten weeks from seed sowing. They have single or double flowers (the single often have lighter coloured foliage) and both dwarf and taller growing kinds are available. *Matthiola bicornis* is the very dwarf annual with dull lilac flowers and a heavenly evening scent. The Brompton stocks are biennial plants blooming 18 months after sowing. All stocks have a distinctive perfume. *Cheiranthus cheiri*, the cottage type wallflower, and *C. × allionii*, the hybrid Siberian wallflower are deliciously scented and very useful early in the spring—at that season their flowers last well and provide colour over several weeks.

The dianthus family is very large and includes the carnations, pinks and sweet Williams. All of them love the sun and the majority are neat and low-growing. *Dianthus deltoides*, the maiden pink, forms neat mats of green and bears magenta-coloured flowers with a thin pencilled line in the centre—brighter colours are now about under the strain named Flashing Light. *Dianthus × Allwoodii* are dwarf and are available in lots of colours. They are usually rather short-lived but this is only to be expected after such prolific flowering. Mrs Sinkins is a very old variety with fat, double white flowers and a lovely perfume.

The delicate blue-flowered *Exacum affine* which is usually treated as an annual and used indoors is scented.

It makes a nice low-growing plant in a window-box and produces a continuous display of small blue flowers with prominent gold stamens.

The flowers of the heliotrope are very strongly scented and of a rich violet-blue. Small plants should be used in window-boxes and other places where their scent will be appreciated. Some light staking may be needed except when they are used in hanging baskets. Some growers are able to overwinter their plants when they can be trained into standard shapes. Roses have been grown commercially in pots and tubs for the production of umblemished cut blooms for many years but their culture has to be studied for good results. The amateur is advised to choose only strong growing varieties of hybrid teas and floribundas. Pots of at least 20cm (8in) diameter must be provided and the trees should be planted up as early in the autumn as possible to allow them to settle down before the winter sets in. Good soil is essential and regular feeding recommended. A watch must be kept for suckers—the alien root-stock on which the cultivated variety is grafted—and these should be removed right back to the base of the shoot. Some sun is essential for rose growing. Roses enjoy all the good things in life and should be carefully tended.

TEMPORARY PLANTS

Some plants normally grown in the home are often used on a temporary basis in containers out of doors with good effect. The *Chlorophytum comosum variegatum* (spider plant) is an excellent example. The elegant variegated foliage of this chlorophytum (and of any of its relatives) adds a light touch to window-boxes. Small rooted plantlets are easily propagated in the home and can be slipped into empty spaces in boxes, pots and hanging baskets when planting them up and older plants which have grown too large for the house can spend the summer and autumn out of doors. The latter should preferably be planted in another container where they will thrive and send out useful plantlets for taking indoors again in September. Valuable too for their lightening propensities, are any of the variegated tradescantias. They are particularly useful for use in hanging baskets and, again, even tiny rooted cuttings quickly establish themselves and grow in a pleasing way. Plants from both of these families help to break up the outlines of containers.

Solanum capsicastrum, (the winter cherry), is one of the best known berried plants and is much used in the home, but is also excellent out of doors in the autumn and early winter. Planted in sheltered window-boxes the brilliant red fruits and dark-green leaves of the solanum will provide a bright splash of colour over a long period.

More expensive to buy for only a limited life, the cyclamen are exceptionally beautiful and one or two tucked into window-boxes, mainly filled with evergreen shrubs and dwarf trees, will dress up a box for between six and eight weeks. Care should be taken to see that the cyclamen are kept moist at the root. All of the slightly tender primulas will provide a splash of colour over a long period. *P. obconica* and *P. malacoides* are the most commonly seen but *P. sinensis* and *P. × Kewensis*, the former with orange, scarlet or blue frilled flowers and the latter with bright yellow blooms and a good amount of silver dust in the foliage, should be grown more often. Primulas also must be kept moist.

The indoor asparagus 'ferns' (they are not ferns at all but members of the lily family are often used in hanging baskets; *Asparagus plumosus* with fine feathery foliage and *A. sprengeri* with needle-like leaves are the best and will do well in shade. They need to be kept well watered

Home Decoration

Placing plants

If you go out specially to buy a house plant, it is more than likely that you already know exactly where you want to place it. If someone gives you a plant, the case is altered because then you have to find a place in your home for it. Light, the source of light, the quantity of light, the warmth of light, the aspect of light are all important to all plants.

Some of those which do not do well in our homes need more than we can give them in the average house. Those which are adaptable and easy to grow find that conditions in a home are not so very different from those of their natural surroundings, even though the means of providing those conditions may differ considerably.

Many of our popular leafy house plants grow naturally in the shade of the jungle forests. They grow in daylight but in the kind of daylight which is filtered down through a ceiling layer of leaves. Surprisingly,

perhaps, this jungle light has much the same degree of intensity as does the light inside our homes. This explains why so many jungle plants make good house plants.

On the other hand, the popular flowering plants, mostly, have originated in sunny open climates and, as we have already seen, the more flowers a plant has the more light it needs when it grows indoors. Sometimes it is impossible to give it the amount of daylight it requires but there are methods of adjusting this, as we shall see.

The same conditions are required by any plant which has some colour other than green. All variegated foliage, leaves of two or more different colours, needs good light. However direct sunlight can cause more harm than good. The pretty scindapsus for instance, placed in strong sunlight will soon develop brown edges to its marbled leaves.

One might think that a windowsill is the natural place for any plant, especially after learning that a plant must have light, but one must realise that even windowsills receive different degrees or amounts of light according to what aspect they face. Fortunately, north, south, east or west-facing, we can find plants to suit any windowsill. Simply bear in mind that the sun pouring in early morning from the east will have nothing like the burning intensity of the sun shining in a south facing window midday or one which faces west on a late, hot, summer afternoon. North-facing windows tend to be both shady and cool and are ideal for many, indeed one might even say most plants, so long as the room itself is warm as well.

You can actually witness the influence of light upon growth. If you leave a plant undisturbed in a window it will, as you may know, gradually turn all its parts to

Previous page
Well-chosen flowering and foliage plants can be very effective in brightening up a corner. From the left: daisies (*chrysanthemum frutescens*) aspidistra (behind lamp), *lilium longiflorum* (in front), *pelargonium* and *hedera*.

Left
You can have plants in flower at all times of the year, even when snow falls thick outdoors! Here, *Euphorbia splendens* towers above an echeveria in bloom, bowls of mixed cactus and succulents and 'Peach Blossom' double early tulips. On the right is a yellow-flowering *Euphorbia splendens lutea*.

Below left
Facing a window in a corridor, *Hedera canariensis* has its roots in comparative shade, *Aechmea fasciata*, tradescantia, croton (codiaeum), anthurium, a poinsettia (*Euphorbia pulcherrima*) which has flowered and the rarely seen *Scindapsus pictus* 'Argyraeus'.

Below
Ficus pandurata. The large, tough green leaves indicate that this fig should be grown in much the same way as the rubber plant. It needs slightly warmer conditions and care with watering.

face the light, and leaves and flowers will show only their undersurfaces when seen from the room. If you want a plant to grow evenly, it is important to turn the plant a little each day, so that eventually all parts receive the same amount of direct light.

We can exploit this tendency. It is possible to grow a great many leafy plants on walls which are opposite to a window or a glass door and these plants will become extremely decorative because they will gradually turn their leaves to face the window. This means that for those people in the room itself, the plants show their best faces.

Fortunately, there are many plants which will grow well this way, all the green-leaved climbers and creepers, for instance. Remember, the greener, thicker, tougher the leaf, the further back from the light the plant can be grown. Bromeliads will also flourish here and if you are so inclined your wall can be decorated by a tree on which a collection of the smaller types of these plants can be fixed. Driftwood, or stripped clean tree branch, or pieces of cork bark made to look like a tree portion, can be used as an anchorage. Alternatively, one can use a good looking plastic mesh and fix the plants on this.

In some situations it is possible to grow variegated plants this way, for instance, in a corridor or hallway where the opposite wall is not really very far from the window. Variegated ivies will roam prettily, especially the large-leaved *Hedera canariensis. Scindapsus aureus* and its varieties can be used for smaller effects. This pretty little scrambler looks well planted at the foot of the large-leaved ivy. Mix it with the dark-leaved plectranthus which has purple undersides to its leaves and will provide contrast.

Another position in which plants look attractive and where, at the same time, they are in a more suitable position, is at right angles to a window. Here, according to the size and style of a room, one can place a shelf, a table, a large container, a group of plants stood on the floor, or a trough.

When they are grouped this way you can often use one or two plants to shield the rest from intense light. Place those which revel in it, a *Euphorbia splendens* or an outsize cactus for example, near the glass and graduate the rest so that those which prefer the shade are furthest away from it.

If you plan to use a trough under or in a window, bear a few points in mind before you install it. Remember that the plants will face outwards in time, if the trough is on the windowsill itself, or even if it is placed immediately below it, unless you are prepared to turn the trough every few days. It is possible to choose plants which look very attractive with the light shining through them. Some of the ornamental begonias, and there are enough of these to give you variety, would be suitable for this purpose and if you have a really warm room in winter, *Iresine* 'brilliantissima' could be gorgeous. If you grow climbers in the trough, and these can look so attractive trained around, or in the case of an unsightly view, on the window, remember that these do best if their roots are not in full light. Either screen the base of the climbers with bushy plants or stand the container out of the light.

Those who know their subject talk of light levels, and the levels of light influence plants in different ways. Light has colour and although a detailed study of this is not the subject of this book, we should say that the colour of light affects a plant so much that it will become drawn or elongated or tight and compact according to the kind of light under which it is grown. Daylight does not offer us many problems in this respect.

How long light shines is another factor in growth, we call it the duration of light. This affects the develop-

ment of flowers so much that light duration is the basis of many horticultural methods used to produce flowers out of their natural season, such as poinsettias and all-year-round chrysanthemums. It affects us in the home in a simple way – we can use artificial light to prolong daylight and thus grow a greater range of plants.

Not all of us want to place plants in a window. In many homes there is not a suitable area in windows anyway and we have to place the plants in other areas about the home. Many of us feel that a corner, a dim hall or some other place could be enlivened if only some plants could be induced to grow there. But what really is the point of doing this if the plants cannot properly be seen? If they are lit some way, you ensure not only that the plants can be seen but also that they will be happier and will look more decorative simply because they will receive more light.

You will find that artificial light, even a reading lamp placed nearby and left switched on for four or five hours, greatly improves a plant's performance. If you have one which appears to have remained static for months, try putting a lamp near it and watch the new

rate of growth. Plants in living rooms often do so much better than plants which grow in rooms which are used only occasionally.

You can improve the light intensity in a room and at the same time direct a little more light on to a plant by a few simple means. Plants grow better where there are light painted walls than they do against dark backgrounds. A strategically placed mirror, or better still a wall covered by a mirror, will reflect light from a window or from some other source, on to a plant.

From these few observations, you will see that it is always a good plan to site your plants with an eye on the room's lighting as well as according to their own light requirements. Generally speaking, our reading lamps give off white light and although plants really have a preference for blue with red light (not to be confused with the colour of light bulbs) when these two colours are properly balanced, the ordinary home light is efficient enough for us to leave the complexities of light colours to the commercial grower. I use only ordinary lights in my own home and house plants grow happily in every room. If you have an understanding of lighting systems, you could possibly work plant wonders.

Opposite top left
Many plants grow best if they are arranged at right angles to a window, with those which tolerate the strongest light placed nearest the glass. Here are ananas or pineapple, dracaena, chlorophytum, sansevieria, *Begonia masoniana* or the Iron Cross begonia, with the blue flowers of browallia nearby, *Begonia rex* hybrid, cyclamen, crotons (codiaeum) scindapsus and vriesia.

Opposite top right
Monsteras and bromeliads add colour and life to a kitchen which has enough space to accommodate them. The humidity and warmth of a kitchen (and even more of a bathroom) often make these rooms good situations for plants.

Opposite below
These plants are growing in a hall which has only one small window. However, white walls and a mirror placed strategically behind the plants reflect what little light there is and so help to increase light intensity.

This page
The monstera is botanically *Philodendron sellou* and like many others of this family, makes a handsome and distinctive climber. It is most effective where it can be given space to display its attractive leaves.

Various forms of lighting can be used from 100 watt bulbs placed no further from plants than 4 feet and no nearer than 2, this is because the bulb generates heat and if placed too close the plants will become scorched; to strip and even spot lights. Fluorescent lighting provides cool light and thus eliminates the danger of scorching. Some plants, such as saintpaulias can be grown entirely under the influence of such lighting where it is not possible to provide daylight for them.

In another section we deal with terrariums or jungle jars, the term which covers all glass containers. Here I should mention that these gardens should never be stood in full sun, yet the plants must receive enough light or they will damp off and die. It is possible to provide them with both heat and light by converting the jungle jar into a lamp. You can buy fitments to fix into the neck of most of these glass containers and these will hold both the light bulb and lamp shade. The important thing here is that by such means the light is directed down on to the plants. As it is more ornamental than useful, the light is subdued and so cannot harm the plants.

Left
Rhoicissus capensis. Strong-growing climbers, especially those belonging to the grape-vine family, should be given plenty of room and encouraged to climb. Given support they will soon cover a wall. *R. capensis* is a strong growing vine with woody stems and leathery leaves. It has attractive red fruit after flowering.

Below and right
The leaves of plants naturally turn towards the most important source of light, a tendency which can often be used for decorative effect. The darker green and the tougher the leaf, the further away from the direct source of daylight will a plant grow. Many climbers can be trained along a wall opposite a window.

Using the same principle, plants can be housed in a cupboard with glass doors, or in an alcove. The important thing is that the plants should never be grouped or grown with a light bulb close under them directing its dry warmth up to the plant's roots.

One of the kindest things plants can do is to bring life to a hearth no longer or seldom used for a real fire. The fireplace, so long as it is draught-proof, is an ideal place to grow plants. Here they can be watered and sprayed without harm. Many of the hearth and fireside accessories make attractive containers. One can, for example, pull out the ash pan under a fireplace, line it with strong plastic or a few layers of cooking foil and plant or plunge in this. Scuttles, coal boxes and hods, log baskets and large preserving pans and others can be filled with a variety of plants. If lighting can be installed the variety of plants can be greatly extended. However, even without this, there are plenty of plants which will thrive at this distance from windowlight, aspidistras, palms, syngoniums, philodendrons, spathiphyllums, bromeliads, sansevierias, for example.

Use plants to their greatest decorative advantage. If you are only just beginning to furnish a home, let them fill in the gaps meanwhile, you can always move them along when you have something more permanent. Let them act as screens, frames, furnishings. Let them mask a dreary scene, take attention away from an ugly or shabby corner. Use them to make a room look taller, wider, homelier and more welcoming.

Containers for them can be as varied as you wish, although it might be more pleasing if you search out only those which go with your general decorating theme. Make sure that the containers suit their setting and that they are deep enough to take the plants and then set about making the plants look as though they really were at home.

Certainly encourage climbers to climb and to do this you will find that strong thread and drawing pins are as good guides as anything else, but remember also that many climbers will also trail prettily. These look best if they can hang down from a pedestal, shelf or torchère. Some, such as ivies, look well cascading from the base of some very formal plants such as a *Ficus elastica* or sansevieria.

Most strong-growing climbers such as cissus, rhoicissus, ivy and several philodendron varieties can be trained to climb up in the corner of two walls and along the top of the wall in one direction or another, or, if it suits you, right round the room. To support the plants, you can stand a cane from the container to the ceiling or you can tie one end of a thread to the short cane to which the plant is already attached. Take this up vertically and pin it securely to the ceiling. Take more thread along the top of the wall near the ceiling or in whatever direction or angle you prefer. The thread is inconspicuous and really most effective. Obviously, it needs to be strong, and nylon fishing line is ideal because this will hold even weighty stems.

If you are going to use plants at high levels do remember that warm air currents rise and that the plants could suffer because of this. Those with lush growing tips such as philodendrons are more likely to suffer than say, rhoicissus. To prevent these from drying out, and so long as this does no damage to surroundings, spray the growing tips, and the rest of the plant if possible, with a little water, rain water preferably, from time to time. Use an atomiser and water at room temperature.

Grouping plants together successfully is not difficult and is never repetitive. Here, near a window framed by a rhoicissus are double tulips, a giant hippeastrum (so easy to grow), a striped vriesia in flower, crotons in a copper preserving pan and a stag horn fern or platycerium. The balance and shape of the group changes all the time as plants grow, flower and fade. It is fun to experiment and put together contrasting leaf shapes, textures and colours. Bulbs often look spectacular against plants grown principally for their foliage.

Right
Varieties of *Tradescantia fluminensis*: 'Quicksilver', top right 'Variegata', bottom left *Zebrina purpusii* is centre left and *Z. pendula* right; all these plants need good light if they are to be well coloured. Tip cuttings can be taken easily from both plants and they should be repotted each year.

Below
Perennials like the shrimp plant, African violets and anthurium to the left will continually produce flowers. Cyclamen, cinerarias and primulas among others can be grown from seed and timed to bloom in winter.

Plant arrangements and dish gardens

In spite of the multitude of flowers on sale in our markets it is a fact that there are more kinds of plants, in other words, a greater variety, than there are cut flowers. Since this is so and since the plants themselves are such good value for money, why not use more of them in the same way that flowers are used, in arrangements about the house? True, a flower arrangement has its own special aura and beauty and can never be entirely replaced, but a plant arrangement will last

Far left
Pot grown eranthus or winter aconites, double tulips and yellow hyacinths arranged with chlorophytum in a shallow trug basket. Driftwood and moss hide and support the bulbs which are planted in potting soil.

much longer and changes shape as the plants grow.

It is one of the best ways of decorating centrally-heated homes for we can provide humidity for plants and so minimise the possibilities of adverse effects from the heat, but we cannot prevent fresh flowers from maturing and fading quickly.

We can make arrangements from foliage plants alone or they can be mixed with shorter-lived bulbous and flowering plants. They can also be grouped with cut flowers which can be refreshed from time to time as they fade and it is worth observing that flowers arranged with growing plants and sharing in the more humid micro-climate around them, do last a little longer than those which are grouped on their own.

Plant arrangements vary considerably, after all; even a trough planted with a number of different kinds or several of one sort, is a plant arrangement. However, we can make more imaginative and decorative arrangements than this.

One can use plants which are left in their pots and these can be plunged into various mediums, as we have already learned, or they can be simply packed round and wedged into position with damp moss or with one of the water-retentive foamed plastics, such as Oasis, which are used in flower arrangement. Alternatively, plants can be knocked from their pots and transplanted. Generally, we refer to the first method as arranging plants and to the second as making a dish garden but, as we shall see, the dividing line is not always absolutely clear cut. Sometimes we used both methods in one container.

We can also make arrangements with cuttings of all kinds, stem, leaf, offsets and stolons, in such a way that these will root in the water, although you can also arrange rooted cuttings, and they will go on growing so long as we remember to feed them with a weak soluble plant food from time to time. This is a simple and effective way of growing little plants and a good way of using any tips you may think it prudent to nip out from a vigorous mature plant. It is also an ideal way for a new indoor gardener to learn a little about propagating plants and growing generally.

The cuttings or plants are held in position by small stones or pebbles. Gravel is excellent for this purpose and is usually easy to find. Any water-tight container will do for this type of dish garden, known as a puddle pot, so long as it is deep enough to hold a good layer of pebbles. All manner of bowls and little bygones such as sauce boats, tureens, lidless teapots and large shells – so long as the water does not spill from these when you move the arrangement – and certain types of flower vases are vessels which can be used.

Generally speaking, the shallower the container the more securely you should anchor the plants.

If pebbles picked up from the seashore are to be used these should be well soaked and the water changed several times to remove the salt. Whenever pebbles and water are used to grow plants always lace them well with nuggets of charcoal to keep the water sweet.

Stem cuttings which will root in water include tradescantia, zebrina and any of this family; small leaved philodendron – unless you are to make a large puddle pot in which case some of the other larger-leaved kinds could be used; ivies, the small-leaved kinds look particularly attractive; syngonium and many other aeroids, plectranthus, peperomia, coleus, impatiens, rhoicissus, cissus, vitis, and even some outdoor annuals such as nasturtiums.

Chlorophytum offsets, especially if you select those whose roots are already well grown will soon begin to grow.

You can use small rooted plants, almost any kind if you do not mind them living but briefly. For more

Previous page left
If hyacinths are grown singly in pots, they can be arranged together or with other plant cuttings when in bud. Here there is a cutting of ivy shoots in the same potting soil. Moss and driftwood cover the bulbs themselves and the soil round them.

Previous page below
Aeroids are diverse in form and habit yet they blend well one with another. In the bowl, still in their pots, are variegated scindapsus and flowering anthuriums. Behind stand monstera and syngonium.

Left
Wickerwork and other non-waterproof containers can be lined with strong sheet plastic or cooking foil to prevent the water from plants escaping and spoiling furniture. Here, still in their pots, are arranged a variegated hibiscus, *Maranta leuconeura* 'Erythrophylla', tradescantia and fittonia – a collection of plants all with striking foliage which complement each other.

Centre left
A piece of driftwood and moss help to mask the pots in which these plants are still growing. The arum-like flower is the bloom of a spathiphyllum. Sansevieria and *Phoenix dactylifera*, the date palm, tower above *Hedera canariensis* on the left and *H. helix* on the right with a tufted chlorophytum at the centre.

Below left
Planted for a Mothering Sunday present this little bowl contains coloured primroses, a hyacinth, ivy and tradescantia. The two latter will go on growing in the bowl for a long time. The flowering plants should be removed when they have faded and be replaced with fresh colour.

Right
A copper preserving pan comfortably holds pots of citrus, pilea 'Moon valley', *Calathea makoyana*, and the tiny-leaved *Ficus pumila*. Moist peat fills the spaces between the pots and generates some humidity, which is necessary for the pilea and the calathea in particular. All these plants should be shaded from direct sunlight.

settled existence choose cyperus and carex, both swamp lovers. Wash the soil from roots before you arrange plants.

Although plants grown this way should be fed, they will never make such large specimens as they would if well grown in soil, but they do live for a long time. They are very dainty, with smaller leaves, more delicate trails and for this reason these little gardens give one the opportunity of using a greater variety of containers for plants than might be the case. And it follows, that this being so, one can use plant arrangements in more varied ways. For instance, such an arrangement in the right container can look delightful on a dressing table or on a desk. Puddle pots make good table centres, especially if you arrange some lovely glowing colour at the centre. This could be cuttings of coleus, some snippets or leaves from some bright-leaved begonia, or even, as a temporary measure, a little posy of fresh flowers. You could also grow or transplant some of the smaller bulb plants such as the pretty little Roman hyacinths which flower before Christmas, or crocus or any type of bulb which will grow well this way. Your choice will have to depend upon size because many of the forced bulbs are tall.

Many attractive flowers can be grown from bulbs planted in pebbles and water. This method seems to suit some narcissi particularly well but crocuses, hyacinths and, nowadays, even one variety of tulips, can be grown this way also. To make sure not only that you buy the correct types and varieties but also that you are kept up to date on new kinds, study a bulb merchant's catalogue and make your selection accordingly.

Any variety of narcissi recommended for indoor growing is almost certain to grow well in pebbles. The bunch-flowered or polyanthus varieties are said to do even better when grown this way than when grown in bulb fibre or soil indoors. Certainly I grow them successfully year after year.

To plant the bulbs, take a fairly deep bowl, the deeper the roots can go, the more securely will the bulbs be anchored, place a few nuggets of charcoal on the floor of the bowl and fill it to within 2 inches of the brim with the pebbles. Sit the bulbs on these, as close as you like so long as they do not touch. The noses of the bulbs should be well above the rim so adjust the level of the pebbles before you add water should this be necessary.

Right
Old fashioned double daffodils grow well in pots of soil. Tall 'Harvest Gold' are growing in fibre. Double tulips, scillas, grape hyacinths and hyacinths will all flower at the same time and can be complemented by cineraria.

Below
Like many other spring-flowering bulbs, crocuses can be grown in water anchored by stones or pebbles. A little charcoal keeps the water sweet. Crocuses are best kept in a cold place until the flower buds show when they can be brought into a warm room.

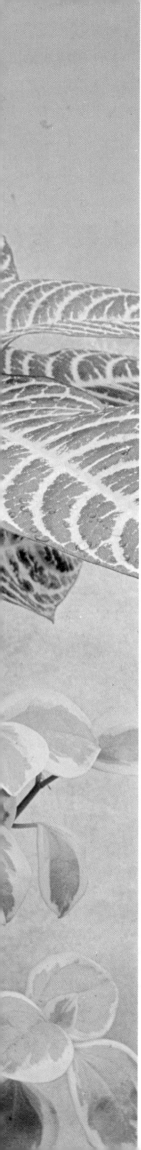

Above
Treat some plants as though
they were flowers and make
some beautiful decorations.
Here the old ironstone tureen
holds a matching cyclamen, a
Begonia masoniana and
cascading over the rim a
Plectranthus oertendahlii with
purple-backed leaves.

Left
Planted in good potting
compost and growing happily
together are *Ficus benjamina,
Hedera canariensis*, with a
vivid poinsettia and striking
striped aphelandra before
them, *Peperomia hederifolia*
and *P. glabella* 'Variegata'
with variegated leaves
scrambling over the rim.

Right
A wonderful variety of textures,
colours and forms can be
brought together in a plant
arrangement. Here at the
centre is a croton or codiaeum,
behind it are sansevieria,
Pittosporum undulatum, and
Hedera canariensis.
Tradescantia and vriesia are in
front with *Hypocyrta glabra* on
the left and aphelandra on the
right.

More pebbles should now be arranged round and between the bulbs so that these are upright and well supported. Pour in water, clean rainwater if possible, so that its level is just under the surface of the pebbles. Place the bowls in a cool dark place until the roots are growing well. This is usually between five and eight weeks according to the type of bulb.

Bulb fibre is also an easy medium in which to grow bulbs and it suits many kinds including all of those which can be grown in pebbles. It should be used moist but not sodden and, once again, the noses of the bulbs should be above the surface after planting.

The critical time for spring-flowering bulbs grown indoors is immediately after planting. The essential factor is that the bowls or other containers should be stored in a cold, dark place until the roots are well formed and the shoots are actually growing out from the bulbs. They can then be brought indoors. This is best done in stages, first into a cool place for a few days, and then into a warmer one and so on. If the bulbs are not treated this way you might find that the flowers are stunted, malformed or unattractive in some other way.

After trying many methods of cool, dark, storage including traditional plunging of bowls out of doors, I have found that the simplest and most effective way is to wrap each bowl inside a black plastic bag and to stand this in the coldest place you have—not the freezer though. I keep mine on the north wall of the garage, indoors. I have kept them outdoors on north-facing windowsills and roof areas, on a cold landing of an outer staircase to a flat and in a cellar. Any of these places will do.

As I said earlier, bring the bowls into the warmth and light gradually and once you have them in a window, give them a quarter turn each day to keep them growing evenly.

Whether you force your own bulbs or buy them ready grown be sure to water them, but once they are in bloom give them very little or they will mature too quickly. Always water the soil around the bulbs and try not to pour water over the bulbs themselves. When you spray your other plants to freshen them, give bulb flowers a little shower as well. They will keep fresher longer.

It is not really a good plan to grow mixtures of bulbs, although it is pleasant to make arrangements of different kinds if these are mature together. As you would expect, bulbs can be easily fitted into all manner of plant arrangements, in or ex-pot. You can plan a bulb and plant arrangement well ahead if when you plant a bowl with bulbs in fibre you also plant one or more empty flower pots. When the bulbs are brought into the warm room, you can then remove the empty pot and replace it with a full one. This could be another type of bulb flower, for instance, crocuses with narcissi, or it could be a flowering plant, such as a cyclamen, or a leafy plant or two.

If the bulbs are growing in pebbles and water you can introduce any of the puddle pot cuttings. If you do not mind being extravagant, you can wash the roots of an anthurium and plant it among the pebbles because this plant will grow happily this way. It will thrive also alone in a hyacinth glass.

To prevent them from becoming spoiled, metal and wooden containers can be lined. Quite often a strong waterproof plastic bag will do—you can cut it or roll it down so that it fits the container and is inconspicuous. Cooking foil offers extra lining and so far as wooden containers are used indoors, if these are precious and not simply plant troughs, it is wise to use foil and plastic.

Incidentally, speaking of plastic bags, those black sleeves, sold as substitutes for flower pots, are often much easier to fit into containers than the rigid pots. If you are building up a stock of small plants for plant arrangements you might care to bear this in mind.

Sometimes a shallow container can be given extra height and so made suitable for a plant with a deep root ball by lining it with foil or plastic and raising it at the back. This subterfuge will be hidden by plants arranged in the foreground. You can also retain the soil by using pieces of cork bark, driftwood and flat shells inside the rim.

The pleasant thing about using plants with flowers, or about grouping flowering plants, is that many containers one might pass over if one were looking for a container for a single plant, or for a collection of green plants, prove to be perfect when flowers are introduced. Old wash basins, which are often highly patterned, are ideal especially in cottage interiors. They are deep enough at the centre to take a large pot with a tall plant yet shallow enough at the edges to take the small pots in which hedera (ivy), tradescantia, plectranthus and other scramblers are often grown and wide enough to allow one to build up a really good collection.

As I said earlier, the dividing line between a plant arrangement and a dish garden is not always clear cut, and using a wash basin could offer an example of this, for I would suggest that where the area near the rim is too shallow to take a small pot comfortably, it might be more convenient and effective to add soil at this point and to plant the scramblers. Alternately, strike cuttings of them and let them root here to be moved later when the arrangement is dismantled.

The types of containers which can be used are legion. They include large soup tureens, coal scuttles, preserving pans, log baskets, urns, pitchers, to mention only a few.

Obviously, one has to be guided by size for a large container filled with potted plants can be very heavy and difficult to move around. One can lessen weight by filling a deep container to the required depth with foamed plastic. The pots can be pressed into this and they will be held at whatever angle is required. A further advantage is that the plastic stays nicely moist, or will do so if it is watered from time to time, and thus will generate a pleasant humid area immediately around the plant. Just one word of warning, plants find this substance so agreeable that after a time they grow down into it, so if you think it time the plants were repotted, examine the pot bottoms from time to time.

Left
Colchicum autumnale (often wrongly known as the autumn crocus). Flowers will grow from this bulb without the assistance of soil or water and in a very short time. Simply stand the bulb in some vessel or saucer to anchor it. After flowering, plant the bulb in the garden where it will produce its leaves in spring and flower again the following autumn.

Right
Plants need not be transplanted when they are arranged. All of these—dracaena, Mistletoe fig, anthurium, cryptanthus and scindapsus are in their individual pots, some of which are raised and hidden by the plants before them. Coccoloba is a plant that will grow very tall and ideally needs space to display its boldly shaped leathery leaves. Very young plants are an attractive addition to an arrangement.

From my own point of view I find tall or pedestal flower vases to be some of the best containers for displaying house plants. Grouped in these, the plants are lifted well above the level of whatever surface on which the arrangement is to stand. They give elegance to arrangements, especially when trailing plants can be allowed to cascade down over the edge for some inches. There is another point to be borne in mind. When you have to move the arrangement you can do so easily and without disturbing the plants in any way, simply by holding a portion of the pedestal.

While bulb bowls are not in use they can hold plant arrangements and, of course, not all of these need be large, often three or four small plants look quite attractive especially if the container is a little out of the ordinary. If you have a choice, bear in mind that a container with sides that slope so that its mouth is much wider than its base gives you a good area of soil surface on which the plants can display themselves. If the container is deep, 4 inches at least, there is room for some roots near the base to reach down to the bottom and for others to be spread out nearer the surface.

Ingredients for a puddle pot are simple: gravel, water and a few nuggets of charcoal to keep it sweet, an attractive container and a selection of house plant cuttings. Arrange the cuttings as you would a vase, with trailers over the rim of the container and an interesting focal point in the centre – a coleus shoot in this case. Strip the stem ends of leaves before anchoring them in place with some of the shingle or whatever other stones are used. Finally, top up with water and feed the plants from time to time.

As the containers you will use have no drainage hole it is necessary instead to install a layer of what is termed drainage material on the floor of the vessel. This provides essential air spaces into which water will be rapidly sucked when the plants are watered. One of the best drainage layers and certainly one of the most simple to provide today is made of small nuggets of charcoal. At one time broken flower pot crocks were recommended but these are becoming rarer and rarer. Stones and shingle may also be used but they tend to make the bowl very heavy.

The first rule for a successful dish garden is to provide good soil. Although the plants will retain their pot soil or root balls, more soil will be needed to pack round them. Do not use soil dug up from the garden or countryside for this may contain harmful pests and fungi. Buy a bag of good potting compost. This is on sale in garden shops and chain stores. Buy small amounts unless you are making many dish gardens because the soil mixture deteriorates during storage.

Before deciding which container you are going to use, examine your plants. The depth at which they should be planted is determined by their crowns, the part of the plant at the junction of root and top. The crown should never be further above or below the new soil level than it was originally.

In the finished arrangement, the soil surface does not have to be level, indeed it is usually better if it is not so. Raise it either in the centre or to one side. A raised soil area gives a plant greater depth for its roots. If you have plants from varied sizes of pots you can plant those from the largest pots in the raised soil area. At this point also, place those plants which like to be well drained, sansevierias, peperomias, succulents and bromeliads.

Having decided what plants you intend to grow together, water them and let them drain well before you begin, that is, unless they have been very recently watered. Knock them from their pots one at a time as you proceed so that their roots are not exposed to the air any longer than is necessary. Before you begin it is a good plan to arrange the plants on the table in roughly the pattern you intend to follow. You will then be able to see what placement is really practical and where the tallest or shortest plants ought to go.

Spread a layer of soil over the drainage layer. Do not make this too deep or you may have difficulty in accomodating the plants. As you arrange their roots on the soil, determine whether and where the soil needs raising. Try to disturb the roots as little as possible.

Below
Sedum sieboldii. A plant that will withstand quite cool conditions and because of its semi-succulent nature can be left for several weeks without water. It dies down in winter.

Most plants should stand upright but if you want some to trail over the rim of the container or to lean away from the centre, tilt them and slip some soil under them to wedge them in place. At the end, see that all the roots are covered with soil. Press this down firmly so that the plant is as solidly anchored as if it has been growing this way always. However, guard against panning the surface, that is making it so hard that water cannot pass through it easily. If it flows off, the surface is too hard.

Make sure that you have left room for watering. The soil level should be at least a ½ inch below the rim, even if it rises in the centre.

Finally, water the plants carefully, preferably by spraying the leaves and the soil surface. It is important that the soil is not made sodden. Stand the arrangement in its place so long as this is not in a very sunny spot.

If after some time, during which the plants have grown well and spread over the surface, you find it difficult to water the bowl it may be best to lower the whole arrangement gently into a sink filled with water or into some other larger vessel. Hold it there until the bubbles stop rising to the surface, then allow the surplus water to drain away. Cacti often need this method of watering but remember not to do this more than once a month in winter.

It is not wise to mix cacti with other kinds of house plants. Fortunately, these make charming arrangements when grown together and you can find sufficient variety among them to make contrasts of shapes and textures. Some succulents go well with them, especially those with bloom on their leaves or those which flower well such as rocheas and crassulas. Sansevierias can be grown with cacti.

Some succulents can be mixed with the majority of the other house plants you are likely to use in arrangements. Again, try rochea and crassulas, *Sedum sieboldii* 'Medio-variegatum', is a prettily variegated plant. Although it dies down in winter it is well worth collecting.

Whether you make a plant arrangement or a dish garden, aim for contrasts. Most groups look their prettiest with a plant or two scrambling over the edge of the container. In the central zones plant rosettes or distinctive broad-leaved plants such as the beautifully marked *Begonia Rex* varieties, calathea, maranta, pilea and some bromeliads. For height and grace there are palms, sansevieria, *Fatsia elegantissima*, ivies trained vertically, dracaenas especially the prettily coloured *Dracaena marginata* and the green and white striped *D. sanderiana*. There are many more.

Below
Most kinds of cacti and succulents will grow well and last for years in a shallow dish garden. In this one a small juniper has been added as a temporary contrast, since it will have to be removed and transplanted later.

Combining plants and flowers

Once you enjoy arranging plants you will not find it a great step to use cut flowers with them nor to add to these two all the accessories and lovely natural materials which are associated with flower arrangements.

You might begin, as I did, from a purely practical need. If a bowl of mixed plants looks a little spent and needs brightening, what could be easier or more instantly effective than to push some kind of water vessel into the soil, among the plants and hidden by them, and then to fill it with a few fresh flowers? You need so few and yet the result is often quite remarkable.

From such a simple beginning, you will find that pot-et-fleur, as such arrangements are called, offers you a most interesting and exciting way of decorating your home. In the first place, you will never be at a loss for basic colours because the plants will provide these. All you have to do is to find the few flowers that are required.

As you would expect, those which grow on plants akin to some of our house plants always look good in pot-et-fleur. These are such flowers as anthuriums, arums, cyclamen, which though they may seem a little expensive at times should last well. Orchids, also extremely long lasting, look delightful with house plants as do any of the smooth-stemmed bulb flowers; in spring, narcissi which include daffodils, freesias, tulips, and later in the year, gladioli, lilies, nerines, *Amaryllis Madonna* (the outdoor plant) and the late-flowering schizostylis.

Many shrubs' blossom looks good, especially in winter or early spring; magnolias, azaleas and rhododendrons, taken from their usual environment and set among exotic house plants have an extremely rich and wonderful effect.

Generally speaking leafy subjects look too fussy and if these are to be used it is usually best to remove most of their own foliage so that the house plants take the limelight. Examples are roses, paeonies, dahlias.

In the same way, soft petalled flowers may not show up as well as you had hoped, anemones and chrysanthemums, for instance.

You can often use a few flowers to emphasise a certain feature of a plant's foliage, colour for instance. Often the underside of a leaf may be vividly coloured and yet, because of all the greens which surround it, this may not be very noticeable. Choose some flower which matches this colour and make a pot-et-fleur and you will see a great difference. Study the plants' colours before you go to shop for the flowers. You will find colours other than greens in stems, stipules, bracts and tendrils.

Use flowers also to accentuate shapes. Irises are attractive when arranged with tall spiky sansevieria possibly because this pot plant's leaves are similar in shape to iris leaves. Arrange pointed gladioli with low

growing large leaves such as begonias. Arrange posies of violets, pansies and tiny cyclamen with little ivies. Use vivid tulips with a vivid cordyline.

Pot-et-fleur can incorporate planted bowls or you can let the plants stay in their pots and arrange them individually. Just the same rules apply as for plant arrangements; you will need suitable containers, a drainage layer and good soil if you are planting the bowl, and plenty of wedging and plunging material if you are arranging plants. If you raise many plants yourself, pot some of these in the black plastic sleeve-type flower pots. As I said elsewhere, you will find these so much more easy to squash into a container than rigid flower pots.

You will need plenty of material for masking and hiding pots and the vessels you use to hold the flowers. The latter can be arranged in many ways. When you fill a bowl you can plant a few empty vessels, deep cream cartons, cigar tubes, small glass or plastic tablet tubes, pointed metal cones which you can buy at the florists' and the plants' roots can find their way round these. You will not then disturb them when you remove the water containers to clean them—flowers die quickly if containers are allowed to become soiled. Keep them as clean as dishes and cutlery. You can also use blocks of foamed plastic inside a small piece of plastic sheeting, this makes it easier to lift out the plastic if you should wish to replace it. After you have made one or two pot-et-fleur arrangements you will soon grasp the essentials.

Of course, many of the plants will hide all the mechanics of the arrangement, but sometimes you will find that a pot rim still shows or the top of a tablet tube appears above plant level. Driftwood, cork bark, coral, sea-fan and sea-shells and dried fungi of many kinds, especially the large bracket-fungi, are some of the accessories you can introduce into pot-et-fleur so that they form part of the design and serve a more useful purpose at the same time.

Do not hesitate either to mix dried materials with your growing plants and fresh flowers. After all, this is nature's way. Dried lotus lily seed heads look extremely lovely used alone or clustered as the focal point surrounded by lively leaves; cocoa palm boats or husks can be arranged with plants other than palms and these will hold flowers, fresh or dried if you wish; so-called dessert-spoons, really the dried ends of agave leaves sometimes sold varnished, will add height and a certain strangeness to familiar plants; skeletonised leaves can be used to back and to throw into contrast those of a more substantial nature.

There really is no limit to the ways you can use flowers and plants to decorate your home.

Far left
Regal lilies, dracaena, *Begonia rex,* blue coco beans, camphor pods, cherries and driftwood. Containers with wide tops are best for plant and flower arrangements. There should be space for small flower pots as well as for vessels for the flowers. All can be effectively hidden.

Left
Tulips and scented pelargonium, ivy and garden arum leaves, *Begonia rex* plant and fruit. Plants, flowers and fruit can be grouped together in many ways to make unusual and highly decorative arrangements.

Harmonising plant and flower colours

In the previous chapter I said that you can often use a few flowers to emphasise some colour in a plant's foliage, and the more you combine and arrange plants and flowers the more you will appreciate the importance of colour harmony.

A simple green plant is likely to suit any setting and if it goes in a green outer pot it will merge discreetly enough with its surroundings. However, you could get much more value from it than that.

Although at first glance they may seem to be so, few leafy plants are in one colour. Even those described as 'green' are unlikely to be produced in one plain definable colour. Such a plant is much more likely to hold many hues of green. It may have tints in its young shoots which are so light and delicate that they seem to offer contrast to the old leaves. Other parts of the same plant may be in deep tones or shades. Often in the oldest leaves there may be a different green on the upperside than there is on the underside. Leaf stipules, tendrils, aerial roots, flowers like those of some of the aeroids, and fruits will extend the variety of hues within this main colour.

Green is a secondary colour of the spectrum, made of a mixture of yellow and blue. In a mixture of plants we can always find some which are more yellow than green and others may have so much blue in them as to be described as glaucous. They all look well together because they are linked by a common colour. Together they make an analogous harmony.

This variation of hue is fascinating and any plant owner will find great enjoyment in discovering just how much variation of one colour exists in one leaf. But there is more to it than that. Many plants, like flowers, have natural colour contrasts and harmonies. Take as a simple example the familiar green rubber plant *Ficus elastica decora*. Often in this plant, perhaps only at certain stages of its growth or times of the year, we can find traces of the most beautiful carmines and magentas. The growing tip may be covered with a vividly coloured sheath. A hue of the same colour, or perhaps a shade, might also be found in the stems or in the raised veins on the underside of the leaf. Many green leaves have beautifully coloured undersides: cinerarias, cyclamen and saintpaulias are familiar examples. Conversely, highly coloured or patterned foliage, begonias for instance, often has plain undersides.

The study of colour is truly fascinating and the purpose of these brief remarks is to suggest that by taking more interest in plant colours we can get greater value from their decorative role in our homes.

Let us refer back to the few simple examples given. It could be that in a furnishing scheme the carmine we see in a rubber plant (incidentally, a natural complementary colour harmony) could give you a lead on what other colours to use in the room where it stands.

Flowering plants in those colours placed near it are likely to have a greater impact and give more pleasure than others. The same applies to flower arrangements, in which, of course, greens can also be blended. Depending on your requirements, containers, some ornaments, pictures, even soft furnishings could follow this guidance.

However, as one can see by the illustrations in this book, plant colour covers the spectrum. Some people have a natural flair for colour, but those who find it difficult to harmonise one colour with another can be helped by the plants and flowers themselves.

If you love plants, then you are bound to admire leaves. As we have already learned, arrangements of different kinds of plants can look very attractive, even when they do not share a flower between them. In a plant arrangement no one colour ever seems to fight or clash with another (although some associations are more exciting than others, as one would expect) and perhaps this is because there is between them the bond of sap—all green brothers under the skin!

The same is true of flowers, but before we deal a little more freely with floral colour harmony I should like to suggest that you experiment with 'flower' arrangements from leaves rather than from cut blooms. A leafy table centre, for instance, is always a good idea. You can keep the arrangement low in stature but very

varied in nature and you can also keep it ever-changing, for it is so easy to take out a faded leaf and slip in some new discovery.

There is no reason why these leaves should be picked from your beloved house plants, although on the other hand there are times when these can be usefully employed. A cyclamen, for instance, which has finished blooming and is beginning to die down is likely to have enough good leaves for you to gather three or four if and when you need them. A rhoicissus, ivy, philodendron, chlorophytum or any plant which is growing just a little too vigorously for your convenience can be pruned from time to time, and there is always the advantage that these prunings can later be treated as cuttings. Indeed, some may even begin to root in water while they are part of the newly created arrangement. This is also often the case with begonia leaves.

Right
The yellow crinkly leaves are cut from stems of forced rhubarb. An arrangement like this uses freshly bought or picked daffodil buds with other blooms. As these fade, new ones can be bought and the roles reversed.

Far right
Simple complementary colour harmony, orange and blue, but by studying the dahlias and using them as a guide we can elaborate and create a more subtle colour scheme. The ligularia leaves and the interior of the dish repeat the tones in the dahlias' centres.

Below
A combination of preserved beech leaves, pussy willow and dogwood stems with fresh variegated kale, wild ivy trails and cuttings from house plants which include variegated ivies and cordyline leaves.

Other leaves are easy to find, even if you have no garden. Preserved leaves can be used with fresh foliage. Fallen leaves can be pressed and fern fronds treated in ways I have suggested elsewhere. Certain everyday leaves that one does not usually consider as material for flower arrangement can be used, for example, cabbage, parsley, forced rhubarb, beet leaves and carrot. Instead of a flower or a flower cluster at the focal point of an arrangement, you can use the thick rosettes from any attractive succulent plant.

Some people find great satisfaction in making monochromatic arrangements, in which all kinds of green plant materials play a role. These may include lichened branches, green berries, seed heads, catkins, stems and buds, and as one would expect, green flowers. Actually there are many green flowers, some of them so lowly and inconspicuous that we tend to pass them by unseen. On the other hand, some are so handsome that keen flower arrangers seek them out. Hellebores and spurges are favourites. Grasses also are green flowers. All of these help us to make arrangements full of interest.

Probably one sees more monochromatic arrangements in green than in any other colour because there are so many green plants to be found, but this should not limit you. You can also try to make yellow, blue, brown, orange, carmine or any other colour leaf ensembles. Better still, mix them and see just how vivid and varied you can make a non-flower arrangement.

Once you have experimented with leafy materials alone you may find it helpful to bring in other accessories. Fruits seem a natural addition. Quite often you can arrange these in a temporary decoration, for a dinner party table for instance, and then use the ingredients for a more practical purpose while they are still at their best. However, there are many other fruits than those you buy to eat, hedgerow and garden berries among them, and there are also many attractive vegetables.

As I have already referred to secondary colours, perhaps it would be helpful to give a few more facts, which should help the arranger to create attractive colour harmonies. The colours of flowers and plants are those of the rainbow, in which there are the three primary colours, red, yellow and blue. From these are derived the secondary colours. If you look at a rainbow you will see how naturally these are made. Blue overlaps with yellow to make green; yellow with red to give orange; and if we could bring the two outer edges together as we do when we make an artificial colour wheel, to make its two edges touch, we should see that when the red and blue meet they make purple.

These, then, are the true spectral colours but, as you know, in plant life and elsewhere colours vary considerably. Just think of the number of reds there are, for instance. Some colours are much more definite than we see in the rainbow through strong light. We say that such colours have a rich or strong tone. When colours have a degree of grey or even black in them we call them shades and, as I said earlier, when the colours are thin, i.e. when they contain much light, we say that they are tints. Then there are all the variations which lie between the true colours, the hues, to which we often give descriptive names, such as jade green, turquoise blue, ruby red, primrose yellow, lavender blue and salmon pink.

Each primary spectral colour has its natural opposed secondary colour which is known as its complementary. Thus orange is complementary to blue, green to red and purple to yellow. You can never create a discord if you put two complementaries together. Think how good a green plant looks inside a red pot.

Sometimes the two spectral complementaries are a

little too strong for some people's taste when used in flower arrangement. They may prefer to reduce one or both colours to a paler tint. In some settings, for example, a green plant might look better in a pink pot than in a scarlet one. Soft apricot flowers might suit a blue room better than bright orange ones and violet delphiniums be more pleasing against pale lemon walls than against buttercup yellow. Don't imagine though that it is necessary to have equal quantities of complementary colour.

Dealing with flowers and plants differs from handling fabrics and paints because, as we have seen, there is certain to be some other colour or hue present, usually green or some hue of it. So when we are making harmonies we always have to compromise and take this extra colour into account. Actually this can be very useful. Green makes a wonderful buffer between one vivid colour and another. Anyone who is undecided can always select a green container and be almost certain of choosing a harmonious colour for its contents. Of course the green of the vessel could exactly match some green in the plants or flowers and then the harmony would be even more pleasing. It is also safe to take tints to their limit, which of course is white, and shades to theirs, which is black. This means that flowers and plants look right in white or black containers.

There are some other safe colours also. When complementaries are mixed together they make what are known as 'broken' colours. These are pleasing, safe, familiar, almost neutral colours, the natural ones of leaf, bark, branch and stone. Orange and blue make a grey, green and red make a brown, and yellow and purple make a tan. You can often see a natural example of the last in a pansy flower, where you will sometimes see yellow and purple and tan all together. Of course these broken colours will vary according to the quantities of one or other colour in them. Take some water paints and mix them yourself to see what results you get.

So far as flower arrangements are concerned, not everyone likes to see contrasts, even if complementary and therefore harmonious. Many people like to see a more subtle blending of hues. As I have already said, monochromatic arrangements are extremely popular and there is no doubt in my mind that, among these, all-white flower arrangements come highest in popularity, but of course this is a matter of personal taste. Whatever your favourite colour, it really is a fascinating pastime to set about making an arrangement which plays on the colour keyboard from its low shades, through the rich tones and up to the palest tints.

An analogous popular colour harmony is that which uses the neighbouring colours on the spectrum. Thus we can have arrangements in which the flowers go from blue, red to purple; from yellow, orange to red; from yellow, green to blue; but with all the nuances of tints, shades and hues. Many familiar flowers naturally produce blooms in analogous harmony.

If you have to buy all your flowers you might find it difficult to make an arrangement with a wide range of related colours. In this case buy flowers in the two or three colours around which you wish to create the harmony and then use other accessories to increase the colour range and provide the other nuances, the tints, tones and shades.

It goes without saying by now, I hope, that some of these could be leaves, fruits and vegetables. The choice and inclusion of these will have to depend very much on the style and character of the arrangement.

Candles are a great help to the colour-conscious flower arranger and it is well worth while collecting and keeping a stock of these. I suggest that they are used for

Left
Making an arrangement like this is a little like painting a picture, one builds it up slowly, introducing light and shade as well as colour. Stems are held in a bowl fitted in the lamp stand. The heavy artichoke was anchored first.

Right
A colour harmony based on some leaf colours. The candles help to bring more of the sap green also found in the variegated kale. The beech is preserved, the maple keys dried. The two flower-like items are the calyces of *Cobea scandens*, an annual climbing plant.

Far right and below
See following page

their colour value alone, but naturally if you wish to light them that is up to you.

If you are making a table setting then you can call in many more aids. Glass and linen as well as candles and fruit can contribute to the colour harmony of the flowers. Even a base on which the arrangement stands can help. Cover or colour it if necessary. Patterned china is often a help in creating colour harmonies, especially simple ones. I have in mind, for example, a few bright orange flowers in a white container which carries matching bands of the flower colour.

As I said earlier, the stem holders such as Oasis make it possible for us to use a plate as a container. If you have one with a patterned or coloured edge, you have a good and useful foundation on which to create a colour scheme. Even if you cannot exactly match the china colour you are almost certain to be able to find either complementary or analogous colours which will set you on your way. Do not overlook the fact that some leaves and other foliage might be more useful from the colour point of view if they are arranged with their undersides uppermost.

Sometimes the colour of the glaze of the interior of a low dish can enhance the floral colour. When flowers are set to one side of such a container and arranged on a pinholder or a block of Oasis, the interior of the vessel is often much more in evidence than the outer surface. This is sometimes worth taking into account when you go to buy or gather your flowers. In the same way, the means you employ to conceal the stem holder can contribute to the colour harmony. Stones, lumps of raw glass, coral and sea shells, can all add one or more hues to the whole.

Do not hesitate, either, to use whole plants as flowers at a focal point in a flower arrangement. You can always slip its pot inside a plastic bag so that it does not get over-watered. Think how attractive a little cyclamen, a variegated cryptanthus or a *Begonia rex* might look under certain circumstances.

Finally, having described so many different combinations and mentioned various combinations encouraging you to mix together plants and flowers, fresh or dried, vegetables, fruits and berries, wood, shells and other accessories, one word of warning: do not forget that it is possible to over-elaborate and that the individual beauty of many plants is often sufficient, depending on their position and type. You can only experiment, and half the joy of plants and flowers is in the fun you can have trying endless variations and combinations to suit your home.

Previous page far right
Christmas colours—red and green—are complementary and we can make a simple yet attractive arrangement by using a handful of evergreens with red accessories. However, the yellow in the holly leaves and the silver down on the senecio prompted the use of silver and gold baubles and honesty.

Previous page below
An arrangement for a summer dining table in which very few blooms are used. Colour comes from the red plastic basket, ornamental kale, eggplant, currant tomatoes, beans, fennel flower, pansies, nasturtiums and three spider chrysanthemums.

All the spectrum colours are represented here in a rich mixture of autumnal flowers, foliage, berries and seed heads. Few of the flowers are one pure colour. Most have one or more hues which blend them all into one harmonic unit.

Plant Health

The care of plants in the house has come a long way from the days of the Victorian housewife who might have had a single aspidistra on a whatnot filling up a dark corner, or the learned gentlemen with a Wardian case full of plants. Little was known then about growing plants under cover, whether in a greenhouse or in the home; a glasshouse was a very modern invention, a curiosity rather than the necessity it very nearly is today, and the cultivation of plants in containers, with protection, was still in its infancy.

But the nineteenth century was a time when thousands of new species of plants were being discovered and sent back to Europe. Their enthusiastic owners experimented with growing mediums, temperatures, light, watering and so on until, mostly by trial and error, and with the help of notes from the plant explorers on the plants' habitat, they were able to grow the new finds successfully. Conservatories became very popular, a status symbol rather like the television set and, with their rather twilight conditions and steamy warmth, were ideal places for plants straight out of tropical jungles. From there it was an easy and natural transition into the house, and so the cultivation of plants in the home gradually increased: their needs became better known, the range of plants widened and the standard of cultivation went up in leaps and bounds.

It was not, however, just an understanding of the plants' requirements that ensured their spread—the discovery of new continents and countries all over the world meant that a much greater variety of terrain and climatic conditions were being encountered. This meant, of course, that the plants themselves were equally varied: climbing, trailing, creeping, epiphytic, growing without water or in water, in forest gloom or desert sun. Some had leaves as brilliantly coloured as flowers; others had flowers as green as the conventional leaf; some, like the orchids, had flowers with bizarre shapes. Some only flowered at night and some were carnivorous and lived on insects. The possibilities for decorating the home with living plants suddenly seemed to be boundless and they became even more popular.

Would-be gardeners who had no garden, or only a tiny one, found they could grow plants perfectly well indoors, provided they chose the right plants for their conditions. This led eventually to the production of the modern and very sophisticated plant windows, specially built into the house, with a heating cavity, plunge beds for the plants, glass partition and maximum light. Such an elaborate construction means that some very temperamental, but highly ornamental plants can be grown; however, it is not essential for an attractive display.

You can still have eye-catching collections of plants all over the house, provided you choose the right ones for the different conditions in the house, and supply the plants with what they need in the way of food and drink, warmth, light and moisture. It helps, too, if you know how to handle plants when potting, pruning or cleaning them, and especially the right times of the year for the various treatments.

Their care may seem elaborate and detailed if you are not experienced in growing plants, but you will find that it is mostly a matter of common sense, of remembering that plants are living things, just as we are, and that they also need water, nutrient, warmth and light, and times to rest. The fact that they do not talk aloud and cannot move does not mean that they are dead, or stuffed—very far from it. In fact a lot of plant owners have gone almost too far the other way, and regard their plants like animal pets, talking to them, fondling their leaves and getting a plant doctor to them at the slightest sign of wilting! But certainly they have the reactions common to organisms with life in them, and should be treated accordingly.

PLANT STRUCTURE

Before I go on to talking about the details of looking after plants, it will help you to understand them if you know a little about the way they work—what makes them tick and what they have inside them.

Plants, like us, are made up of millions of cells containing sap (the equivalent of blood), but they do not have a bony framework. Each cell is a tiny bag, mostly of cellulose, containing water in which are dissolved mineral nutrients, and all sorts of other chemical compounds. There are different kinds of cells which do different jobs—for instance, one group carries water containing the minerals up the plant from the roots, another acts as a transport for the carbohydrates formed by the top growth, some form woody tissue, others are a special type called cambium cells which are constantly dividing so that the plant gets bigger, and so on.

A living plant with the sun shining on it will be a hive of activity, though it may look as though it is just a lifeless object. The roots will be absorbing moisture from the soil; the leaves and stems will be taking in carbon dioxide from the air and producing oxygen and sugars in its place and the leaves will be giving off water vapour. Cells will be enlarging and dividing so that the size of the plant increases, new leaves are produced, flowers appear, and seed and fruit grow.

When you consider that a plant not only pursues most of these processes continuously, but moderates them and adapts itself according to whether the sun is shining or not, the temperature is going up or down, moisture in the soil or atmosphere is increasing or decreasing, and attack by pests or disease may be occurring, just one plant is little short of a miracle in itself, especially as it may have soft, vulnerable tissue. Plants have developed tremendous powers of endurance and adaptability to help them survive in spite of being immobile, and even one such delicate and complicated mechanism merits a good deal of thought and consideration of its needs.

Feeding

When a plant feeds, it does so in two ways. One is by absorbing some of its food through its roots. The food which is taken in by this process consists of particles of mineral nutrients, such as phosphorus, magnesium or potassium. In order to be absorbed, however, they must be in solution—in other words, a plant drinks part of its food. These nutrients must be dissolved in the moisture contained in the soil or whatever is the growing medium in which the roots are anchored, and this moisture is then taken into the root cells.

This process will continue quite satisfactorily, provided the concentration of the solution in the soil is more dilute than that in the root cells. If the soil solution is more concentrated, as happens when too much fertilizer is added to the soil, the liquid in the root cells flows out of the roots into the soil moisture until both are at the same concentration. As a result of the roots losing moisture like this, they begin to dry up, stop working and die, and because of this the top growth—the leaves and stems—are short of mineral nutrient and also stop growing, become discoloured, (usually brown) and die.

So you see, understanding this particular aspect of the job of the roots helps in knowing how much food to give a plant...

The other way in which a plant feeds is by the process known as photosynthesis. The Greek word for light is *phos*; synthesis also comes from Greek words, meaning putting together, and photosynthesis is the putting together of water and carbon-dioxide from the air, in the presence of light, to form sugars and oxygen. The sugars are then sent round the plant to be used where they are needed, or stored as starch; the oxygen is given off into the atmosphere. Photosynthesis stops in the dark, and the plant becomes very much less active; it could be said to be resting.

But if it is kept in the dark it will die, because there is another process going on at the same time, called respiration, which does exactly the opposite to photosynthesis. The plant would therefore lose its sugars altogether and so could not live.

There is not very much that we can do to influence the amount of food the top growth manufactures, except by altering the quantity and quality of the light. Some plants are very much affected by the length of time they are in the dark and the number of daylight hours they are subjected to. For instance, chrysanthemums will only flower in what is known as 'short-day' conditions, and commercial growers make use of this tendency and manipulate the quantity of light so that they flower all year round. Poinsettias are affected in the same way; unless they are given short days in the autumn they will not produce their coloured bracts at Christmas.

The temperature also has some effect on some plants; the warmer conditions are, the more likely they are to flower, especially some of the tropical shrubs. Warmth encourages ripening of shoots, as well as of fruit, so that they produce flower buds rather than leafy buds.

It is possible to grow plants in 'light cabinets', which are glass cases with legs, with neon strip lighting at the top, and quite often built-in heating, controlled at the

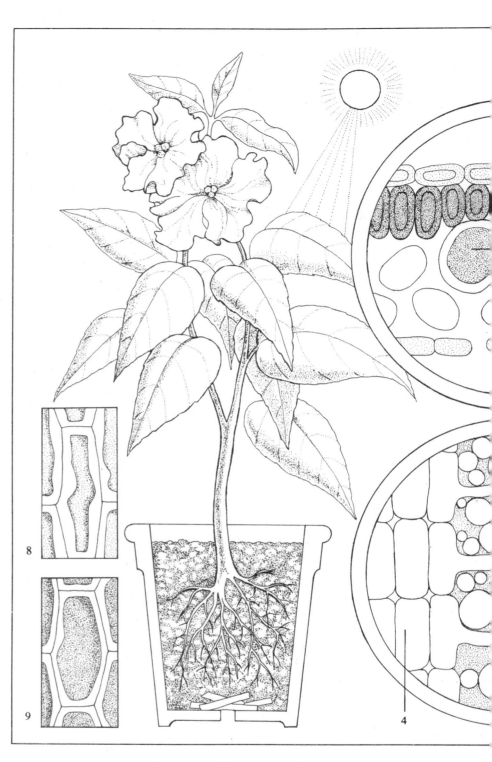

right temperature by a thermostat. Warmth and light can therefore be easily controlled, but such cabinets are expensive, and in any case may not be convenient.

However, quite a lot can be done to regulate the amount and type of food the roots absorb. We have already seen that if more fertilizer is added to the soil than specified, it does not do that much extra good, but quite the opposite. The roots lose the liquid out of their cells and gradually dry up and stop growing. The same kind of thing can happen if the right amount of fertilizer is used, but it is mixed into a rather dry soil. What moisture is present will then have much too concentrated a solution and, in order to right the balance, that in the roots will move outwards. The botanical name for this process is osmosis.

Soil Structure

The amount of food taken in by plants is determined in another way, by the structure of the soil; that is, the way in which the soil particles hold together. If they are tightly packed against one another, it is difficult for the excess moisture in the soil to run through it.

Photosynthesis. The root hairs (1) absorb water droplets (2) from the soil (3) and pass it to the root cells (4) (see lower inset). When cells lose water and become flaccid (8), the plant wilts, but normally the cells are turgid and full of water (9). The water then travels through the stem and into the leaves. Simultaneously the leaf pores (5) absorb carbon dioxide from the air (see upper inset). Light shining on the leaf activates a green substance called chlorophyll which is contained in cells called chloroplasts (6). The chlorophyll splits the water molecules into hydrogen and oxygen; the hydrogen combines with carbon dioxide to form sugar and starch, and this food then travels through the leaf veins (7) to the rest of the plant.

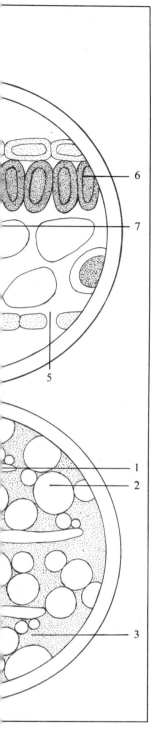

Staying where it is means that after a while, it gets stagnant—the secretions produced by bacteria and other tiny creatures in the soil accumulate, so do those given off by the roots, and the water gradually becomes poisonous to the roots.

A lot of long-standing water also means that the air, and therefore the oxygen, in the soil will be proportionally less. As the roots need oxygen, as well as mineral nutrients, to live and lengthen, it is obvious that this is another reason why the soil structure needs to be right. The kind which is compacted and tends to be wet all the time usually has a lot of clay or silt in it, and feels sticky when it is wet.

The reverse of this is the sandy soil, in which the particles are comparatively large, unlike clay and silt. They do not cling tightly together, being of a different chemical nature, and so water runs away easily, taking with it, naturally, most of the plant foods. The result is the roots are left not only dry, but starving. A plant can wilt in both these types of soil, because the roots cannot work properly; too much moisture produces the same result as too little. If a plant is too dry, however, the leaves usually wither when they wilt, whereas a waterlogged plant either keeps its colour or turns yellow and does not dry out—it simply flops permanently.

Because the type of soil is so important, a lot of experimenting went on when plants were first grown in pots, with all kinds of soil mixtures, in which a variety of ingredients were tried in varying proportions. Gardeners swore by their own recipes, which were deadly secrets, but eventually a mixture was produced in England which is still used today. It was one which suited all sorts of plants and in which they would grow well, and it was called the John Innes potting compost. It was composed of (hence called compost) loam—which is a good well-structured soil to start with—coarse sand, and granulated peat, that is, peat which will go through a sieve of a particular mesh, together with a measured quantity of fertilizer and chalk. In the U.S. the University of California and Cornell have developed mixes.

A plant has different parts to it; just as we have legs and arms, stomachs and livers, so a plant has roots and stems, leaves, branches and flowers, fruit and seeds. They are not such complicated organisms as we are, but each part needs different kinds of food in order that it can maintain itself, develop, and help the other parts. The basic foods consist of a variety of minerals, each specific to a particular part.

Kinds of Food
Roots thrive on a diet of phosphorus, particularly the tips of the hairs found on roots. Without it they do not grow; a seedling will die, and many kinds of adult plants which suddenly go short of phosphorus turn purplish at the edges of the leaves, have a generally bluish-green tinge, and stop growing.

The green parts of the plant, the leaves and young stems which contain chlorophyll, the green colouring matter, must have nitrogen and magnesium. Without them, the plants get spindly, the stems turn pale green, stop growing, and the green of the leaves gradually fades to pale yellow all over. A nitrogen deficiency is very serious. If you water a plant too much, the nitrogen being particularly soluble, is easily washed out of the soil, and that is the reason why the lower leaves on many plants in constantly wet soil turn yellow.

The flowers, fruit and seeds are only produced when a plant is mature, and maturity is associated with the mineral nutrient potassium. It has what is called a 'hardening' effect on the plant; growth slows down when it is applied to the compost, and the plant's internal mechanism switches over to flower production rather than leafy growth. Provided it then continues to receive potassium, it will develop seeds and fruit and finish its life cycle, for good if an annual, and for the season if a perennial.

This discussion is all very much simplified; the feeding processes, and indeed the growth processes generally, of plants are extremely complicated, and interact on one another. Too much or too little of a nutrient can cause trouble, and the absorption of one is affected by the presence or absence of another. It is better if they can all be absorbed together, as they would be in Nature, otherwise one part grows at the expense of another. Some nutrients are preferred by plants to others, for instance tomatoes will absorb potassium in preference to magnesium, even though the latter may be present in the soil, and so the plant suffers from a deficiency. Moreover, the three nutrients detailed, nitrogen (N), phosphorus (P) and potassium (K) are only the 'big three'; there are at least twenty 'trace' elements which are also essential, but needed only in infinitesimal quantities, and also the in-between kinds, like calcium and iron and so on.

Container-grown plants are totally reliant on their owners to supply them with the food and water they need, just as pets are. Growing in the open ground, their roots can forage all over the place and absorb the essentials as required, but once they have exhausted the soil in a pot, you must give them completely fresh soil, a bigger pot, regular feeding, or a layer of new soil (a topdressing) on top of the old. They also have no control over their heat and light; for instance outdoors in hot sunny places, plants have adapted themselves so that they are the type known as cacti, but if you put a cactus in a cool dark part of the house, it can do nothing about the situation and will die.

Hormones
One very important group of compounds in living plants which has not so far been mentioned is that consisting of the hormones. The increase in the size of the plant is due to the division of cells, and division is stimulated by the auxin hormones. These occur in the tips of shoots and roots and, besides making the plant grow, direct which way it shall grow. If a plant is lit from one side only, it bends towards the light; this is because more auxin is produced on the shaded side so that growth is faster on that side. The uneven growth results in the plant leaning so that it gets all the available light possible. These hormones also have a marked effect on inducing cuttings to root more quickly and easily. Ready-made preparations are available, and can help in the propagation of difficult plants such as holly.

Another hormone called florigen is responsible for the changeover from leaf production to flowers. Petals and coloured bracts are only modified leaves, coloured mainly so that they are attractive to pollinating insects or animals, but these and the male and female parts of a flower will only be formed if florigen is present. Here we come back to the effect of light on plants, because florigen itself will only occur in certain plants according to their day-length category. For instance, the 'short-day' chrysanthemum mentioned earlier will only produce florigen when the plant is subjected to 8 hours or so of daylight. Others will only produce florigen under long-day conditions, and yet others are not affected at all, and are said to be neutral.

Finally, there is a group of hormones which actually slows down a plant's growth until it virtually stops, and these are found in seeds, and are associated with dormancy of mature plants in winter.

Plant care

troughs, window boxes, urns, tubs and so on, all in various sizes. Whatever you use, it is important that you choose the right size for your plant.

If you pot a plant in too large a container, the roots cannot make use of all the water in the soil and you will be faced with the problem of stagnating, 'sour water', as you would be in a badly-drained soil. When potting-on a plant use a pot or container whose diameter is about 2.5–4cm (1–1½in) larger than the soil-ball of the plant. For instance a plant in a 10cm (4in) pot could be moved into a 13cm (5in) size. Once a plant has reached its maximum size, it is repotted, into the same size container, but with as much fresh soil as possible.

The only exceptions are cacti, which are very slow growing, and plants which grow quickly during the early part of the spring and early summer, for instance tomatoes or chlorophytum. Some plants have shallow, fine root systems, and do better in half pots known as pans; African violets and some of the begonias are examples.

PLANT CARE

You can see from all the previous paragraphs that a plant is very much a living, breathing organism, which needs to be supplied with the right kinds of cultivation all through its life if it is to be healthy, well-coloured and ornamental. None can be ignored without eventually being harmed, even the long suffering aspidistra and the apparently lifeless cactus. Never forget that, inside the plant body, there is a great deal of activity going on, and that water, food, air, warmth and light will all be needed in various quantities and combinations by the plant all the time.

There are all sorts of ways of treating plants in containers so that they are always fit, also various methods of treatment, unfortunately often used, through ignorance or carelessness, which result in damage or death. One of the most important aspects of container growing is potting, transferring the plant to a new pot or other container and ensuring that the soil mixture and the container in which it is growing are suitable.

Containers

The container should always have a hole or holes in the base so that when the plant is watered, any extra water can flow out of the pot, instead of sinking to the bottom and staying there, getting sour and poisoning the roots. The container can be more or less any shape, and made of all sorts of materials, though the traditional container is the terra-cotta clay pot. This comes in various sizes from 5cm (2in) in diameter, measured across the rim at the top, to 45cm (18in); depth will vary from about 5cm (2in) to 35cm (14in). Clay pots are very good and still preferred by many people; they are porous and soak up a good deal of moisture, and therefore the soil in them dries only slowly and steadily. They are long-lasting, with care, but are much heavier than plastic pots, and more difficult to keep clean; drainage material is needed in the bottom.

Plastic pots are the same shape and colour, but very light-weight, and thin-walled; they have several drainage holes in the base instead of the one of the clay pots, and also need drainage material. The soil in them remains quite wet for longer, but then suddenly and quickly becomes almost completely dry, so watering plants in these pots has to be done differently from those growing in clay pots. It need not be done quite so often, but when it is, more will be needed.

Besides clay and plastic, pots can be made of expanded polystyrene, which is very light, retains warmth and is long lasting provided it is treated with respect, otherwise lumps are easily broken off it. They can also be of peat, black polyethylene sheet, rigid coloured plastic, fibreglass and cardboard. These materials are used for other kinds of containers, too, such as

Potting

Most plants are moved into different pots in spring, just as they are starting to grow after the winter rest. The need for repotting will be shown by the roots either coming through the drainage holes, or penetrating to the outside of the soil-ball and covering it. If you are not sure about the need for potting, turn the plant and pot upside down with your right hand across the soil surface and knock the rim of the pot against the working surface. The soil ball will fall out into your right hand, complete.

The day before you repot, water the plant, so that it has taken up plenty of moisture in reserve, while the roots recover from the shock of pruning and breakage involved in potting. If there are many long roots wound round and round the outside, cut them off so that they extend a little way beyond the soil ball, and also cut off dark brown or black roots which are discoloured all through, as they will be dead or rotting. A healthy root is usually partially or completely white, particularly the tips. When you are potting, be careful not to damage the root tips, which are slightly pointed; you will remember that it is at the root tips that most of the activity of the roots goes on.

See if there are any root aphids present and deal with them (see p. 182), and then put the plant into its new, clean container. If it is a new clay pot, soak it in water for several hours beforehand. Put a little soil into the bottom first, on top of the drainage material if needed, and then sit the soil ball on this. Adjust the quantity of new soil, so that the plant will be at the same height as it was in the previous pot, allowing a space for watering at the top of 1–2.5cm (½–1in) depth, and fill in soil round the sides, keeping the plant in the centre and holding it steady. Firm the soil down with the fingers, bang the pot gently on the working surface to settle and level the soil, and then water. Put the newly potted plant in a warm shady place for a few days to let it recover—treat it as a hospital case, in other words—and then move it back to its old home.

Soil Mixtures

You have already seen how important the growing medium is, especially for container-grown plants, and you can make your own potting mixture yourself, instead of buying it ready made-up. Suggested proportions are seven parts loam, three parts granulated peat and two parts coarse sand, all by volume, mixing 125g (4oz) base fertilizer and 20g (¾oz) ground lime-

Repotting. Above, left to right: roots growing out of the soil indicate that repotting is needed; the plant is knocked gently out of the pot; any particularly long roots are snipped off. Below, left to right: compost is put in the bottom of the new, larger pot; the plant is put in and the rest of the compost packed round it; the surface is pushed firmly down round the plant's stem.

stone to each bushel of the mixture. Fortunately fertilizers and soils can be bought from garden shops or centres. If you can get sterilized loam so much the better, otherwise you may find unexpected plants coming up from seeds in it, or there may be pest or disease which can infect the roots.

You can vary the proportions of the ingredients of your compost as you become more experienced in dealing with plants, and discover their particular needs. Cacti, for instance, like very porous soil, and need only a little food, so you can put more coarse sand, and even some grit in, and decrease the quantity of peat and/or loam, and fertilizer. Bromeliads, on the other hand, grow perched on trees in their natural habitat in very shallow rotting vegetation, so they do better in a very peaty mixture, again with not very much fertilizer.

Bulbs will grow in bulb fibre; a mixture of six parts of loose bulk peat, two of oyster shell and one of crushed charcoal. However, as it has no food in it, the bulbs will not be able to store food or form flower embryos for the following season and will have to be thrown away, unless you liquid-feed them during and after flowering until they die down. Even so, they will not be as good the following season.

A modern alternative to loam-containing mixtures is the soil-less mix, consisting of peat and sand only, usually in the proportion of three to one. It is sold ready mixed, sometimes with nutrient added, and with instructions as to use, and to when more plant food should be added. The need for an alternative medium arose because loam has become very short and varies greatly in its quality. It has the advantage of being naturally completely sterile and is light in weight. Some plants grow very much better in it than in the older type of potting mixture, and it is particularly good for rooting cuttings.

However, if you cannot obtain any kind of potting soil, there is a way of overcoming this. For some time it has been known that plants will grow in water only, provided it contains nutrients, and a method for growing container plants has been developed from this, in which clay granules are used. These are porous, light in weight and about the size of a marble or a little larger, and support the roots. The plants can be grown in a single container of granules and nutrient solution, or in a pot containing granules, placed in another, in which there is nutrient. The nutrient solution reaches to the level of the bottom of the inner pot, through which the roots emerge into the solution. Many container-grown plants do better with this system of hydropot or hydroponic cultivation.

Some plants do not like a soil which contains lime; they will only grow in one which has an acid reaction, or acid pH, so you should make one up without it, or ask for one for ericaceous plants. The *Ericaceae* include the azaleas, rhododendrons and heathers, all of which are calcifuges (lime-haters).

Light

By doing all this, you will have given the roots the very best conditions for them to develop in and so the top growth will be good. The growing media are, however, only part of the plant's environment. The light and the temperature are also very important, separately and interacting. Light, as we have seen, has an effect on the green colouring of plants, on the amount of growth, on the food manufactured by the leaves and on the development of the flower-inducing hormone. Most plants will grow in average home lighting, but will grow better if their light requirements are more precisely supplied. Some plants only need a little light; they are happier in shade and one of these is the rhoicissus, which climbs beautifully and remains a good dark green with large leaves if kept out of the sun. In the sun, it grows very slowly and the leaves turn a sick yellow-green and curl at the edges.

However, if you kept a cactus in the same place, it would never get any larger, it would never flower, and

eventually it would die. A healthy cactus needs all the sun you can give it—a south facing window-sill is ideal —and, provided you water it in spring and summer, it will then enlarge, grow more spines or get hairier, or flower profusely and brilliantly, depending on the species.

These are extreme examples, but even so most plants have different light requirements. There are some rough and ready guides to these given by the plants themselves; in general flowering plants need a good light, including sun.

Plain green-leaved plants will live in good light or some shade, variegated-leaved ones like a good deal more. Climbers and trailers are all right in some shade, bromeliads will grow in a good light or dappled sunlight, being forest plants growing high up in trees. Orchids vary, but they also are often forest epiphytes and like some shade. African violets are very fussy, and the amount of light they prefer is best found out by trial and error, trying them in various situations, but never hot sunlight.

Temperature

In the same way that most light conditions will do, but can be improved on, most home temperatures will ensure the continued life of a plant, but better results will be obtained if you can give exactly the right one. Whatever the temperature, a steady one is the best; the same at night as during the day. Temperatures which constantly go up and down inflict unnecessary stress on the plant—it has to keep adapting itself to the changes, mainly by the amount of water it absorbs and transpires—and so energy which could be used in growing is lost to adapting. A very common cause of ill-health in house-plants is the severe dropping of the temperature at night in winter. The living rooms are over-heated during the day, but heating is lowered too far or turned off at night, at the same time as the outside temperature drops, and the continual severe alternation gradually weakens plants, especially those that need higher temperatures. With such plants it is better to give them a slightly lower temperature all the time than one which is right some of the time. Draughts, even warm ones, do a plant no good, and doors which are constantly opened and shut will mean frequent changes in temperature, too. Outdoors, plants can cope with such changes to some extent, as their roots are not confined, and a lower temperature generally means less light, and therefore less internal activity in any case. But plants in containers are very vulnerable, and so we come back to their reliance on you to get their growing conditions right.

In spring, summer and early autumn, normal temperatures will suit the majority of plants; in winter they will do best if the minimum is 7°C (45°F) and no lower. This is because winter is a time of dormancy and rest, while the daylight is short and dull, and the plant's growth processes are only just ticking over. Quite a lot of house-plants in fact are better if kept at 10°C (50°F) or above in winter, a fact which is not as well known as it ought to be. The more attractive plants are often the exotic but tropical kinds, and unless you can maintain the warmth at this level or above in winter, the plants will become weak at best, and may lose their leaves or die at worst. If you are propagating them by cuttings, slightly higher temperatures are needed than those in which established plants live, to induce the production of roots. Seeds also need more warmth, otherwise they will not germinate.

Humidity

It has been found that the dry atmosphere central heating creates in modern homes is harmful to human beings and to furniture. It is not quite so widely realised though, that plants are not happy in it either, with a few exceptions; most of them need a moist atmosphere. But it is one of these invisible necessities, unlike the need for water or food, and is easily forgotten. Lots of house-plants come from hot, damp forests, where heavy downpours of rain are frequent, and if they have to do without the humidity this creates, they weaken and die, especially in high temperatures. All plants lose moisture as water vapour through pores (stomata) mostly in the leaves, on the underside, and if they lose it very quickly, in hot weather or high indoor temperatures, the roots cannot replace it fast enough.

No one is going to put up with the equivalent of heavy downpours of rain in the sitting room, but you can give your plants localised humidity in various ways. Probably the quickest and easiest is a short burst with a mister every day, two or three times if you can manage it. A mister is a sprayer producing water in very fine droplets and is ideal for enveloping the plants in a cloud of moisture.

Another method is to put the plants in a second container, larger than the one in which they are growing, and to pack absorbent material in the space between the two. It can be anything which will hold water: peat, newspaper, rags, or the flower holding material called Oasis, and if packed in moist, water vapour will be constantly evaporating up round the plant. Or you can put shallow trays of water close to the plants; the more water surface there is, the more there is to evaporate.

Humidity control. The pots of African violets (left) stand in a water tray; the larger dieffenbachia is kept sufficiently moist by using a mist spray.

Another idea is to stand the container in a plate containing water, but with gravel beneath the container, so that it is raised out of the water.

Whatever you do, don't stand the plants on a shelf over a radiator; it is much too hot and dries up the soil very quickly, so that the plants are more or less baked as well as being especially short of humidity.

Another indirect way of providing dampness for plants with large leaves is cleaning them. A great deal of dust and grit settles on the leaves of rubber plants, for instance, and this chokes the stomata and the plant cannot 'breathe'. Regular sponging with a clean wet cloth does wonders for their appearance and health.

Watering

Plants and animals are all said to have evolved from the sea; a large part of a plant consists, like us, of moisture, and this is partly why we all need humidity to supply liquid indirectly. But we all also need water supplied for direct drinking, which plants take in through their roots.

You will remember that the balance of water in the soil has to be very carefully maintained so that the soil is not so dry that the plant is short of water, nor so wet that there is no air. In one's enthusiasm to make sure that the plant does not dry out, one tends to over-water, and it is just as quick a way of killing a plant as to under-water it. You must gear the watering to the plant's needs; it will tell you itself when it needs water, which will be at irregular intervals and in irregular quantities, depending on the temperature, light conditions, humidity, season, rate of growth, type of soil mixture, and size of plant and container. Do not, whatever you do, water at regular intervals, giving the same amount of water every time.

When you think the time to water has come, but are not quite sure, you can make several tests. The weight of the pot is one guide; a light one means that there is little water present. If the soil's surface is lighter in colour than the underneath, and feels dry to the touch, then water is needed. A clay pot, if tapped with a wooden pencil or stick, will make a high ringing noise if dry, but will produce a dull thud when wet. Finally, if the plant is much in need of water, it will have a generally limp appearance, if not actually wilting. The leaves will all be starting to turn downwards at the tips, the colour will not be as bright as usual, and it may even be dropping flowers.

Once you have decided the plant needs water, then give it water which is at room temperature, preferably rain water, otherwise water which has been boiled or softened. At the top of the container, there should be a space between the soil surface and the rim, of at least 1cm ($\frac{1}{2}$in) depth, more if the container is a large one. This space should be filled up with water, pouring it on fairly quickly before it has a chance to soak through appreciably. Then, when it has soaked through, and the extra has been allowed to drain out, don't give any more. Provided you have been watering the plant correctly before this, the new moisture will have soaked evenly all through soil mixture, and the plant can be left alone until the next watering.

If you are doubtful about the need to water, as a last resort, you can always turn the pot upside down and tip the plant out into your hand, to examine the soil ball. If it proves to be fairly dry, put it back and give two waterings; if very dry put it in a bucket of water so that the water level comes up over the soil and leave it there until bubbles of air stop coming up from the soil surface. Then take it out and allow it to drain.

Whatever you do, don't give little dribbles of water; this is worse than useless, as it only wets the surface, and the main part of the roots never receives any water. Eventually the soil gets so dry that it shrinks away from the side of the pot and the water which is given simply runs down the resulting space and straight out of the drainage hole, without doing even a little good.

Feeding

As with watering, so there is one way to feed, the right way, and it can coincide with watering because the plant has to 'drink' its food. The mineral nutrients which are usually provided in powder and liquid fertilizers are the three most important ones, nitrogen (N), phosphorous (P) and potassium (K)—the roles each of these play is described elsewhere in this volume. However, there are also some minor ones, such as magmesium and iron and the 'trace' elements, called this because they are needed by the plants only in minute quantities, of the order of parts per million. Mostly these occur naturally in soil mixtures, and there is no need to supply them in special feeds.

But the 'big three' are used up fairly quickly by most plants, and it is often necessary to supply more of them, though the plant may not necessarily need repotting. For instance, if the roots reach the edge of the soil ball by about the end of July, potting it into new soil and/or a larger pot could be damaging. This is because the plant will not be producing new root growth for long enough to penetrate the soil ball well and use all the moisture, before winter dormancy starts. So we come back to the old problem of stagnant water.

In general, the food already available in a soil mixture will be sufficient until about July, if there was a spring potting, but after this it is a good idea to start liquid feeding. Each proprietary feed will have different directions for use and different dilution rates, because the percentages of each nutrient in each will vary. Whatever they are, they should always be carefully followed; never, never give a stronger feed than is specified; you will do more harm than good, and end up with a sick plant. Incidentally, you should not ordinarily feed a sick plant, that may also harm it, like giving steak to someone with pneumonia.

Always liquid-feed a soil which is already moist; feeding a plant in a dry one will result in osmosis in reverse, giving desiccated roots. Feed little and often for the best results; you can feed at half strength at half the time interval suggested by the makers without any harm, and some plants may prefer it. Continue to feed until autumn and then, if the plant is one which becomes dormant in winter, stop feeding completely.

There are variations on this general practice; some plants grow very fast and are greedy feeders; they will need feeding long before July. Others need feeding at different times, especially the bulbs, which quite often have different flowering times and different life-cycles. This is when it pays you to know what part of the world your plants come from and what their natural habitat is.

Some need more nitrogen—these include the plants grown for their attractive leaves—and others do best with a higher proportion of potassium, mostly the flowering and fruiting kinds. You can get proprietary liquid fertilizers which will cater for these needs, and as the percentage of each nutrient will be shown on the fertilizer container, you can choose the most suitable one.

Plants growing in soil-less mixes will need feeding almost from the beginning; fruiting kinds often need feeding from the time the first fruits have set and begun to swell. Some plants hardly need any food at all, even in the soil mixture; these include the bromeliads, the cacti and many of the alpine plants.

How to prune correctly.
Above left: the cut is too close
to the bud. Above right: the
cut is too far away. Below left:
the angle of the cut is wrong;
it should face the same way
that the bud just below it is
pointing. Below right: the
correct way.

Pruning

With all this care and attention to the best ways of looking after plants, they are likely to grow rapidly into large specimens. You can keep them under control to some extent, and help them to flower more profusely, by cutting back some of the shoots. The climbers, in particular, may need a good deal of pruning.

The best time to prune most plants is towards the end of winter, just before they start to grow again in spring. If you cut a good strong shoot which was produced the previous year, back by about half its length, it will probably produce three or four new ones in the coming season, all of which will want pruning the following year. If a plant begins to get out of hand by doing this, then one or more of the oldest and strongest shoots should be completely removed, back to where it originates on the main stem. This will thin out the growth, prevent the production of new shoots in that particular region, and decrease the height.

In general, the harder you cut a shoot back, the more vigorous will be the new growth which results, provided the plant is healthy. If you take off only the tip, the top 8cm (3in) or so, not very much growth will result and you are more likely to get flowers. Weak shoots are the ones which need really hard pruning, so that two-thirds, three quarters, or even more, of the previous season's growth is removed. This stimulates growth, provided there is ample food for the roots to absorb and the plant is not short of water or light.

At the same time as you prune to manipulate the production of new growth, the dead shoots, the really weak ones, which simply waste the plant's energy, and any which are crowding the best growth can also be removed. If you are uncertain whether a shoot is dead or not, scratch off the outer layer of skin or bark with a finger-nail. If the shoot is alive there should be a green layer just below the surface. If it is dead, this layer will be brown, the stem will be brittle and break easily, and it will be dry and quite likely slightly shrivelled on the outside as well.

Pruning applies mainly to the shrubby and climbing plants, but some of the smaller, herbaceous kinds can be treated in late spring and early summer, by taking out the tips so as to encourage a bushier shape. The aluminium plant, *Pilea cadierei*, is one which is much improved by doing this, so is the busy Lizzie, *Impatiens wallerana*, and the tradescantias.

Whenever you make a cut on a plant, do it just above a dormant bud or the junction of a shoot with the parent stem; do not leave a stub, because it can become infected and result in the rest of the plant rotting and for the same reason always make the cut clean, without any snags or tearing.

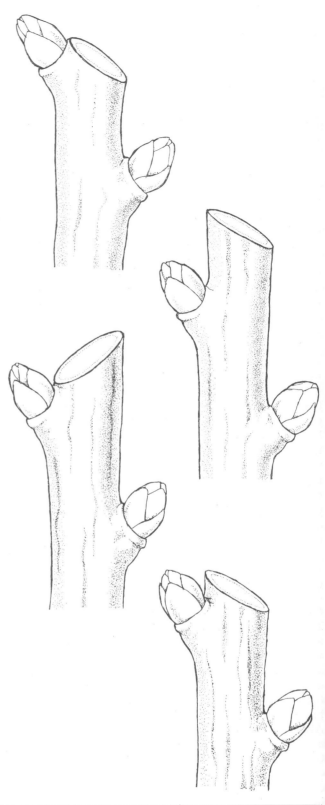

Shapes achieved by careful
pruning. From left to right:
bush, half-standard, cordon,
espalier.

SPECIAL METHODS OF CULTIVATION

So far, we have talked about the details of the right ways to care for plants generally, to ensure their health and vigour, and therefore greater beauty. However, there are one or two groups of plants which have special needs and will grow better if treated accordingly.

Cacti

One of these is the cacti, plants which have adapted themselves, of necessity, to living without rain for months at a time. Their cells are of a kind which can hold much more water than ordinary plants, they are often covered in hair or wax and the mostly rounded shape is one which ensures that they have the smallest area possible, in relation to the volume, from which to lose moisture. So, if you water them normally, all that will happen is that the roots and the base of the stem will rot fairly quickly. In winter, or whenever they are resting, cacti need not be watered at all, or given only a moderate watering about once a month. In spring and early summer, most of them receive heavy spring rains, when they absorb a great deal of water, and then flower. After that, during the summer, there may be very infrequent downpours, so that if you forget them, it will not matter too much.

Cacti also like to be baked in the summer, so that they get as much light and heat as possible—this is the condition which ensures flowering the following year—but do not need much nutrient. Although it goes against the grain, a gritty rather poor soil is the one to provide, and there is no need to liquid feed. Moreover, they will not need repotting so often, perhaps every two years or less, as they grow slowly. Cacti often produce widespreading but shallow roots, in their attempts to absorb as much moisture as possible when it is available, before it gets burnt off by the hot sun, so pans rather than pots will give the best results. Humidity is something which can be forgotten altogether—the last thing they want is a damp atmosphere.

Care of Bromeliads

The bromeliads, too, require special treatment. They are the plants such as the aechmea, the billbergia, and the vriesea which have funnels or 'vases' in the centre, and which are epiphytes. They constitute a collection of plants with very varied habitats. A good many of them come from forests, where they grow high up on branches and in the forks of trees, especially in South America; and they also have adapted to their peculiar conditions. What rain does reach them filters down through the leaf and branch cover, and the arrangement of their leaves ensures that it runs down them and collects in the funnel in the centre. Vegetation and insects also fall into this funnel and slowly decay there. As you can imagine, the growing medium is sparse, consisting of rotting leaves, twigs and similar debris and, as it is almost non-existent, the bromeliad roots are therefore few and small.

Any sunlight they receive is through the gaps in leaves and branches; there is a fair amount of warmth and humidity, though they are surprisingly amenable to dry atmospheres.

There are others which grow directly on the ground, amongst rocks and pebbles, where temperature at night drops to freezing. These are the kind found growing high up in the Andean mountains. Yet others come from deserts and subtropical steppes, but all are adapted to growing where there is a lack of soil and moisture for the roots.

Bromeliads should therefore be given most of their water via the funnel, and liquid fed occasionally in this way too. The funnel should never be allowed to dry up, even when the flower starts to appear through it, though the level can be allowed to drop when the plant is resting. The soil mixture should be very peaty, and kept moist, but not saturated, using pans as with cacti, and putting the plant in a good light. Northern European sunlight filtered through a window will not be too strong except possibly at midday.

Holiday Care

Other instances when you will have to depart from the general care of plants are when you are away on a vacation, and during the winter or resting season of the plants. When you go away during the summer, most plants are growing and flowering, and the main problem will be the watering. If you cannot get a friend to do this for you, there are various ways of supplying water sufficient to keep them alive at any rate, even if not applied at ideal times and in ideal quantities.

Groups of plants, placed on trays or in large shallow bowls, the old shallow stone sinks, zinc baths and so on, can be packed round with really wet peat or rags, and black polyethylene sheeting placed over this and round the soil in the pots so that it covers them completely, but leaves the plants free. An absorbent length of wick with one end in the soil and the other in water is another method. It is possible to obtain self-watering pots and troughs which can be filled up and left for several weeks, and there are also separate gadgets which can be put in individual pots to do the same service.

There is also a special kind of absorbent plastic matting, mainly for use in greenhouses, but there is no reason why it should not be used temporarily for indoor plants. The matting is soaked and the containers put on to it; it then remains moist, as water is delivered to it through a tube attached to a container of water at a higher level than the plants and matting. The matting will need to be on some kind of moisture-proof surface or in a shallow tray or bath. Provided the plants are in a good light and unlikely to be subjected to cold, they will be in reasonable condition when you return.

In winter, the problem will be not so much water, unless you are leaving the central heating on, as cold, and the best that you can do is to put the plants in a group away from windows, and hope that low temperatures will not occur for long or be too extreme.

When a plant is dormant or in its resting season, its needs are much different to when it is growing. Much less water, sometimes practically none, no feeding, and a lower temperature (but not freezing), are the essentials. You can assume that this will be during winter, though the South African plants are often exceptions and do things the other way round.

Plants can be kept adequately watered during your absence by using a length of wick leading up into the compost to absorb water gradually from the tray.

177

Propagation

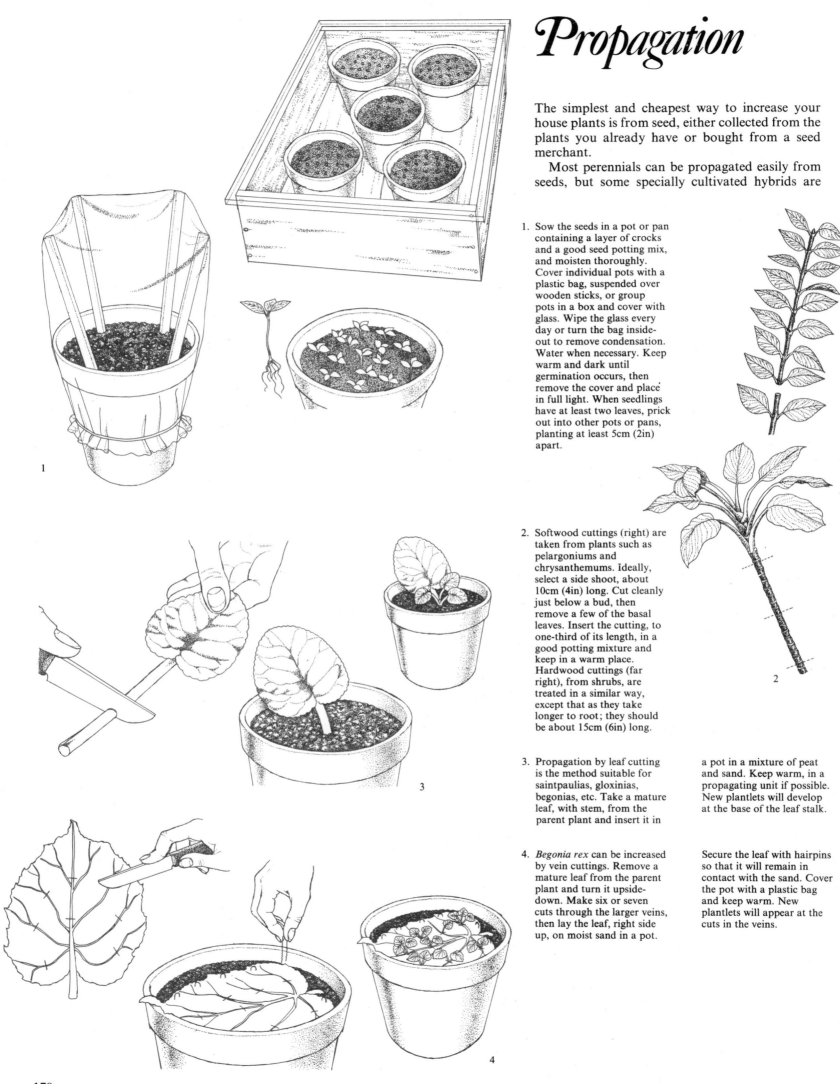

The simplest and cheapest way to increase your house plants is from seed, either collected from the plants you already have or bought from a seed merchant.

Most perennials can be propagated easily from seeds, but some specially cultivated hybrids are

1. Sow the seeds in a pot or pan containing a layer of crocks and a good seed potting mix, and moisten thoroughly. Cover individual pots with a plastic bag, suspended over wooden sticks, or group pots in a box and cover with glass. Wipe the glass every day or turn the bag inside-out to remove condensation. Water when necessary. Keep warm and dark until germination occurs, then remove the cover and place in full light. When seedlings have at least two leaves, prick out into other pots or pans, planting at least 5cm (2in) apart.

2. Softwood cuttings (right) are taken from plants such as pelargoniums and chrysanthemums. Ideally, select a side shoot, about 10cm (4in) long. Cut cleanly just below a bud, then remove a few of the basal leaves. Insert the cutting, to one-third of its length, in a good potting mixture and keep in a warm place. Hardwood cuttings (far right), from shrubs, are treated in a similar way, except that as they take longer to root; they should be about 15cm (6in) long.

3. Propagation by leaf cutting is the method suitable for saintpaulias, gloxinias, begonias, etc. Take a mature leaf, with stem, from the parent plant and insert it in a pot in a mixture of peat and sand. Keep warm, in a propagating unit if possible. New plantlets will develop at the base of the leaf stalk.

4. *Begonia rex* can be increased by vein cuttings. Remove a mature leaf from the parent plant and turn it upside-down. Make six or seven cuts through the larger veins, then lay the leaf, right side up, on moist sand in a pot. Secure the leaf with hairpins so that it will remain in contact with the sand. Cover the pot with a plastic bag and keep warm. New plantlets will appear at the cuts in the veins.

not always suitable and should be grown from cuttings. Some seed-raised plants can be very slow-growing; hence cuttings are a better method of propagation for these. Thus the most common method of propagation is by cuttings from either leaf or stem.

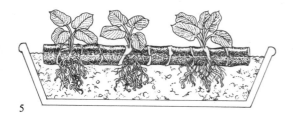

5

5. Stem cuttings are made as follows: Divide a leafless stem into sections, each containing a bud. Make a cut above and below each bud and remove a small strip of bark from opposite the bud.

Place the cut stem flat on the soil and keep warm. Small plants will form at each bud. Other propagation methods are leaf and vein cuttings, air layering, and soil layering.

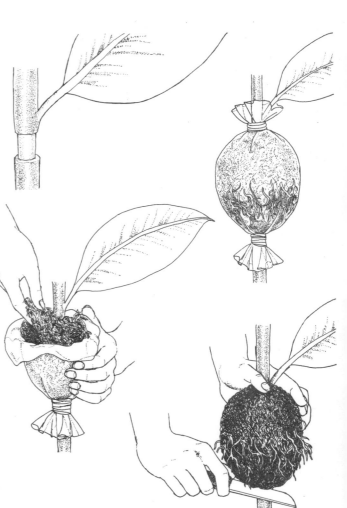

6

6. Chlorophytum and *Saxifraga sarmentosa* are two plants that multiply by sending out runners from which new plants grow. Propagation is therefore, a simple operation. Place the parent plant, in its pot, in a tray containing potting mix and pin down the plantlets with hairpins. Alternatively, pin the plantlets down in separate pots. These new plants will soon take root.

7. Air layering, which can be used to increase camellias, hibiscus or *Ficus elastica*, is suitable for plants which have become very tall and lost their lower leaves. Slit the bark just below a leaf node, then remove the bark, as shown. Rub the area with rooting powder and pack moist sphagnum moss around it. Tie a piece of plastic around the moss.

Small roots will grow from the plant through the moss and will be visible in about three weeks. When the moss is filled with roots, remove the plastic and cut the stem below the moss ball. This can then be planted up in a new pot. If this method has been used to produce a more attractive plant, rather than to propagate, the parent plant may be discarded.

7

Plant troubles

Given the optimum conditions in which to grow, plants would not have any physiological disorders—troubles occurring as the result of faulty watering, wrong compost, etc—and they would be so constitutionally strong that no pest or disease could get a real foothold.

However, with the best will in the world, things go wrong, and a plant may be short of food at a crucial time, or given sun when it wants shade, or you may buy a plant which is already infested in some way. It is often very puzzling when confronted with a trouble on a plant, to decide what has caused it, and why; once you know the reason, the remedy is generally simple.

A crucial part of diagnosing plant troubles is observation, noticing every single point about a plant which could be abnormal. Another is keeping a record, mental or otherwise, of how you have been caring for it. Container-grown plants are likely to be attacked by only a few pests or diseases, compared with their counterparts growing in the open ground, and the main difficulties come, as you might suspect, as a result of giving the plants the wrong care. When this is done, the whole plant weakens, and such plants are much more prone to assault by pests and invasion by fungus or bacterial disease, and will suffer more severely than strong, healthy plants. In particular, dry atmospheres and dry soils—with the exception of cacti—are a major source of plant weakness.

Let us suppose that you have a plant ailing for no apparent reason. By a process of elimination, it should be possible to pinpoint the culprit without resorting to calling in an expert, and deal with it accordingly.

Leaves turning yellow and falling off.

DISORDERS
The causes of 'physiological disorders' in plants are all tied up with the way the plant lives, feeds and drinks, and their appearance means that you have not cared for the plant in the way that suits it best.

Leaves
Discolouration of the leaves, whether the leaves are green or otherwise coloured, and unnatural or early fall, are nearly always a sign of these disorders; flower buds, flowers and fruit that do not develop or drop much too soon, occur because the plant is too weak to mature them.

To take the leaves first, the main barometers of health, the following are common symptoms of container-grown plants.

1. Leaves whose green colouring has become pale or even yellow, all over the plant. Such a plant will probably also be growing slowly, it may be rather spindly and with leaves which are smaller than normal. Not enough light or lack of nitrogen in the soil are the two possibilities here; you may have put the plant in a corner far away from a window; the light provided by a northern winter may not be strong enough; the

Brown spots on leaves.

plant may be one which is provided with intense sunlight in its natural home and the summer has not been sunny enough so far north of the equator, or it may not be receiving light for long enough during the day. Lack of nitrogen can be remedied either by potting into a fresh soil, if the roots are cramped, or using a liquid fertilizer with a high nitrogen content as shown by the analysis.

2. Green leaves at the base of the plant which turn yellow and then fall. An occasional basal leaf or two will do this, in the normal course of events, but those which do it suddenly and quickly mean that the plant has either been over-watered, or there has been a considerable and sudden drop in temperature, or the plant has been subjected to persistent cold draughts.

3. Green leaves which turn yellow or almost white, but do not drop. These are a sign that the plant is one which prefers an acid soil, and is being watered with alkaline or hard water. The iron and magnesium which the plant needs for the green colouring agents in its leaves and stems are present in alkaline soils in a form which is unavailable to acid-soil-loving plants, so the green gradually fades, and eventually the plant will stop growing though it retains its leaves. Change to using rain water, or water which has been boiled and allowed to cool. If it does not improve, repot into fresh soil.

4. Green leaves which are variegated yellow or white changing to plain green, often rather pale. Not enough light; most widely contrasted variegation will be obtained by putting such plants into plenty of light.

5. Coloured leaves becoming faded, or all-green; also lack of light, but may be too much water and feeding as well. Plants grown for their coloured leaves will often have better colours if their soil mixture is kept slightly on the dry side.

6. Brown tips and brown edges to leaves of any colour. Usually a dry or insufficiently moist atmosphere, and one of the commonest problems, especially if combined with a fairly high temperature as found with central heating. Draughts and alkaline soils are other possibilities, depending on the plant.

7. Brown spots on leaves. Very common, and due to various causes, such as: cold if the plant is a succulent one or with fleshy leaves, or a cactus; feeding too heavily especially if foliar feeds are used, or if dry fertilizer settles on the leaves; trouble at the roots due to a poorly structured compost so that it is always soggy or too dry.

8. Leaves which are wilting and flabby. Commonly due to not enough water, but can also occur with over-watering, because the roots are drowning and not absorbing water to be conveyed to the top growth.

9. Fleshy leaves which turn brown at soil level, rot and collapse; cold and/or too much water; sansevierias are prone to this trouble.

10. Lighter coloured patches on hairy leaves. These are due to drops of water lying on the leaves after watering and, if the conditions are cold, leads to rotting. The velvety leaves of African violets sometimes become white in blotches—this is thought to be due to watering with cold water instead of at room temperature.

11. Light brown papery patches on leaves. Due to sun burn, especially on thin or young leaves, as a result of standing the plant in brighter sun that it can stand. Camellia leaves turn bronze in the centre if put in a sunny place.

12. Green leaves which turn grey-green or are minutely speckled yellow, and then slowly wither and fall; red spider mite.

13. Leaves blotched and spotted irregularly yellow, also curled and distorted; aphids.

14. Leaves with black patches on the surface which can

easily be rubbed off; scale insect, but may also be caused by aphids.

15. Leaves with white powdery patches on upper and lower surface; mildew. Occurs on specific plants such as begonias, in dry atmospheres and where there is dryness at the roots.

16. Leaves with brown patches which have grey fur growing out of them; grey mould. Due to too low a temperature, possibly combined with over-watering, or letting water lie on the leaves.

17. Thickened leaves with a white grey covering is sometimes seen on pot azaleas, and is due to a fungus disease called azalea gall. Remove the affected parts and treat the plant with benomyl systemic fungicide; review your cultural care which may have weakened the plant.

18. Beige-coloured wavy lines and blisters on the upper surface of leaves; leaf-miner. Cinerarias and chrysanthemums are very common victims.

19. Large holes in leaves; slugs, especially if it is the lower ones which are damaged, or caterpillars.

20. Irregular silvery white streaks and patches on the surface of the leaf. Due to the feeding of a small insect called thrips (thunder bugs); damage usually not very serious.

21. Pale green or white speckling which becomes patchy on the upper surface of leaves and imperceptibly increases. Attack by leaf hopper, more troublesome outdoors and in hot weather.

Flowers and fruit

Troubles to do with the buds and flowers are almost as frequent as leaf damage, but not as varied, for instance:

1. Buds and flowers dropping. Can be due to a dry atmosphere, using cold instead of tepid water, draughts, not enough water, moving the plant, turning it away from the sun, and giving too much water. The start of the flowering period is a crucial one, and you should be particularly careful with watering, humidity and evenness of temperature at this time.

2. No flowers produced at all. Something is fundamentally wrong with your care of the plant. Bulbs are especially prone to this. With any plant, it must be mature and healthy before it will flower but even provided this is the case, it will need in most instances, warmth and light to ripen the shoots and potash to ensure full maturity so that the growth switches to flower rather than leaf production. Too much water and too much nitrogen give a very soft, leafy plant which grows vigorously but never flowers. Slow it down by giving it less water, more light and potash feeding. You may also have pruned off all the shoots with flower buds!

Many bulbs come from hot countries and are accustomed to a hot, baking sun during their period of rest; without it they will not lay down a flower embryo ready for the following season. Some such as daffodils, start to form the new flower quite soon after the old one has died. While this is happening, the leaves remain green and healthy, and it is important to continue to feed the plant until the leaves die down naturally, to keep them going so that they can supply food to the developing flower, as well as building up a store. During summer the bulb has a short rest, but becomes active again in autumn, when the roots start to develop, and this continues slowly all through winter. If you are forcing bulbs for Christmas, you must therefore make sure they never run short of water while they are in the dark, otherwise the roots cease to grow, and when the flower does emerge, it will have brown florets, or be stunted and malformed—it may not emerge at all.

Shrivelling or falling fruit can be due to a dry atmosphere as well as lack of water in the soil, and if the fruit is badly shaped, a dry atmosphere at pollination time could have been the cause.

Stems

The stems or trunks of plants do not often show signs of trouble; it is the leaves which react most, but you you may sometimes see small brown, grey or black raised spots on the bark or skin, very often associated with black patches like soot and/or stickiness on the leaves. These raised spots may also be present on the under surface of the leaves, and are in fact scale insects.

You may also see what looks like small dabs of cotton wool on the stems, particularly at the junctions, and low down on leaves of bulbs where they emerge from the neck. Such plants are likely to be growing slowly; the cotton wool is a protective covering for a pest called mealy bug, which is greyish, slow moving and shaped like a miniature woodlouse.

Stems may turn brown and rot at soil level but, as with fleshy leaves, this is due to cold and/or over-watering; it may be followed by the appearance of grey mould on the rotting parts.

Complete plant

If the whole plant has a generally 'tired' appearance, that is, limp but not wilting, not growing, and is rather a sickly dull grey-green in colour, it may be infested with a pest on the roots called root aphis. This is dark grey, with white meal covering it, but it will be necessary to turn the plant out of its container to confirm your diagnosis.

Some plants react to too much water in the same way, without necessarily having a change of leaf colour, and examination of the roots will often show that they are dark brown all the way through, easily broken off, and stunted, with hardly any of the fine, feeding roots. Healthy roots should be white, strong and plentiful, changing only to light brown when older.

General Pest and Disease control

If you decide that whatever trouble you are faced with on your plant is not due to the wrong care, but is caused by a pest or disease, there are various ways of dealing with these. Quite often, you will stop them in their tracks simply by removing the most heavily infested parts of the plant, back to clean growth.

Some insects which adhere closely to the plant, such as scales and mealy bug, can be scraped off with a knife, doing this carefully so as to avoid injury to the plant, and placing a sheet of paper beneath the plant to catch the pests.

Some pests can be treated biologically, that is, there are other insects with the rather nasty habit of feeding on them, which can be put on the plants. For instance, the parasitic wasp *Encarsia formosa* is parasitic upon whitefly 'scales' (larvae) and is an excellent control. Similarly the predatory mite *Phytoseiulus persimilis* feeds on red spider mite and wipes out large populations most effectively.

There are, of course, chemicals which can be used to destroy pests and disease. Resmethrin is one of the newest and most effective of these; it is related to pyrethrum, but is even safer, as well as being more powerful, and destroys many sucking insect pests. Pyrethrum can still be used but will need to be applied more often; derris is another 'safe' kind, but remember that it kills fish, bees and other pollinating insects, so if you use it outdoors, do not spray plants in flower.

Malathion is a phosphorus-containing insecticide with a short persistence, very effective on sucking insect pests. It is not as safe as those already mentioned, but is not dangerous. The main difficulty is that as with

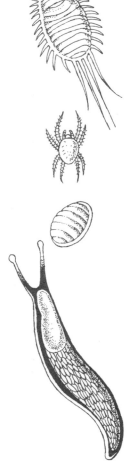

Plant pests. From top to bottom: aphid, leafminer, mealy bug, red spider mite, scale insect, slug.

those above strains of some pests are becoming resistant to it. It also has an unpleasant smell, especially when used as an aerosol, and is not suitable for any of the marrow family, crassulas, ferns, petunias, pilea species, and certain other plants which will be named on the container. Dimethoate is another phosphorus-containing insecticide, less safe, which has a systemic action; when applied to a plant, it is absorbed through the leaf into the plant's sap, and remains effective for several weeks.

Sevin (Carbaryl) can be used on caterpillars (and many other chewing insects), but they are rarely present on container-grown plants in such numbers that they need to be chemically treated rather than hand-picked.

For the fungus diseases mildew and grey mould, treatment with benomyl will be effective. This is a new systemic fungicide, which is absorbed into the plant and kills the disease from the inside, remaining effective for several weeks. Otherwise you can dust with flowers of sulphur or spray with any approved chemical fungicide after removing the worst affected parts, when mildew is the problem.

These chemicals are avilable as sprays, aerosols and dusts. Aerosols are convenient, if expensive; the chemical is very concentrated, so it is sufficient to envelop the plant in a mist; do not hold the spray too close otherwise they will be scorched and browned. Dusts can be disfiguring and are not easy to apply evenly; sprays are effective and relatively cheap, but must be diluted and applied exactly as the makers instruct, otherwise plants may be damaged, or the trouble not controlled. Remember that both sides of a leaf should be treated—the underside is generally the place where the majority of pests live and feed.

THE MAIN PESTS OF INDOOR AND CONTAINER GROWN PLANTS

Aphid species
Aphids are tiny insects, coloured green, black or red and 8–15mm (1/16th–1/8th in) long, found clustered on the tips of shoots and on the under surface of young leaves, in late spring and early summer. They are present also for much of the rest of the year if there is warmth and food available. They are mobile, but do not in fact move very much, and feed by sucking the sap out of the leaves and stems through needle-like mouthparts, with which they pierce the plant tissue. Their feeding results in the leaf losing its green colour and becoming pale or yellow in patches, and distorted and curled. Growth of the new shoots slows and the plant becomes weak, as its moisture is progressively removed. When adult, they become winged and fly to other plants to lay eggs and start the life cycle again. Each aphid casts its skin, or moults, as it grows, three or four times, and takes about a month to become adult. They excrete a sticky, transparent substance called honeydew, which should be wiped off the leaves. Control is by spraying with resmethrin, pyrethrum, derris, nicotine sulphate, malathion or dimethoate, all available in proprietary products with trade names.

Leafminer
Pale brown or pale green wavy lines on the upper surface of a leaf are characteristic of this pest, but its feeding may also produce pale brown blisters. The larva is a minute maggot which lives just below the skin of the leaf; if an affected leaf is held up to the light it is often possible to see the silhouette of the maggot. Badly affected leaves wither and fall, and the plant becomes weak and is disfigured; cinerarias and chrysanthemums

are frequent victims. It is best to remove the badly infested leaves and burn, and then spray the plant with dimethoate. The adult is a fly, also tiny, and rarely seen.

Mealy bug
Sap-sucking pests, like the aphid, mealy bugs are like miniature woodlice, dark grey and covered with a protective white, waxy, almost fluffy coat. They are mostly immobile and feed at the joints and tips of plants, and at the bases of leaves of bulbs. Hippeastrums can be badly infected as the bugs get down into the neck and are difficult to reach. Painting them with a brush dipped in methylated spirits is a good way to deal with them; removal with the point of a knife is another, otherwise spray forcefully with malathion to penetrate beneath the waxy coat, and repeat once or twice more, to control newly-hatched eggs.

Red spider mite
This can do a great deal of damage before it is noticed, the first symptom to the inexperienced person being the leaves falling. The mite is minute, and really needs a hand lens to be seen clearly; it is round, pale red to transparent and lives in great numbers on the under surface of the leaves, close to the main vein. With it there will be what look like white insects, but which are the white skin cast, as the mites moult and grow bigger. When there are a lot of mites, webbing is also produced. They take four weeks to complete their life-cycle, and there may be eggs, larvae and adults present all the time. Leaves become speckled, yellow or grey-green, gradually turn brown and wither, and then drop. Flowers also drop. The mite is rather difficult to control; derris will do it but needs to be sprayed repeatedly at two or three-day intervals. A more thorough method is to use malathion or dimethoate, or the predatory mite can be used, where supplies are available. Infected plants should be isolated as soon as discovered, until cleared. The mites thrive in hot, dry conditions, so spraying the plants daily with clear water and maintaining a humid atmosphere should keep them at bay.

Root aphids
These are the same kind of insect as the above, which have adapted to living in the soil, on the roots of plants, from which sap is removed in the same way. They are dark grey, with white meal covering them, this white coating being the first obvious sign of their presence. Bad attacks can kill the smaller plants. If infected, all the soil should be washed off the roots with warm water, taking particular care just below the crown, the plant repotted in fresh, clean soil, and then watered two or three days later with a solution of malathion. Examine the plants in a few weeks to make sure that there is no further outbreak.

Scale insects
If you discover brown, black or grey spots, oval, round or shell-shaped, on the stems, bark, or underside of leaves, these are scale insects. They are motionless, and feed beneath the protective scale in the same place all their lives. When adult, they may emerge and move to a fresh place where they lay eggs. Many also move around after hatching. Sometimes they are not noticed until black patches appear on the leaves, a sooty mould living on the sticky honeydew excreted by the scales as they feed. By this time, the plant will be growing poorly if at all, with a dull, limp appearance. Bay trees and citrus fruits are especially popular. The scales should be scraped off with a knife on to a sheet of paper below the plant, as thoroughly as possible, and the plant then sprayed all over, including the bark

with malathion or dimethoate. This should be repeated twice more at about 10-day intervals.

Slugs
Mostly a trouble on outdoor plants, grown on balconies, window-sills and terraces. They feed at night, so that holes in leaves appear mysteriously, without any obvious cause, and hide during the day beneath containers, in the bottom of pots and in nearby cracks in brickwork, stone walls and so on. Bait with poisoned pellets, or hand-pick when seen.

Whitefly
Tiny, snow-white flies living on the underside of leaves, usually the youngest to start with, but spreading to the older ones. The immature stages ('scales') and the eggs are flat, round and transparent, barely visible, and feed by sap removal. Feed on all sorts of plants, especially tomatoes, Martha Washington pelargoniums and fuchsias. As with others, remove the worst affected parts and destroy, and spray the plant with resmethrin as the makers instruct. Alternatively use the parasitic wasp *Encarsia formosa*, if obtainable.

There are several other insect pests which may cause trouble, but usually not much. Ants may nest in containers and disturb plant roots; they also move aphids about. Woodlice occasionally eat roots at the bottom of containers, and feed on seedling roots; thrips (thunder bugs) occasionally take the skin off flower petals, and leaf suckers and leaf-hoppers feed like aphids, and leave pale green patches on leaves. All can be treated with derris or malathion, and ants, which are killed by resmethrin.

Fungus disease is unlikely, but grey mould (*Botrytis cinerea*) sometimes appears. A grey fur grows out of affected parts of leaves, stems and flowers, following a previous injury. Brown rotting follows, or leaves may yellow and fall. Cyclamen and saintpaulias are often infected. Cold and damp conditions encourage its spread; keep the plants warmer, and with a less moist atmosphere and soil mix, remove affected parts, and spray the plant with the systemic fungicide benomyl.

Mildew, a white powder produced in patches on leaves and stems, may appear on certain plants, especially if they are on the dry side at the roots. Leaves die, and plants cease to grow and can be killed. Benomyl, flowers of sulphur, or mildex are all effective, applied to plants after removing all the infected parts.

If you have a plant which is sick, it needs to be literally regarded as a hospital case. It will not be able to stand normal stresses and strains in the form of changes in light, temperature, watering and humidity. You should therefore keep it in a shaded, steadily warm but not hot place, misting it frequently, and if necessary enveloping it in a plastic bag to maintain humidity. Any dead or dying parts should be completely removed; also any parts which are heavily pest or disease infested, and the plant sprayed with the appropriate control. Watering should be very carefully done—less will be needed than usual—no feeding, and no moving the plant at all, until it shows signs of recovery in the form of new growth, and a much better colour.

I have described all the troubles possible on container and indoor plants, but do not think you will be constantly having to deal with major damage and outbreaks for most of the time. Indoor plants do not very often get attacked by pest or disease, and many will survive unusual conditions of care fairly successfully. Plants are most adaptable—it is just that, if you give them what they really need, you will have a much more attractive and longer lasting plant.

Plant Terms

Aerial roots Roots produced usually from the stem above the soil, but may be from other above-ground parts of the plant. They are used to enable the plant to cling to a support, or to absorb moisture as well as support it.

Air-layering A method of propagation used if ordinary layering is difficult. A suitable stem is cut so that the cut slants upwards diagonally but only partially severs the stem, and is then bound with moist sphagnum moss or peat and polyethylene sheet until roots are produced from the cut.

Annual A plant which completes its life cycle within one year and then dies. The life cycle is from the time when the seed is sown to the time when the plant flowers and sets seed.

Aroid A plant which is a member of the family *Araceae*. This family forms a very mixed collection of plants, mostly tropical, often with aerial roots, and many make good house-plants. The flowers are calla-like.

Axil The angle formed between a stem and the organ, usually a leaf-stem, which arises from it.

Bark The hard, often rough outer covering of the trunk and branches of trees and shrubs, which protects the vulnerable cambium layer beneath it.

Biennial A plant which completes its life cycle over two years and then dies.

Bleeding Plants are said to 'bleed' when liquid flows from an injury, such as a pruning wound. It should be checked at once with a prepared tree paint or shellac on woody plants.

Bract A collection of modified leaves at the base of the flower, usually green and leaf-like, but sometimes coloured and shaped like the petals, or tiny and barely visible.

Bromeliad A member of the *Bromeliaceae* plant family. Nearly all are epiphytes, and are characterised by a central funnel or vase, through which they absorb most of the food and water that they need.

Bulb A kind of bud whose fleshy leaf bases store food while it is inactive, e.g. daffodils. Bulbs are generally underground organs.

Cambium The thin layer of cells beneath the bark or skin which is constantly dividing, and which increases the size of the plant. Beneath the bark it is coloured green.

Chlorophyll The green colouring matter in plants without which they cannot carry on photosynthesis.

Compost In England, as used for plants in containers, a mixture of ingredients in which the roots are planted. The conventional composts consist of a mixture of loam, peat and sand, chalk and fertilizer, in varying proportions. The new soil-less composts contain peat and sand, with or without food. In the U.S. the term is reserved exclusively for a humus made of decayed plant parts.

Corm A storage organ like a bulb, the food, however, being stored in the fleshy base of the stem, *e.g.* some begonias, gladiolus.

Cutting A portion of a plant, mostly the stem, which is cut off and induced to root at the cut end. Stem cuttings for pot plants are generally of the 8cm (3in) tip of a new season's shoots. Leaf cuttings (saintpaulias and begonias), and root cuttings are also possible.

Deciduous A plant which sheds its leaves every year is said to be deciduous; applied to trees and shrubs.

Epiphyte A plant which lives on other plants, but which does not absorb food or water from them (*epi* = upon; *phyton* = plant).

Fertilizer A liquid or dry powder substance containing one or more plant foods.

Fibrous-rooted Some plants are said to be fibrous-rooted, to distinguish them from others of the same genus which have tubers instead, such as the begonias. The fibrous roots are many and fine and are those through which the plant absorbs its food and water.

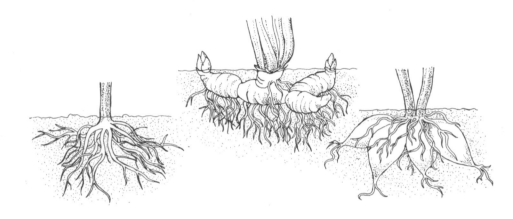

Different types of root. From left to right: fibrous root, rhizome, and tuber.

Genus A group of plants whose flowers, fruit and seed are botanically similar, but different from those of other genera within the same plant family and usually composed of several species. Such a group would have been descended from a common parent.

Humidity Dampness in the atmosphere, essential for good plant growth.

Leach Washing nutrient away through the soil by watering or rain.

Lime A substance contained in soils which makes them non-acid or less acid in reaction; it always contains calcium. Some plants cannot grow at all or do not grow well in soils which contain free lime, e.g. azaleas.

Node The point at which a leaf or flower joins the stem.

Oasis A type of expanded polystyrene, coloured green, which absorbs a great deal of moisture, yet still retains its shape and firmness when dried out.

Offset A miniature edition of a plant, usually produced at its base, which can be detached to grow into a new plant, exactly the same as the parent. Bulbs are plants which reproduce in this way.

pH A numbered scale whose values indicate the degree of acidity or alkalinity of a soil or compost. It is counted from 0–14, 7.0 indicating neutrality. Numbers lower than this show acidity, higher mean alkalinity.

Perennial A plant which lives three or more years, producing flowers and seed usually in its second and successive seasons. The top growth dies down completely in most cases after flowering, but the roots sprout again the following year.

Plunge Of potted plants, when they are buried up to the rim of the pot in soil or peat in an outdoor border, or indoors, to keep them cool and moist or, while they are resting or ripening, to prevent them becoming too hot and drying out.

Photosynthesis The process by which green plants manufacture oxygen and sugars from the carbon dioxide of the air, and water, with the help of energy supplied by sunlight.

Pot-et-fleur A combination of potted plants and cut flowers to make the most of both, and in which plants and flowers can be replaced as the arrangement grows or dies.

Potting-on The moving of a plant into a larger container; repotting consists of moving it into a similar-sized one.

Respiration The process by which carbon-dioxide and water are given off and energy released as a result of the oxidation of sugars within the plant. It is the reverse of photosynthesis.

Rhizome An underground or nearly underground stem, usually creeping, often mistaken for a root, but which has buds on it, sprouting to produce shoots and flowers.

Runner A stem which produces plantlets with roots at each node.

Species A member of a genus which, when grown from seed, will be the same as its parents—it is said to breed true. The specific name of a plant is the second name, the first the generic name. Varieties of a species do not breed true; they differ from the species in details such as flower colouring, height, size of flower and so on.

Stolon A stem which roots at its tip, where a plantlet is produced.

Stomata (singular, stoma, or stomate) The pores of a plant, mostly on the underside of leaves, but some also on the upper side, and occasionally on the stem, through which water vapour is given off. They close in dark or very hot conditions.

Succulent A plant with thick fleshy organs which retain a lot of moisture; such plants grow where conditions are dry, and include the cacti.

Systemic Materials which are absorbed into the sap or system of a plant and circulate through it; applies to weedkillers, insecticides and fungicides.

Tuber A swollen root or stem, usually formed under ground, which stores food while the plant is resting.

Turgid Swollen with as much moisture as the organ concerned will contain.

Transpiration The giving off of water vapour from the leaves by plants, which goes on continually.

Vase The central hollow formed in bromeliads by the leaves, in which rain collects.

Terrariums and Bonsai

Terrariums

Previous page
Terrariums provide a miniature ornamental greenhouse for plants in the home.

Left
A specially designed case with a regulator for ventilation, placed on a deep drip tray, provides a perfect atmosphere for plants and enables one to grow some of the more temperamental kinds, even when the arrangement is stood in a warm, dry place.

Below
A large brandy glass-type container makes an attractive jungle jar and is easy to fill. Almost any deep glass will serve the same purpose even if it is slightly colour tinted. Jungle jars seldom need watering. In this one are selaginella, fern, *Begonia rex* and carex.

Terrariums or jungle jars as they are sometimes called are extremely decorative and even appealing but apart from these qualities they can also play a useful role. In them it is possible to grow many plants which cannot be expected to do so well outside the glass walls, in rooms where the atmosphere is dry and the temperature sometimes fluctuates. Of course, it is possible also to grow similar plants within the glass as are on the outside, but if a terrarium offers you the choice of

adding to your collection of house plants, why not take it and have a new arrangement to place as well?

Some of the more choosy plants you can expect to grow – and can buy – are species of selaginella which are mossy and fern-like and carpeting; *Nertera depressa*, another carpeting plant with tiny leaves and little orange berries, many kinds of the tender ferns such as the wiry-stemmed maidenhairs, miniature tender palms, crotons, fittonia, calathea, maranta, peperomia, pellaea, pilea and pellionia.

Some of these you will recognise as being good room plants under certain conditions and the important thing about using these in terrariums is that they are fairly slow growing. They also provide colour and texture contrast. It is possible to fill a bottle with just one type of plant, say a colony of bromeliads or ferns, but usually they look more attractive when the plants are mixed.

Unless you know your plants well, do not be led into thinking that if a plant is small and has small leaves it is bound to be suitable for this type of garden. Helxine now known botanically as *Soleirolia soleirolii*, sometimes called baby's tears, has the tiniest leaves yet it would soon take over the entire bottle. The same applies to the creeping ficus, to tradescantia and zebrina. Of course, if you find that a plant is growing too rapidly you can always take it out and pot it in the usual manner and grow it elsewhere. If you have a terrarium for several years, this becomes necessary.

Jungle jars have become so popular that today special glass containers are being produced for this purpose. Unlike the old-fashioned glass carboys these are made with necks large enough to allow an arm to reach down inside. Another and easy-to-fill jungle jar is an outsize brandy balloon type glass. Storage jars and even wine and cider jars and bottles can be used, so long as it is possible to plant them.

The glass is usually clear but it can be tinted, light brown, light blue and green. The important thing is that it shall be clean and kept clean.

If the neck of the glass is large enough for you to insert your hand, planting will offer few problems but when you are filling a jar which has a narrow neck you should be both careful and patient.

First group the plants in the way you hope to see them in the jar. I suggest that you slope the soil, so keep this in mind, remembering that this will heighten any plant you set at the top of the slope.

If you cannot insert your hand you will need to improvise a tool or two so that you can make a hole for the plant, guide the plant into the hole, cover it and firm the soil round the plant afterwards. Often one thick stick will do the lot but more often it is helpful to lash a kitchen spoon to a cane to use to dig out holes. An old-fashioned wooden cotton spool on the end of a cane will make a neat little rammer with which you will be able to pat the soil round the plants. These should always be set firmly in the soil otherwise their roots will not be able to absorb nourishment and they may sicken and die.

As with all containers, troughs, large bowls, dish gardens, a drainage layer is essential. The safest thing to throw or pour in is charcoal which is so light in weight that it cannot crack the glass. If you use small pebbles such as pea gravel, do not pour this straight into the jar on to the glass base, but first pour in a thin layer of peat to cushion the impact of the stones.

To fill a carboy, make a funnel or cylindrical chute of strong paper or card. Insert one end of this into the neck of the jar. First pour in the peat, then the gravel and lastly the soil.

This drainage layer needs to be quite deep, 2 inches

Top
Planting a terrarium. Make sure that the inside of the glass is sparkling clean before you begin work. Strew a few nuggets of charcoal on the floor of the container before adding some sand for drainage.

Slope the soil slightly. This is easily done if you put the lowest plant in first near the front, cover its roots with soil and put the next plant in position. Be sure to secure the roots of each plant and at the

end gently ram the surface to firm it.

The little cryptanthus has been tied to a mossy branch and arranged out of the soil. The selaginella and tiny fern will carpet the soil, while the shrubby variegated euonymus and carex rush will provide contrast of shape and colour. Selaginella has small, scale-like leaves like a tiny fern and the species that are low growing and creeping are ideally suited to the cool humidity of a terrarium.

or so for a large carboy and proportionately less for smaller jars.

Soil composts should not be too rich or the plants will grow too fast. The amount of soil you use will depend upon the size of the container; you should be able to see more glass and plants than soil but it is the depth of the plant's roots which should guide you. These must be properly planted.

To get the soil in the right condition so far as moisture is concerned, calculate how much you need, take about one third of this amount and spread this out on newspaper to dry. Spray the other two thirds until it is just moist, uniformly so, and when you take a handful and squeeze it gently it should just cling together.

This dampened mixture should go in first. The dry mixture follows to form a top dry layer which should help to seal in the moisture.

As with dish gardens, water the plants beforehand and allow them to drain thoroughly. Knock them from their pots in turn. If the aperture of the glass is very small it may be necessary to shake off any loose soil from the roots so that the plant can be slipped in easily. The leafy portion is no problem because this naturally contracts as it is pushed root first through the opening. To make sure of this, hold the plant by the tips of its leaves, or if it is tall, gather its branches or leaves up near its centre stem, so that this top portion is made really slim. Make a hole in the soil, tilt the jar and aim for the hole. This actually, is easier than it sounds. Direct the plant into the hole with the stick or with the spoon. Make the hole for the next plant directing the soil round the roots of the first plant. Ram the soil down before tilting the jar for the second time. Continue this way until all the plants are in position.

Inevitably, some soil particles will dirty the inside of the jar. It is not wise to spray these off with water, which seems the natural thing to do because the soil will be made too moist. A feather duster fixed to a strong piece of wire, which can be bent as required, is the easiest way to clean the glass. If the plants' leaves have soil on them, lash a fine paint brush to a cane and clean them.

If the soil is properly moist the plants should settle in and you should not need to water it for some weeks. If the balance is right you should see a little condensation or dew on the interior each morning. However, if this seems excessive—so much that there are several runnels and large drops on the glass, there is too much moisture in the soil and it would be prudent to remove the moisture from the glass to prevent it running back into the soil. Lash a tissue to the end of a wire or the bow of a coat-hanger to do this. When the time comes that you see no condensation, this is an indication that the soil needs watering. To do this, gently spray the interior glass. This will help to clean it at the same time. Do not feed the soil or the plants will grow too well.

Bonsai

Miniature trees which are perfect copies of large forest trees have been grown by the Japanese for at least 800 years under the name of bonsai. Many kinds of tree are suitable: most conifers, such as pines, spruces, firs, junipers and cypresses, and several broad-leaved kinds, such as beech, oak, birch, willow, rowan and elm.

Bonsai can be bought from nurseries, but it is far more satisfying to grow them oneself, starting from a seed or seedling. It should be planted in a good potting mixture in early spring. When the seedling is growing well, it should be given its first root pruning. The seedling should be removed from the pot and any large roots cut back – the finer ones can be left as they are. Repot it in the same container with a new potting mixture. At the same time, the top growth should be checked by pinching back the tips of the side shoots. The tip of the leading shoot should be removed only when the main stem has reached the length required for the mature tree.

By the third spring the tree can be put in a permanent container. Root-pruning should be done every year and the top growth carefully trained by means of weighting, tying or wiring, to mould the tree into the desired shape, as a replica of the full-grown specimen.

A row of miniature pine trees, carefully trained as bonsai to imitate the shape of the forest tree.

190

Index

ACKNOWLEDGMENTS

The publishers would like to thank the following individuals and organizations for their kind permission to reproduce the photographs in this book.

A–Z Botanical Collection 37 above, 41 above right, 57 above left; Agence Top 7; Bernard Alfieri 30–31 above, 31 below left, 34, 63, 66; Julia Clements 148 centre; Connaissance des Arts (R. Guillemot) 140 above right; W. F. Davidson 42–43, 67; Douglas Fisher Productions 50; J. E. Downward 49 below, 54–55, 56 above; Melvin Grey 185, 190; A. Huxley 28 below, 72, 145 above; George Hyde 32, 57 above right, 56–57 below, 59 above, 61 centre and below; Jackson and Perkins 27, 38 below; Leslie Johns 1, 4, 26, 29, 30 below, 36, 37 below, 38 above, 40, 41 left, 43, 44, 45 above and below left, 45 right, 46, 46–47, 48, 49 above, 51 above and below, 52, 58, 60 above, 62, 64, 65 above and below, 70, 89, 90, 91 left and right, 92, 93 above and below, 94–95, 95, 96, 97, 98, 99 above and below, 100 above and below, 101, 102 above, 102–103 below, 103 above, 104 above and below, 105, 106 above and below, 107, 108 above and below, 109, 111 above left and right and below, 112, 113, 114, 115, 116, 117, 118, 119, 120, 138 above and below, 140 above left, 140 below, 142 above, 144, 145 below, 146, 147 above and below, 148 above and below, 149, 150, 150–151, 153 above and below, 154, 155, 156, 157 above and below, 159, 160, 161, 162, 163, 164, 164–165 below, 165 left and right, 166 above, 166–167 below, 167 above, left and right, 168, 186–187, 187, 188 above and below, 188–189; Giuseppe Mazza 8; Bill McLaughlin 39, 69, 137, 142 below, 143; N.H.P.A. (Bernard Alfieri) 59 below; Octopus Books Ltd. 2–3; Wilhelm Schact 139; Kenneth Scowen 52–53, 158; John Sims 25; Harry Smith Horticultural Photographic Collection 71, 141, 152; Spectrum Colour Library 28 above, 31 below right, 32–33, 35, 41 below right; W. J. W. Unwin Ltd. 60 below, 61 above; Werner Wolff 110.

Drawings by Virginia Nokes and Prue Theobalds